'67 Ford GT40 Mark 4

'67 M5A McLaren F1

'63 McLaren Zerex

'59 F1 Cooper Climax

'71 M8F McLaren CanAm

CW00672249

McLAREN MEMORIES

McLAREN MEMORIES

A BIOGRAPHY OF BRUCE McLAREN

EOIN YOUNG

Haynes Publishing

First published in 2005 by HarperCollins*Publishers (New Zealand) Limited*
First UK and US edition published in August 2005 by Haynes Publishing

A catalogue record for this book is available from the British Library

ISBN 1 84425 119 5

Library of Congress control number 2005921911

Haynes North America Inc., 861 Lawrence Drive, Newbury Park, California 91320, USA.

Haynes Publishing, Sparkford, Yeovil, Somerset BA22 7JJ, UK.
Tel: 01963 442030 Fax: 01963 440001
Int. tel: +44 1963 442030 Int. fax: +44 1963 440001
E-mail: sales@haynes.co.uk
Website: www.haynes.co.uk

Front and back cover photos by Tyler Alexander
Inside front cover photo courtesy of Grand Prix
Spine photo by Lester C. Nehamkin
Inside back cover photo by Frank Shacklock
Designed by Murray Dewhurst
Printed and bound in Australia

Foreword
Sir Jack Brabham

I first met Bruce and his parents when I went to New Zealand for the first New Zealand Grand Prix in 1954. Geoff Wiles of Redex introduced us and in no time at all I was working on my Redex Special in the McLaren garage workshop in the Auckland suburb of Remuera. Bruce had just left school and had been on an engineering course, so we had a common interest straight away.

It wasn't long before Bruce was driving in hill climbs and local car club events. When I went to New Zealand again in 1956–57, I took two Coopers out there and Bruce's father bought the Bobtail 1500 cc sports car off me for Bruce to drive. Bruce had a lot of success driving that Cooper and then a single-seater and he won the New Zealand Driver to Europe competition. He raced in Europe in 1958 and did extremely well. At that time Roy Salvadori was my teammate in the Cooper Formula 1 team, but I knew he was leaving us to drive for Aston Martin. I phoned John Cooper from New Zealand and we soon had Bruce installed as my teammate.

Bruce did a terrific job for us and in 1959 on one great weekend at Sebring Bruce won his first Grand Prix and I clinched my first World Championship. We backed this up with another successful season in 1960, but unfortunately the formula changed to 1500 cc in 1961 and our winning streak was over.

I left the Cooper team at the end of the 1961 season and Bruce took over as the number one driver; he went on to engineer and drive for Cooper until he decided to build cars of his own.

He formed a team of his own in 1964 and his McLaren CanAm sports-racing cars would totally dominate the North American series until 1970. He had also built a car for the Indianapolis 500 in 1970 and I flew back to Heathrow with him the day after the race. We talked long into the night about our plans for racing and discussed when it would be right to retire. Which just made the tragic news of his death two days later testing a new CanAm car at Goodwood, so much harder to accept. He was a good friend and a good man.

There could not be anyone better than Eoin Young to write this personal story of Bruce and his racing career.

Contents

Acknowledgements

This book of memories was fuelled by the columns that Bruce and I wrote together and I syndicated to magazines and newspapers internationally, with *Autosport* as the UK outlet. The columns were eagerly awaited by readers, who relished Bruce's way of getting it down on paper in a manner that no mere journalist could capture. As a fan you wanted to be there. Reading Bruce's column, you felt that you *were*. I wasn't really a ghost writer; I just tidied his thoughts and put them on paper. It wasn't a job, it was a delight in that I always got to be first to read the McLaren columns. Now I've written the *McLaren Memories*.

Thanks to Bruce's sister Jan, who runs the Bruce McLaren Trust in Auckland, for providing a complete set of the columns to use as reference. I had kept many of them, but by no means all, so Jan's assistance has been invaluable in the writing of this book. Thanks also to Peter Foubister at Haymarket Publications for his co-operation.

Bruce seldom regarded writing his column as a chore. He wrote one after most major races. If things were going badly he didn't write a bad column, he simply decided that perhaps it was better not to write one at all and we might go for a month or six weeks until track fortune picked up and he got back to getting his thoughts on paper. Bruce was always disarmingly honest. And amusing. On occasions he would dictate into my tape recorder while relaxing in the bath. You could hear the background splashing, and his giggles when he remembered a funny story from the race weekend.

Thanks also to Milan Fistonic, who has always fielded my seemingly incessant requests for information and background material from his extensive motor racing library in Auckland. I would hate to have me as a friend, but I'm sure that's been said by other people on other occasions.

Pete Lyons provided magical quotes on his appreciation of CanAm racing and an incredible description of riding in a CanAm McLaren at Riverside, for which I give my thanks. He also made available some of Tyler Alexander's photographs. Check Pete's web site on www.petelyons.com.

Thanks to the Peters, Grant and Ward, for ongoing good company while I was working on this book. Peter Grant (a.k.a. Baldric) loaned me his collection of *Automobile Year* annuals, which have been invaluable for checking race details from events where Bruce perhaps hadn't done as well as he wanted, and so had not produced a column about the race. The pedantic Peter Ward kept me on the straight and narrow with his proofreading. Early evening libations with the pair of Peters at the Brewers Arms in Merivale often helped to fan my enthusiasm to get back to the laptop ...

The Bruce McLaren Trust is due further thanks for the very special album of photographs of Bruce from his baby days through those painful years recovering from Perthes' Disease. These seldom-seen family photographs were generously made available for this book.

Conversion table

1 inch	25.40 millimetres
1 foot (12 inches)	30.48 centimetres
1 yard (3 feet)	91.44 centimetres
1 mile (1760 yards)	1.61 kilometres
1 pound	453.60 grams
1 stone (14 pounds)	6.35 kilograms
1 ton (2240 pounds, 160 stone)	1.02 tonnes
1 brake horsepower (bhp)	0.746 kilowatts (kW)
1 gallon	4.55 litres
1 US gallon	3.79 litres
1 acre	0.40 hectare

Preface

Bill Bryce, a New Zealander and a long-time friend of Bruce's, was first to arrive at the horrifying scene of the crash at Goodwood on that fateful second day of June 1970, but it would be thirty years before he told anyone about that numbing experience. Bill died late in 2003 after a long battle with cancer, but before that, he talked to me about that day, almost as a confession, though he had committed no crime.

Bill was the Bry of Brymon Airways, an aviation company that he and Chris Amon, the New Zealand racing driver, had established in Britain. On 1 June 1970 he was having a gin and tonic with Barry Newman, the next-door neighbour of Bruce and Patty McLaren, who lived in the elegant and expensive Burwood Park, not far from the old Brooklands Track in Surrey. There was no fence between the two homes. Newman and McLaren were good friends and Newman had even helped fund New Zealander Howden Ganley into a Formula 3000 McLaren drive — a move that eventually led to a Grand Prix drive with BRM and later Williams and March.

'We realised that Bruce had arrived back from Indianapolis that day, so we wandered across the lawns for a drink,' recalled Bill. 'Ron Smith, Bruce's testing manager, was there and we talked about what had happened with the McLaren team at Indianapolis a couple of days before. They were due to test the new McLaren CanAm car at Goodwood the next day and when I told Bruce I was delivering a plane to the Isle of Wight he suggested that we drop in for lunch at the circuit.

'The next day we went down to Fairoaks airfield in Barry's Rolls-Royce

— Barry and his chauffeur were coming with me for the flight. We jumped in another plane for the flight home and we were over Portsmouth when Barry reminded me that we were to call in to Goodwood for lunch with Bruce.

'We saw the orange CanAm McLaren come out of the pits as we were circling the airfield to land and we parked up by the control tower to walk across to the pits. I remember we were chatting, it was such a nice day, and we could hear the car lapping. Then all of a sudden there was silence, absolute silence, and at that point the noise hit us — a huge *whoompph!* when the car hit the concrete marshal's post. We were halfway there, so we ran as fast as we could and we were first on the scene. It was just bloody carnage. The car was at least a football field of bits lying strewn about. It had slammed off the circuit at high speed into the marshal's post and just exploded.

'The gearbox was on fire on the circuit and Bruce was very close to it so we pulled him away from the burning magnesium. One thing that stuck in my mind was that his driving boots had come off in the crash. I was trying to get his helmet off, but I was shaking like a leaf. I was trying like hell but I couldn't undo the buckle. His chest was thumping up and down and when the other guys arrived I shouted at them to give me some bolt-cutters so that I could cut the helmet strap, but they pushed me aside. I said, "But he's still moving…he's OK." I don't remember who it was, but someone just shook his head sorrowfully and said, "No…he's dead."

'Barry and I looked at each other and we ran back to the plane. We fire-walled it all the way to Fairoaks and dashed back home in Barry's Roller. We arrived at Patty's just as Phil Kerr (one of McLaren's managing directors) got there in his car. I heard him phone Bruce's father in Auckland and tell him that Bruce had had "a bad one". He said that he didn't know how bad, but that he would keep him in touch.

'I gestured to Barry to go outside because we obviously knew more than they did. I said to Barry, "Shall we tell them?" and he said, "No…" '

It appears they never did, as the fatal news came through on the telephone and then the bad accident became a death. The awful news had overtaken the need for Bryce and Newman to elaborate on it.

'I remember being out in the garden the following evening,' said Bill. 'Chris Amon was there and Denny Hulme, with his hands burned and bandaged and he was talking and talking. He was talking and crying and saying "I wish it had been me and not him…" over and over again.'

Introduction

Bruce McLaren was the victim of too much technology too soon. Today, 35 years after his death, aerodynamics in motor racing is an accepted, highly advanced science. In June 1970 it was a black art. Fellow New Zealander and former leader of the Ferrari Formula 1 team, Chris Amon, remembers those early days of wings in racing. 'We used a suspension-mounted rear wing on tall struts on our Ferrari in the 1969 CanAm series and then they were banned. On the day he was killed, it would have been Bruce's first test for the McLaren team with such a large body-mounted wing. You can imagine the huge leverage from the wing at the back of the car and with the body section fixed at the front edge, hinging back from the middle of the car, all that downforce was doing was trying to rip open the engine cover…

'It was a thumping great wing mounted between the tail fins and it would have been putting huge stresses on the forward fixing pins. I'm not entirely sure that anyone in those days would have worked out how much downforce a wing like that was generating or how much stress it was putting through the pins.'

On 2 June 1970, Goodwood was bathed in sunshine as Cary Taylor, a mechanic who had raced his own Brabham in New Zealand, warmed up the CanAm car while Bruce tested the Formula 1 car Peter Gethin was to race at Spa in place of Denny Hulme. 'I'd been trundling around in the CanAm car, running the engine in, giving it a general shakedown,' said Taylor. 'Bruce was flicking round the circuit in the Formula 1 car, in and out of the pits, having a good time. On one lap I gave the sports car a big handful out of the chicane and spun it. I took it easier after that. Bruce came past me with a big grin...'

At 10.45 Bruce drove out of the pits for the first time in his new M8D CanAm car they had christened 'The Batmobile' — a reference to the high side fins that sloped up both sides of the tail, a broad wing slung between them. After a standing lap and a flyer he headed for the pits.

The 7.5-litre 630-hp aluminium Chevrolet V8 engine was bolted to a plate directly behind the cockpit, acting as part of the chassis. Two hip-hugging seats were scooped into the aluminium riveted monocoque box that formed the frame of the car and also accommodated 64 gallons of pump petrol in bag tanks. Every ounce of the 1420 lb car was purpose-built for pace. In first gear the dial directly in front of the driver would show 6500 rpm when the car hit 110 mph.

There was more high-speed oversteer than Bruce liked and he mentioned to testing manager Ron Smith that the special flat-bottomed steering wheel they had made for the Indianapolis cars would be better than the normal wheel, with its fat, leather-bound round rim. The Indy wheel was more comfortable on the tops of his thighs in the wriggle-fit cockpit.

The mechanics raised the wing just a fraction to increase the downforce and try to curb the oversteer. Bruce went out again and after four laps, two of which equalled his earlier time in the 3-litre Formula 1 car, he came back to the pits to have the wing angle raised another notch. He said the sports car felt a lot softer everywhere compared with the precision of the open-wheeled Grand Prix car at the same speed, so the crew checked the fat Goodyears, pressuring them at 22 psi all round. They put tape under the front duct of the nose to check the possibility of grounding, and as an efficient test driver Bruce rattled off the instrument readings he had checked on his way in to Woodcote on the last lap. Oil temperature 90°C. Water temperature 70°C. Fuel pressure 140. Oil pressure 60.

Another four laps for a best of 1:12.2 and he was back for a further notch on the wing. The official lap record was jointly held in perpetuity by the Flying Scots, Jim Clark and Jackie Stewart, in their 1.5-litre Formula 1 Lotus and BRMs, respectively at 1:20.4 (107.46 mph) when the 2.4-mile circuit closed. It had been closed down because officials felt that the track would not cope with the power and speed of the 1966 3-litre Formula 1 cars.

Taking advantage of the stop the McLaren mechanics filled the tanks just to the top of the first layer of safety foam. That made it about 20 gallons on board. After a further six laps with a best of 1:10.8 (122.03 mph) Bruce reported that the high-speed oversteer had been cured. Instead, he now had a trace of understeer. He was pulling only just over 6400 rpm on the straight and he wondered what had happened to the other 200 rpm. He thought he might be losing time coming out of Lavant corner on to the straight, so he asked for adjustments to the rollbars front and rear. Another five laps and he came back to say that the handling was better and he was back up to six-six again on the straight.

The oil temperature was up five degrees but the other instruments were normal. They checked the tyres and shock absorbers to see why the car might be oversteering at Madgwick corner, just after the pits.

At 12.19 by Ron's pit watch, the big orange-finned McLaren rumbled away down the pit lane. Another few laps and they would stop for lunch. All was well as Bruce twitched the tail coming out of the chicane and set off on his flying lap.

He never completed it. At 12.22 p.m. he was dead; killed instantly when the car left the road just after the left-hand kink on the main straight and slammed into a marshal's protective embankment on the right-hand side of the track. An investigation of the scattered wreckage showed that a section of the tail had lifted at around 170 mph, causing immediate and total instability and a situation that was beyond human control.

Cary Taylor remembers the terrifying silence after the crash. In the pits they heard the deceleration and the brakes going on and then the huge impact. 'He would have got down in the cockpit the instant he realised it was gone. He always did. He was never very big in the cockpit anyway. He'd have corrected automatically, jumped on the anchors and ducked.

'There was no ambulance at the track so we jumped into the old Land Rover they had there. There was no fire when we got to the site, just the huge impact in the mid-section of the car. Bruce had been flung out. He was lying at the side of the track and he appeared to be uninjured externally, but he was like a rag doll. I imagine the force of the impact would break every bone in your body.'

In one shocking instant, Bruce McLaren, the young New Zealander who led the Cooper Grand Prix team, won the Le Mans 24-hour race for Ford, dominated CanAm sports car racing in North America and won a Grand Prix in his own McLaren car, was gone. He would be mourned by those in motor sport, but the loss would be felt more strongly by his family, especially his young wife, Patty McLaren.

'He'd been away about a week at Indy and had arrived back the afternoon before he went to Goodwood,' said Patty McLaren-Brickett, recalling that fateful day. 'Denny [Hulme] had been badly burned during practice at Indianapolis and his hands were still bandaged, so Bruce took over the CanAm testing. I said I would go down to Goodwood with him, but he said no, that it would be tedious and there would be lots to sort out, so I got up and made his breakfast and sent him on his way. He drove to Goodwood in his Mercedes with Ron Smith, who was doing the timekeeping. Our daughter Amanda and I were going to spend the day with the Ouvaroff family in Richmond. Their eldest boy had been born just a couple of weeks apart from Amanda.

'We were about to leave around lunchtime when Phil Kerr arrived. Initially I was told that Bruce was very badly injured, but not that he was dead. The phone call from Goodwood had come through to Phil at the factory and he came straight to the house. Then more and more people arrived and I knew that Bruce had been killed. I saw Denny there later and I remember him sitting with his head in his bandaged hands, sobbing and sobbing and sobbing.'

Phil Kerr, joint managing director at McLaren with Teddy Mayer, said Ron Smith had phoned from Goodwood around midday. 'He told me there had been an accident, that Bruce had gone off the circuit and it didn't look good. At that stage they were waiting for the ambulance to arrive. There wasn't one at the track. He said he would call me when he knew more. I went down to the workshop to tell Teddy and we decided that I would go to the house just in case. It was just so traumatic…awful…

'It was mid-afternoon by the time I got the final news and I called Bruce's parents in New Zealand. In those days you couldn't just pick up the phone and dial New Zealand. Sometimes you had to wait hours in a queue, but I got through to Pop and Mrs Mac at four in the morning.

'I had gone back to the factory but then I got a call from the house asking me to get back there because Denny had arrived and was in bad shape. He had been up in London having treatment for his burns and he must have heard about it on the news.

'While I was at the factory Teddy and I called the mechanics together and told them what had happened. We told them all to go home and said that nobody was expected to come in the next day. Teddy and I decided to regroup the next day because the Belgian Grand Prix at Spa was only five days away. We knew we didn't have Denny and now we didn't have Bruce. We told all the staff to take the next day off, but the incredible thing is that between 7.30 and 8 o'clock the next morning, *everyone* turned up. To a man. That's when I realised, if you ever needed proof, that anybody would do anything for Bruce. They must have talked to each other and said Bruce would have expected them to be there, so they all turned up. There were about 60 on the staff at the time.'

Chris Amon was driving back from the March factory in Bicester when he heard the news about Bruce. 'It was a lovely afternoon and the Belgian Grand Prix was due to run the following weekend. I was wandering back through the Oxfordshire countryside and had the radio on when it came over the news. I stopped the car, got out and just stood there for a while. There are some events where you always remember where you were and what you were doing, and that's one of mine. I'll never forget that day. I think I was numb, really. When things happened to me during a race, adrenaline took over for a while. But just driving along the road and not pumped up at all, it was a stark reality. I guess I had to go through the process of taking it on board and accepting it.

'For quite a while before that day I hadn't seen all that much of Bruce, apart from the odd party at his house. I'd gone to Ferrari and was living in Italy. But I'd just spent the thick end of a month with him at Indianapolis and that made it even more devastating for me. I'd quit the Indy project a week before the race…'

Amidst the sudden shock of Bruce's death, formalities still had to be followed. It was a time when others rallied to help, as Phil Kerr recalls. 'Louis Stanley, the boss of BRM and a strong man in this sort of situation, had heard about Bruce on the news and took over all the arrangements for Bruce to be taken to the funeral home and for the flight to New Zealand. I was really so grateful to him for that.'

Bruce McLaren's funeral was held in Auckland on 10 June and was followed a fortnight later by a memorial service at St Paul's cathedral in London, where close to 1000 turned out to honour the Kiwi who had given so much to motor sport. He is buried at Waikumete Cemetery, Auckland.

This book is a collection of memories, not a formal biography. The memories of Bruce McLaren are mine and those of others who knew him well and appreciated what a fantastic chap he was. He was worthy of the description of Rob Walker: a gentleman in terms of one word as well as two.

1 **Boyhood blues**

Bruce Leslie McLaren was born on 30 August 1937, the middle child in the McLaren family, seven years younger than his sister Pat and ten years older than his sister Jan. His father, Les, who was always known as 'Pop', had three brothers and they all competed in local motorcycle races. There had been motors in the McLaren family for as long as anyone could remember. Les's father, Bruce's grandfather, had started a bus and truck transport business before the First World War and Les himself owned and ran a service station and garage business in Remuera. The first sporting car Bruce could remember in the family was a four-seater Singer Le Mans, which soon gave way to a larger 2.5-litre 1935 SS1, forerunner to the Jaguar. It wasn't long before Pop started racing the SS1 in club events.

'When I was nine or ten, I was always drawing racing cars,' recalled Bruce. 'I suppose that was the beginning of my interest in being a draughtsman. All my other interests were physical and, being a New Zealander, I was especially keen on rugby. I was captain of the Junior School football team — looking back it was a lousy team, but at least I was the captain! I was second-best boxer in the class — the other chap was bigger than me…'

Bruce's sporting career came to an early halt when, aged nine and a half, he felt a sharp pain in his left hip. It happened during a polio epidemic so Bruce was presumed to have contracted that dreaded disease. After several days in bed and an unsuccessful anti-polio regime, he was sent for an X-ray. It was not polio; it was worse. Bruce was diagnosed with Perthes' disease and there were fears that he would never walk again.

Perthes' disease, also known as Legg-Calve-Perthes' disease, was described around 1910 by Legg, an American, Calve, a Frenchman, and Perthes, who was a German. It is characterised by loss of circulation to the head of the femur (the ball of the hip) in a growing child, resulting in death of the bone cells in the head of the femur. This is typically followed by revascularisation over a period of 18 to 24 months. During the period of revascularisation, the bone is soft and liable to fracture under pressure, causing collapse of the head of the femur. Untreated, over time, the head of the femur heals and remodels in the collapsed position, resulting in a non-spherical shape, which leads to stiffness and pain.

Perthes' disease is not preventable because no one knows what causes it. In Bruce's day, children with Perthes' disease were treated by keeping weight off the affected joint, by either crutches or prolonged bed-rest. Today, treatment is less extreme, with surgery, braces or casts being used, depending on the extent of the problem.

Bruce was moved to the Wilson Home for Crippled Children in Auckland. 'When I arrived at the Wilson Home, I was put in a Bradshaw frame, with my legs encased in a thick elastic plaster with weights dangling from the end,' Bruce noted in his 1964 autobiography, *From the Cockpit*. 'As I was putting no pressure on my hip, there was no real pain and I soon became used to enforced idleness.'

His mother, Ruth, who died at Easter 2004, aged 97, remembered those worrying days. 'There was no treatment. He lay on a thing called a Bradshaw frame, with big bike wheels and they just wheeled him everywhere. He lay on that for two years and never came off it. He was washed on it, educated on it, the whole lot.'

At the Wilson Home there were four or five other lads of Bruce's age also confined to these frames and the boys soon discovered that they could reach the big rear wheels and achieve covert self-propulsion. Of course there were races around the hospital grounds and in the unstable vehicles accidents were inevitable. Bruce described one of the most spectacular shunts. 'One morning we decided to try something new, so we hitched three or four bathchairs into a train and crept out into the grounds. There were ramps instead of steps and these were ideal for a bit of extra acceleration. We pushed off down the first slope and were soon gathering speed. We were going very fast off the second ramp when the horrible thought struck me that there was a slow right-hander at the end of the drive and we were all bearing down on it at high speed. There was no question of slowing our ungainly entourage, or making the corner in any respectable fashion, so we had our accident in a straight line.

'It was a colossal pile-up, with bathchairs going in all directions, but I had the biggest crunch of all. My Bradshaw frame whistled off the chair and launched me feet first into a flower bed. Panic reigned as we struggled to get my frame back on the chair, the flower bed restored to near-normal and ourselves indoors before the matron arrived. I don't think anyone ever found out about that little dawn escapade.'

Bruce spent his tenth and eleventh birthdays at the Wilson Home. Then came the day when he was allowed to get up. 'The doctor told me to stand, not to try to walk, but just try to stand normally. My legs had been hanging in the air for a couple of years and I suppose I must have forgotten how to stand on my own. I levered myself up until I figured I was standing quite naturally. The doctor looked serious and had a technical discussion with the nurses. This unnerved me a little and I looked down to make sure my feet were pointing the right way. The main trouble turned out to be that I was holding my legs straight. I'd forgotten that when you stand up, your knees are slightly bent and no one had thought to remind me. I relaxed the muscles and everyone, myself included, breathed a sigh of relief. But it seemed the weights on my left leg had not been completely successful and that leg was a little shorter than the right.' For the rest of his life Bruce wore a built-up heel on his left shoe, and when he wore racing boots he walked with a distinct limp. It was one of those things that you came to accept and never noticed, but today, watching film footage of him walking down the pit lane, it's easy to see how pronounced the limp was.

His elder sister Pat considers that Perthes' disease made Bruce 'a very understanding boy. He spent two years on that Bradshaw frame and while he was always involved in the high jinks, I thought he changed from a happy little boy to a very deep, thoughtful little person and that remained with him all his life...it made him more aware of other people's suffering, it brought out a depth of compassion in Bruce, and his ability to help and talk with people.

'His hip affected him in that he limped and when he was very tired he had a bit of a rolling gait. It also gave him the occasional headache, because his spine wasn't quite straight because of having one leg shorter than the other. I suppose that if he had lived he would have had a hip replacement.'

While Bruce was in the Wilson Home his father entertained the idea of replacing his SS1 with a new XK120 Jaguar sports car and he brought along the lavish illustrated sales catalogue for Bruce to look at. Les had been trying to convince himself that he could afford one. He eventually dropped the idea, but that XK120 catalogue would change Bruce's life and eventually turn the McLaren name into fame in Formula 1.

'It had a magnificent cutaway drawing of the 3.4-litre twin cam engine and I pored over that drawing,' Bruce recalled. 'For a long time it meant nothing more to me than an intricate mass of cogs and shafts, but after reading the specification sheet and putting two and two together I began to realise how an engine worked.' He was eleven and from then he began to take an interest in cars and their design.

He got hold of a miniature 1 cc model aeroplane engine and stripped and rebuilt it so often that it eventually wore out. 'When I was ready to go back to school in 1951, I enrolled in an engineering course at an Auckland college where the main subjects were maths, science, English and history and where part of the curriculum was engineering workshop practice. In other words, we were taught to use a file, a hacksaw, a lathe, drills and so on.' His ability must have been noticed, for he went straight into an 'A' stream. But even then Bruce's goal was a career as a civil engineer, not a motor engineer. That would come.

Now that Bruce was mobile again, his father took him to local car club hill climbs and beach races, but it was apparent that the SS1 was not really suitable as both a racing car *and* family transport. Les looked around for something purpose-built and within his budget.

He found an Ulster Austin Seven, the two-seater competition version of the ubiquitous 750 cc Austin Seven 'people's car' of the 1920s. Herb Gilroy had raced the car locally and had dismantled it for one of those comprehensive rebuilds that never seem to happen when the end result is likely to be little better than the original. The little racing car arrived as boxes and bags of bits and Bruce helped his father rebuild the vehicle and eventually drive it. Sister Pat remembers the Austin turning up on the back of a truck. 'There were all sorts of odd bits in boxes and sugar bags and I know mother and I looked at it and looked at each other and wondered what the boys had got themselves into…'

Bruce later compared his early experiences with those of Colin Chapman, whose first racing cars were based around the same Baby Austins. Bruce believed firmly that anyone who had grown up with an Austin Seven was certainly equipped with the Right Stuff.

'Part of my training at secondary school was technical drawing, so I had some good basic training in that, but my favourite subject was what we termed engineering mathematics — mathematics applied to the broad scope of engineering. I became good at that partly because I was interested and partly because there was nothing else to do at the time. I couldn't play sport for a while, though I eventually got back to swimming and rowing, so the only hobby I could have was something connected with the school. I gravitated to the subjects that applied to motor racing and engineering — horsepower formulae and centrifugal force formulae and all the things that covered the design of a racing car.'

Bruce was still too young to drive on the public highway so he rode his bicycle to school. 'Thrashing around on my bike and swimming were the only sports in which I could take part,' Bruce later wrote. 'The doctors had warned against anything like rugby. Cricket was permitted, though it never appealed to me, but the biggest blow was the veto on rugby. This was goodbye to an ambition that dated back to my primary school days. Like most youngsters in New Zealand, I'd had visions of becoming an All Black.'

The Ulster Austin project was the ultimate way for Pop and Bruce to work together, for Pop to be able to pass on his nous and knowledge to his son, lessons that would never be taught in a technical college.

'It was a wonderful relationship,' Pat recalled. 'What more can one say. It was a great father-and-son thing. They respected each other and as Bruce got older and obviously knew more about cars and engines and such than Dad did, Dad would listen to Bruce. It was a sort of role reversal really. They held each other in such high esteem and respect.'

Pat remembers life at home in those days: 'If you enjoyed having your dinner with motor racing parts on the table it was a very good era. I'm sure many a time neither Dad nor Bruce knew what they were eating because they were more interested in how they could get a little bit more speed out of this little piece that fits in here…they were always doing something to it. Life revolved around that Austin Ulster.'

Bruce's lack of a driving licence was regarded as of minimal importance as far as the Ulster was concerned. He learned the complexities of car control, hurtling around a makeshift figure-of-eight circuit skirting the lemon and plum trees in their garden in a well-to-do suburb of Auckland. It must have helped that the next-door neighbours were the Fowlds family and the Seabrook Fowlds company were Austin agents who would later import Austin Healey sports cars for Ross Jensen and Les McLaren — and Bruce — to race at Ardmore.

Pat went for only one ride in the Ulster; Bruce was at the wheel. 'I had one very hair-raising ride going up and down Upland Road. I wasn't quite sure that we'd get round the corner, but we got back to the front gate safely and I vowed and declared then that that would be the one and only ride I ever had in it. And it was…'

Les McLaren's first drive in the Ulster was along similar lines, as Bruce later recalled: 'Pop set off on his first trial run and I waited anxiously at the end of the drive for his first impressions. When he eventually brought the smoking Ulster to a halt he was pale and shaken. It was the most diabolical racing car he could imagine. Sure, it went all right, but it wouldn't stop, it wouldn't steer and, as for the handling…words failed him!' He was all for selling it there and then, but Bruce persuaded him to keep the car and let him look after it. Fortunately, Pop relented.

As a little lad on his trike, Bruce had gathered something of a reputation among the mechanics in the McLaren Service Station around the corner from the family home. Pat said he liked to work beside them, fixing his tricycle with the very spanner a mechanic was about to reach for. In contrast, the Ulster was mainly worked on at home in the back yard. 'I suppose some of the mechanical work was done up at the service station, but I don't think it really affected the running of the business.'

Bruce had been taken out to the family beach house at Muriwai Beach on a travelling version of his Bradshaw frame but with the Ulster Austin up and running Bruce and Pop were sharing the drives. Pat: 'I think Dad got as much of a kick out of racing the Austin as Bruce did. When Dad realised that Bruce was a little bit lighter and could go a little bit faster, then Bruce drove in more and more events, with Dad giving him encouragement and helping him mechanically.'

The most important date in the junior McLaren mind was his upcoming 15th birthday, which meant two things: he could get his driving licence and then with his road licence he could qualify for a competition licence. It seemed only logical to Bruce that he rack up some road miles in the little Austin in order to gather experience before taking his test and to this end he took to a few dawn trials on local streets.

'One early morning I had to call Pop out for mechanical rather than legal aid,' Bruce wrote in 1964. 'I'd risen at some ridiculously early hour and found the car difficult to start. An under-bonnet check showed both fuel and ignition systems operational, but the engine still refused to fire. I rolled the car down the drive and hopped in to let it trundle down the road. I was nearly at the bottom of the hill before it fired and then everything happened at once. It went charging up the other side, locked solid and skidded to a halt. I had no idea what had happened and, fearing the worst, Pop helped me to tow the Ulster home behind the workshop truck.

'It turned out that I'd over-richened the mixture in my attempts to start the car and the neat petrol had washed all the lubricating oil off the cylinder walls. When the engine fired there was no film of oil between the piston and the wall and the engine seized. Pop was not amused. He told me that if I insisted on these early-morning sessions, I should restrict my test area to within pushing distance of home.'

By the time his anxiously awaited 15th birthday finally arrived, Bruce had abandoned his original idea of taking his driving test in the little Ulster. 'I didn't suppose a noisy little Ulster Austin with virtually no brakes, questionable steering and highly suspect suspension would impress the Traffic Inspector, so I borrowed a friend's 1949 side-valve Morris Minor. I was nervous at first — isn't everyone? — but after driving him round the block a couple of times, doing a few turns and a reverse and answering the stock questions from the road code, he gave me a column of ticks and I had my licence. At last. Now I was ready for racing business.'

2 First races

If Bruce's first drives had been around the circuit he'd laid out in the garden at home, his first official competitive event as a licence-holding racing driver was actually up the drive at the family holiday home at Muriwai Beach, some 25 miles northwest of Auckland. Pop had laid gravel on the new drive, which climbed just over half a mile to the house, and it occurred to him that it would make an ideal private venue for a club hill climb. He arranged an event with the Auckland Car Club, but when the day for Bruce's competition debut arrived, Pop was in hospital, having developed a nasty gallstone problem.

'Not being able to give me a last-minute lecture, Pop settled for a few well-chosen words from his hospital bed, the general message being that if I so much as scraped a guard, the Ulster and I would part company for good.'

Bruce set the fastest time in the 750 cc class, just beating Phil Kerr in an Austin Nippy. It was one of those serendipitous events that punctuate the lives of many great people. Phil would, in time, become an important figure in the McLaren career.

'We first met in 1952 at a car club hill climb,' he recalled. 'It was Bruce's first event and it was my first event as well. We were the youngest guys there and we just got talking. We got on very well that day and I soon started turning up at the family service station in Remuera.'

They were two boys with a bond of motor sport that would stay with them for the rest of their lives. Bruce introduced Phil to Jack Brabham and he helped to manage the Brabham empire before switching to join Bruce and become joint managing director of McLaren Racing at Colnbrook in 1967. Even in 2005 Phil remains connected to McLaren, running a web site about the team from his home in Albany, Auckland.

'It was clear from early on that Bruce was naturally inclined towards motor cars,' notes Phil. 'Bruce's engineering expertise was more obvious than anything else early on. He just seemed to have a natural affinity with motor cars. We were very lucky that Harold Bardsley, the foreman at Les McLaren's workshop at the service station, was immensely helpful and taught us a great deal. Pop was absolutely incredible too, so we were being taught by two very talented and very competent men.

'We both had Austin Sevens then and I suppose in a way you could compare that with young drivers starting their careers in karts today. Karts didn't exist then. In our spare time we always seemed to be either working on our cars or reading the overseas magazines. We used to go through them cover to cover and talk about overseas drivers and cars and races for hours on end. It helped that the overseas drivers we read about used to race in the Grand Prix at Ardmore and we volunteered to be crowd marshals. This meant that we would be on the right side of the crowd, closest to the track so that we could watch the races as close as possible. You can imagine what happened when a couple of teenagers tried to tell a crowd of boisterous race-goers what to do. We took the easy way out and sat down to watch the race, while the crowd behind happily sorted themselves out. We couldn't have realised it at the time, but being that close to the local and international drivers and cars was a huge influence.'

After that first hill climb Bruce visited Pop in hospital to deliver the results and assure him that the Ulster was still in one piece. 'I also wanted to reassure myself that its ownership was now on a permanent basis. I wouldn't say that a hot Austin Seven is a short-trip ticket to a Formula 1 racing car, but that Ulster taught me a lot. There was the obvious learning of car control, but there was also the importance of careful maintenance and preparation. Painstaking work in the garage before a race meant the difference between winning and failing to finish.

'One of my first lessons was to tackle one job at a time, do it thoroughly and be satisfied with the result before moving on to the next.

'We modified the Ulster so much over the three years I used it that by the time we parted company it was barely recognisable as the car I had been given, while its performance was so far removed that it might have been a different car.'

During the first year the car seemed to get worse rather than better, but performances improved and it became apparent that the young McLaren was learning from his mistakes. Harold Bardsley schooled Bruce in the arts of the lathe and the welding torch, and when Pop scoffed at Bruce's suggestion of replacing the twin SUs with a single Zenith carburettor, Bruce fabricated his own new manifolds for the SUs. 'These worked extremely well and after that, Pop became more co-operative when I came up with the odd inspired thought.'

They flattened the rear springs to cure the oversteer and reverse-curved the front spring. Bruce then suggested converting the car to independent front suspension, but, he said, 'Pop convinced me that a really good beam-axle layout was better than an indifferent independent set-up.'

To begin with, Bruce and his father both drove the car and could compare each other's performances. Bruce's first real race win, as opposed to gymkhanas and hill climbs, was on Muriwai Beach in 1953. 'Pop tried the car first and when he brought it back to the pits he looked a trifle grey. Apparently he preferred a car with brakes! I had become so used to the anchorless state of the Ulster, that I probably would have found myself in trouble with brakes that actually worked! Ettore Bugatti once said something about brakes not being essential as they slowed the car down, and I agreed with him.'

The Ulster must have been accustomed to being shared as when Phil Kerr had problems with his Ford Ten special at a Muriwai hill climb Bruce offered him the Ulster to drive. Phil immediately turned in a time 2 seconds faster than Bruce's best. Honour was more or less restored when Bruce equalled Phil's time in his next climb, but it was clear at that stage that Bruce and Phil were more or less on a par and this parity was maintained for a few more summers. When the Driver to Europe scholarship was announced in 1958, Phil was one of the finalists on a short list of three.

But that was still down the track. Phil was training to become an accountant and Bruce was at university studying engineering.

Pop was a founder member of the New Zealand International Grand Prix Association, a group formed to stage a Formula Libre race on a circuit laid out at the Ardmore airfield, 20 miles south of Auckland.

The first Grand Prix — in 1954 — attracted a good field, but the results turned to chaos when Horace Gould in a Cooper Bristol, claimed that he had won the race after completing 101 laps, saying that he had refrained from passing Australian Stan Jones on the final lap because he knew Jones was a lap behind. The lap-scorers did not agree with Horace, and Jones was declared the winner. That was just the beginning of the confusion and arguments raged for weeks before Jones was eventually and finally declared the winner in his Maybach Special, a car powered by a 4-litre straight-eight engine taken from an abandoned German Maybach scout car found in the Western Desert. Stan's son, Alan, later gained greater fame in racing when he won the World Championship for Williams in 1980.

The Grand Prix was a pivotal point in the career of Bruce McLaren. Jack Brabham, who had won the New South Wales and Queensland road racing titles in his Cooper Bristol with sponsorship from the additive RedeX, came to New Zealand to participate in the Grand Prix. It was Jack's first trip overseas and he was happy to let RedeX help his budget by arranging for him to stay with an Auckland family. Les McLaren supplied RedeX at

∧
An immobilised Bruce outside the family home at Upland Road, with sister Jan and the dog for company.

∧
The Bradshaw frame. Even this wasn't enough to keep Bruce and his Wilson Home
compatriots out of trouble.

∧
Despite the practical difficulties, Bruce's family tried to include him in activities wherever
possible, including visits to the beach house at Muriwai.

∧
Bruce cruising down the Muriwai hill climb course in a Bobtail Cooper.

∧
The 1957 Teretonga grid featured Ernie Sprague (Maserati 4CLT), Bruce McLaren (Cooper) and Ron Frost (Cooper).

> Bruce taking the
Austin Healey for
a spin on One Tree
Hill, Auckland.

∧
The 1958 Clellands hill climb wasn't a great success for Bruce, but was redeemed when he
met future wife, Pat Broad.

∧
Bruce's first Grand Prix victory was at Sebring in 1959. Teammate Jack Brabham ran out of fuel.

∧
The 1959 New Zealand Grand Prix podium featured (left to right) Stirling Moss (first), Jack Brabham (second) and Bruce McLaren (third).

∧
The real thing. Bruce McLaren, racing driver, 1959.

^
Bruce drove the Lycoming Special to fourth place in the 1960 Wigram race in the New Zealand series.

>
Cooper days —
Bruce (left) with
John Cooper, 1960.

∧
The 1962 Teretonga grid was an all-Cooper affair featuring Bruce (47), Stirling Moss (7), Jack Brabham and Lorenzo Bandini.

∧
Bruce loved driving the Mini Cooper, seen here at Pukekohe in 1963.

his garage, he had a spare bedroom and so it made perfect sense for Jack to stay with them. For Bruce, this was like the opening of a garage door.

In his autobiography, *The Jack Brabham Story*, Jack recalled that 1954 Grand Prix: 'During my time there I met and stayed with an Auckland garage-owner and keen racer named McLaren, who had an even more enthusiastic young son and budding racer named Bruce — a young man I would come to know very well.'

For that inaugural 1954 Grand Prix, the Austin agents in Auckland, Wellington and Christchurch had each been supplied with one of the shapely new four-cylinder Austin Healeys to enter for their chosen local driver. Ross Jensen had been selected by Seabrook Fowlds to drive for the Auckland car and he managed a creditable seventh overall. Billy Fowlds, of course, was the long-suffering McLaren neighbour in Remuera. The Austin Healey was eventually put on the market and it was suggested that Les McLaren might be interested in it. The fact that it was being offered for sale because the latest racing version of the Austin Healey — the 100S ('S' for Sebring) — was on its way to New Zealand for Ross to race was not a deterrent for Pop.

Pop had never been comfortable with the little Ulster and while it was an ideal grounding for young Bruce, his father still hankered for a 'proper' drive, a car to enter in the 1955 Grand Prix. The Healey provided a perfect project. The car was completely stripped for a mechanical makeover. 'Everything that moved was polished and balanced,' wrote Bruce. 'Chrysler pistons were fitted, along with Buick cam followers and pushrod gear and Chrysler exhaust valves. The ports were opened out and highly polished and a special twin-pipe exhaust system made up and fitted. A full-length under-tray was made and cast iron brake drums were refitted with plenty of cooling holes and big scoops on the back plates to draw in cooling air.' Colin Beanland remembered that they unlocked first gear on the transmission, which was originally a four-speed gearbox — on the Austin Healey only the top three gears were used. The result was a competitive sports car that would be a class-winner for the next three seasons, often heading the 100S Healey in sprints, and making a best top speed of 128 mph.

In the 1955 Grand Prix the car ran strongly, but Pop had to retire when the teeth stripped from second gear. Bruce recalled in *From the Cockpit* that this was probably a blessing in disguise, because they had planned a refuelling stop and had reckoned on pouring in 8 gallons in about five seconds, but they discovered later that the tank wouldn't accept more than a gallon every 10 seconds. 'In other words, it would have been a case of one in the tank and seven on the ground, splashing around the hot exhaust…it hardly bore thinking about!'

Meanwhile, McLaren Junior was still using the Ulster, which had been tuned to the point where the Austin now rode on a trailer and Bruce was back on his bicycle. When the cylinder head cracked, Bruce was able to demonstrate his engineering skills, building another using the head of a 1936 Austin Ruby saloon. 'I filled all the combustion chambers with bronze, then re-cut them with rotary files, keeping as closely as I could to the specifications laid down by Sir Harry Ricardo, the famous engine designer. To my everlasting amazement and pride, the Ulster went better than ever and was timed at 87 mph, regularly turning in times under 20 seconds for the standing quarter mile.'

Bruce's first circuit race was on the Ohakea airfield north of Palmerston North. It was also the first time that Bruce and his father raced together. Bruce always maintained that there were 'some 40 cars on the front row and another 30 cars in the second'. The grid *was* a wide one with 15 cars on the front row, 15 on the second and 14 on the third and back row. Given that grids were usually 4-3-4 on airfield tracks or 2-2-2 on road courses in New Zealand then, it probably seemed to McLaren Junior, who had qualified last, on the back row, that there *were* 40 cars across the grid. Ron Roycroft was on pole with the P3 Alfa Romeo that Tazio Nuvolari had driven to an amazing win against the German Auto Union and Mercedes teams cars on the Nürburgring in 1935. Pop was in the centre of the second row alongside the Healey 100-4s of John Seabrook and Graham Cowie and Laurie Powell's Ford V8 special. Bruce and Pop were both listed as retirements in the Ohakea Trophy, but Bruce did finish third in a handicap race.

After three years, though, Bruce felt the Ulster had served its purpose. With it, he'd learnt the basics of racing and the detail of discipline and preparation, so when a Ford special became available Bruce decided that it was time to 'move up'. He sold the Ulster for £280 and borrowed £30 to buy the Ford for £310. Pop was probably glad to see the back of the little Ulster, but his plan to race the Healey in the 1956 Grand Prix went awry when he ended up back in hospital and then home again but under doctor's orders not to even think abut driving in the race. The car was ready but the driver wasn't, and Les needed a suitable replacement. Bruce said he didn't think his name was originally high on Pop's list, but he put up a worthwhile promotion within the family and so was entered for the sports car race. It was no dream debut. A gearbox problem in practice resulted in Bruce's first all-nighter to effect repairs and then a blown head gasket resulted in his retirement from the race. In fact, the engine had nipped momentarily in the middle of a corner and Bruce thought the steering had failed. He pitted for Pop to check the steering, but it was fine. Pop suggested it was perhaps an engine problem, but Bruce couldn't see that an engine problem could affect the steering and went back into the race…only to realise that Pop had been right and the engine was running roughly. To cap it off, the all-nighter caught up with Bruce and he slept through the Grand Prix that afternoon.

In March 1956 father and son went down to Ohakea again where Pop had entered the Austin Healey for himself and Bruce with the proviso that whoever set the fastest lap in practice would get to race. Bruce solved that problem forever with a lap that was fastest by 7 seconds and from then on Pop took on the role of entrant and proud father.

In 1957 the McLaren plan was to run the Healey in the full New Zealand series starting with the sports car race before the Grand Prix at Ardmore. The series started badly. Ken Wharton had brought out a 250F Maserati and a Monza Ferrari sports car and had entered for the Grand Prix and the sports car race. He was leading the sports car race in the Monza when he ran wide and clipped a pylon. The Ferrari somersaulted down the pit straight in front of a stunned crowd that included Bruce's mother. That the accident had happened at all was bad enough, but she thought it was Bruce in the Healey. The Ferrari was No. 64 and Bruce's Healey was No. 46. Ken Wharton was wearing a yellow sweater. So was Bruce. Wharton was killed when he was thrown from the cockpit and the Ferrari crashed to a halt upside down. For that instant Mrs McLaren thought the worst. Bruce never wore a yellow jersey again. He never raced with No. 46, either. From then on, when he raced in New Zealand his car was No. 47.

That year Bruce was fifth at Ardmore and third at Levin. At Wigram he led the race until Jack Brabham came past in his centre-seat Cooper sports racer and Bruce settled into a race with Ronnie Moore, the speedway rider, in his 1100 cc Cooper sports car. Then the Healey went off song and he pitted to tell Pop he thought it was a duff spark plug. Pop didn't agree, but he changed the plugs and sent Bruce back into the race. The car was still off-song, so Bruce retired. That was when they found that one of the pistons was wrecked and they had major repairs to make before the race at Dunedin the following weekend where he finished third. On the Ryal Bush road circuit near Invercargill Bruce detected another misfire and when they set about an engine check back in Christchurch a con rod clattered through the side of the block. The 1957 Healey racing programme ended on a down note, and it looked as though Bruce would be passing up his racing career and going back to engineering.

A month later the future brightened.

3 The first Cooper

The 1500 cc centre-seat Cooper sports racer that Brabham had driven to beat Bruce in the 1957 sports car races had been left behind in New Zealand for sale. With the demise of the Healey, it was suggested to Pop that the Cooper might be a good replacement. A deal was done and Bruce's Ford special — which he had never really liked — and the Healey were both sold, and the Cooper bought. It was the start of Bruce McLaren's career as a real racing driver, although there were perhaps few who appreciated it at the time.

In fact, no time was wasted. The Cooper arrived on a Friday and it was entered in the Horahora hill climb the following day! It was tipping with rain and the climb was heavy, but Bruce won the 1.5-litre class and was entranced with the way the car performed. 'It was a dream to drive. I'd never experienced such responsiveness to the controls and right from the start I felt at home in the driving seat.'

The FWB four-cylinder Coventry Climax engine developed 100 bhp at 6000 rpm and was virtually bulletproof, which was important so far from the factory.

The first race meeting in which Bruce could drive the Cooper was at Levin, but it clashed with an important university test. Bruce had been told by his professor that he was spending too much time on his motor racing and not enough on his studies. He would have to decide on his priorities. He did. That weekend he won three races at the Levin circuit and his engineering degree was put firmly on the back burner. During that season the Cooper set new records in every hill climb in which it ran and there were pie-in-the-sky plans to enter the sports car in the 12-hour race at Sebring.

Colin Beanland remembered going for after-dark runs up the northern motorway. 'I sat on the token seat space on the left-hand side of the centre-seat sports racer, sitting on a piece of board on the alloy floor, with my right arm draped over the chassis tube. You had to wear goggles because there was no windscreen. Those trips were *great*.'

Bruce had been in constant touch with Jack Brabham in England and learned that Jack would be able to bring him a Formula 2 Cooper fitted with a stretched 1750 cc version of the Formula 2 Coventry Climax engine to race in the 1958 Grand Prix. It had already been a busy car, first serving the Cooper team in Formula 2 and then being driven to fifth in the British Grand Prix by Roy Salvadori, after it had had a 2-litre engine fitted. For himself, Jack was bringing out a Cooper with a Climax engine enlarged to 1960 cc.

In anticipation of his new vehicle, Bruce sold his existing Cooper to Merv Neil and while he waited for the single-seater to arrive, he went back to his studies. He was 21, and there was a further challenge afoot. Grand Prix promoter Buzz Perkins let Bruce know that they were funding a Driver to Europe scholarship in 1958 and with the single-seater Cooper, Bruce's chances of winning the award would be vastly increased.

As it turned out, the first single-seater car Bruce drove was not the Cooper but a rather special 3-litre 8CLT Maserati, one of two cars built for Indianapolis but never raced there. It was in effect a bigger version of the 1500 cc supercharged 4CLT Maserati Grand Prix car, fitted with two of these engines joined together end-to-end with a carburettor and supercharger for each half. The two cars had been brought out from Modena by a wealthy New Zealander, Lebanese-born enthusiast Freddie Zambucka, in a deal that also included a 6C Maserati. The Maseratis were painted black with a silver stripe and when Freddie died suddenly of a heart attack, the cars were taken over by Frank Shuter, who planned an attempt on the New Zealand land speed record.

Bruce had time on his hands between his exams and the Cooper arriving, so he took on the task of making one of the 8CLT Maseratis a runner after its long period in storage. The methanol fuel had jellified in the system, which had to be completely dismantled and cleaned out. Phil Kerr helped with the resuscitation project and he remembers the day they fired it up. 'The noise was deafening. We decided that we should give it a blast since we'd got it working, so we trailered it out to Ardmore. There was nobody there to tell us not to, so we fired it up and took turns driving it around the runways. We had an absolute ball. It was the quickest thing either of us had driven at that stage!'

Bruce remembered it as a monster. 'The long gear lever sprouted up in the centre of the cockpit and was cranked to the left. The blown 3-litre engine had miles of power in a straight line, but it was a bit unpredictable around corners. It had four speeds and it would spin the wheels at anything up to 140 mph.' The 8CLTs were said to have topped 200 mph when they were tested in Italy.

The Coopers landed in New Zealand just before Christmas 1957 and later, when Jack arrived, they went out to try the cars at Ardmore. It was Bruce's first drive in a single-seater Cooper and he had no notion that he would soon be a works driver.

'Jack led me around for a few laps and I had a marvellous time following his lines and hanging the tail out when he did. Then I was waved on and Jack sat on my tail and followed me. When we pulled in at the pits, I was told off for hanging the tail out too far — a case, I thought, of the pot calling the kettle black…'

Meanwhile, Phil Kerr was company secretary for an outfit that imported tuning equipment and also built Buckler sports cars under licence to the factory in Britain. Before the Cooper arrived, Bruce spent much of his spare time helping Phil and another friend, Merv Mayo, who both turned out to be his opposition for the Driver to Europe scholarship. Colin Beanland was also involved with Phil and Merv and when Bruce turned his attention to the Cooper, Colin was appointed his chief mechanic. It was to be a long-lasting working relationship and friendship that would eventually see Colin working at the McLaren Engines operation in Indianapolis.

The 1958 Grand Prix at Ardmore early in the New Year was run as two heats followed by a final. Bruce started in the second heat, running against Jack in his Cooper, Roy Salvadori in a Connaught and Ross Jensen in the ex-Moss 250F Maserati. Bruce finished second to Jack in the first of several one-twos they would repeat in summers to come.

But for the final, trouble struck the fledgling McLaren equipe before Bruce had even made it to the Grand Prix grid. To warm up the engine and transmission, the car was hoisted on a quick-lift jack and left with the engine running and wheels spinning. That was when the gearbox gave a terminal clatter and the warm-up ground to a halt. Repairs were out of the question with just 23 minutes before the race start. Fortunately Brabham had the answer; he loaned Bruce the spare gearbox he had brought out for the Cooper of English driver, Dick Gibson.

Everyone helped remove the graunched gearbox and bolt the new transmission in its place. There was an empty space on the front row of the grid but the officials were on McLaren's side. When the start time arrived an announcement was made that oil had been found on the course and that there would be a delay.

'No one was quite sure where the oil was, but an official car set out to look for it...then they *found* some oil...and a little bit more and then, of course, they had to let the cement dry.'

There may well have been oil on the circuit, but it was more likely that the race organisers had bent over backwards to give their local boy his best chance. As the flag dropped, the final bolts were tightened, oil was dashed in, and Bruce set off, wheels spinning, half a lap behind the field. It took him eight laps to climb to eighth place, passing ten cars on the way. Then the engine misfired, which meant a seven-minute stop to change the plugs. Back in the race — and at the back of the field again — the Cooper was running well when it suddenly baulked into neutral. Bruce grabbed it into a gear and kept going, but when it happened again and again, Bruce headed down the pit lane. The bolts holding the bell-housing had worked loose after the frantic refit, all the oil had gone and the gears were glowing hot. The Cooper clattered ominously as it was pushed away.

Bruce sat glumly on the pit counter with his family and watched Jack win the race from Jensen's Maserati, but he also imagined his chances at the racing scholarship going down the drain. His depression lasted until the prize-giving dinner in Auckland that night. Bruce was announced as the winner of the inaugural Driver to Europe award, an endowment that would finance him into the start of the rest of his racing career.

Bruce went on to win the race for New Zealanders at Levin and to get a close look at the performance of Archie Scott-Brown in the works Lister-Jaguar sports car. 'The way he could throw the Lister round, despite the physical disability of his unformed right arm always amazed me. Brabham seemed a certainty to win at Levin, which was a real Cooper circuit until Archie confounded everyone, Jack included, by keeping the Lister right on the tail of the 1960 cc Cooper. Archie passed me with little bother just before the straight and I sat behind him as long as I could, watching the Lister swinging from lock to lock to lock as Archie played continual correction to keep the car pointing the right way through the tricky bits, then crabbing away from the corner under acceleration.' Bruce finished third behind Jack and Archie. Later that same summer in his first European race at Spa, Jim Clark also saw the speed of the Lister-Jaguars when Masten Gregory and Archie blasted past him. Recalling that race, Jim said that he was gaining confidence in the D-Type Jaguar as the race went on. 'I was coming down to Burnenville corner and the car actually felt as if I was drifting and I was not concentrating too hard on what was coming up behind me. Suddenly there was an almighty howl of sound, a blast of wind, the whole car shook and Masten went steaming past like a bat out of hell. He was well out in the lead with the Lister-Jaguar all sideways, his arms crossed and fighting the steering. I remember having a sudden twinge of shock and thinking "To heck with this, if this is motor racing I'm going to give it up now." ' Fortunately for motor sport enthusiasts, neither Clark nor McLaren gave up easily.

In New Zealand, the fast open Wigram airfield circuit was next in the series. That this race could happen at all was something to consider. It was an operational New Zealand Air Force base and had gained the race by order of the Prime Minister of the day in 1949, Peter Fraser. The Air Force management displayed little enthusiasm for this international motor race that disturbed one weekend a year. The race organisers moved in on the Friday evening, laid out the circuit with hay bales and marker drums, ran both practice sessions and the race on the Saturday, and then cleared the airfield so by night it had returned to flying duties.

Bruce's opposition at Wigram included Stuart Lewis-Evans and Roy Salvadori in Connaughts. Salvadori was to be Bruce's Cooper teammate in Europe that summer and Bruce was fascinated by him. 'I really liked Roy. He is the epitome of smoothness and calmness, though his nickname "Smoothadori" did not stem from his prowess in a racing car. The average New Zealand racing driver has six big races a year if he is lucky and regards a spin as a black mark and a shunt of any magnitude as a hint that he should retire. I suppose this was my outlook in the early years and I well remember Roy walking back to the pits after nearly writing off the Connaught and himself as well at Wigram, and saying with disarming nonchalance, "I've bent it…".'

Archie won at Wigram, while Bruce retired with a broken crown-wheel and pinion. The following weekend at the wharf-side Dunedin circuit the McLaren sang-froid looked as though it was unravelling. Bruce crashed twice in two laps during practice but his team repaired the Cooper and he finished second, behind Jensen's 250F Maserati and ahead of Archie's Lister. He was second again to Jensen at Invercargill's Teretonga Park, the southernmost race circuit in the world. Next stop south was Antarctica.

Similar to Zandvoort, the Teretonga circuit was only a year old and the smooth riverbed shingle of the surface was very slippery to the point where Bruce fitted his Cooper with Michelin X tyres on the rear and racing Dunlops on the front. He wondered later whether this was the first time Michelin Xs had been used on a single-seater Formula car.

In fact, Teretonga is where this book of McLaren memories really starts for me. The next event on the McLaren schedule was a loose gravel hill climb at Clellands Hill near my home town of Timaru, then a popular holiday beach town on the coast midway up the east coast of the South Island. I wrote a weekly motoring column and race reports for the *Timaru Herald* and I can still remember the overwhelming diffidence with which I approached Bruce. His sister Pat lived in Timaru and, aware of my interest in racing, used to phone me when she received letters from Bruce. He was my hero and I wasn't quite sure how to start the conversation. I wanted to offer to show him around my home town the following weekend. He was disarmingly affable, a quality that would stay with him throughout his career. I didn't call him Sir and I didn't stand with cap in hand, but that was how I felt until he put me at my ease.

In those days, you could stroll through the pits and talk to the drivers and mechanics. I had a small camera that I carried with me and I snapped everything that looked interesting. To my embarrassment when I look at that early photograph album, I see that I wrote 'McClaren' in the caption. I never did *that* again…

To cope with the loose-metal surface of Clellands Hill, Bruce had locked the differential by filling it with plumber's lead, which worked well enough to break a half-shaft on the second start. It was the first and only time my name appeared in the same programme as Bruce McLaren. I was entered in my mother's Austin A30, which had been fitted with twin carburettors and a straight-through exhaust. There were two cars in my class and the other didn't show up, so I was a class winner. Bruce was beaten by the Stanton Special, a car of heroic proportions with a supercharged air-cooled Gypsy Moth aero-engine fitted amidships. The driver and constructor, Maurie Stanton, sat well forward, almost between the front wheels and held the New Zealand land speed record with this car at 173.8 mph.

That evening Bruce and I went to the Saturday night dance at the Bay Hall beside the beach, in his father's 2.4 Jaguar saloon. This was in the day when any sort of Jaguar, even the small-engined 2.4-litre, was regarded as a motorcar close to Rolls-Royce in local esteem. The girls stood on one side of the hall and the boys congregated on the other side, sometimes nipping out for a sly drink in the car park, a necessity in the days of 6 o'clock closing. Indoors or out, I took pleasure pointing out to my mates that I had beaten Bruce in the hill climb.

Bruce was a handsome young man and he took a fancy to a pretty blonde girl, Pat Broad, who had won a number of local beauty contests and was the class of the evening. He had a dance or two with her and then asked me the form for escorting her home. The idea then was that you requested the last dance and if you were accepted you were first in line to drive the young lady home. Bruce somehow got wrong-footed on this arrangement and Pat told him she had already promised to go on to a party. She had obviously made an impression on the young racing driver because he decided that we would drive the Jaguar around the town in the early hours of the morning to try to find the party. We failed. The next morning he telephoned to ask if I would telephone Pat and ask if it was OK for him to telephone her. Serious stuff. They went for a drive, as one did in those days…and four years later they got married.

But in 1958 there was a final race to run in New Zealand before Bruce left for Britain. It was a national event at Ardmore, which Ross Jensen won yet again, clinching the Gold Star as national champion. Bruce had to stop for a plug change and finished fifth.

Both Bruce and Colin Beanland were to make the trip to England. Bruce was 20 ('And a young 20 at that,' he would recall) and Colin was 22. 'Bruce could probably have managed building the Cooper on his own, but I was asked if I would go over with him and I was delighted to accept,' recalls Colin. 'There are plenty of problems when you start out in racing, especially in a new country, a whole new experience and way of life. There are a million things that go along with racing, even just for someone to push-start the car and show pit signals. The races were short, but it was always good to be kept informed of race progress. Bruce and Les had to buy the new Cooper and money didn't grow on trees in those days. I agreed to buy a car that we could use as general transport and as a tow vehicle to save Bruce that part of the financial commitment. If I'd have gone to England on my own, I'd have still bought a car to run around in, so all it meant was buying something more powerful to tow the race car and trailer.'

The Cooper was shipped to Sydney, where it was loaded on the *Orantes*, an elderly vessel that had been used as a troopship in the First World War. Bruce and Colin flew from Auckland to Sydney, decked out in their black NZIGP blazers — with a fern leaf pocket badge — and natty clothing donated by sponsoring Auckland department stores.

'The publicity began to snowball as departure day drew near, and on 15 March 1958, we were swept out to the airport to be bundled on the plane amid a swarm of photographers, reporters, friends and both our mothers, who cheered us by making a bad attempt to cover up the fact that they were crying…'

The *Orantes* stopped to load cargo in Melbourne, where Bruce received a letter from Pop to say that an entry had been arranged in a Formula 2 Cooper at Aintree on 15 April which meant that Bruce would have to leave the boat at Aden and fly the rest of the way. He was granted permission to go down into the hold, where he spent an hour with the Cooper, removing his tailor-made brake and clutch pedals and his St Christopher medal. Salvadori and Brabham were both longer in the leg than Bruce, so by taking his special pedals he'd save time getting his works car to fit.

In Melbourne they stayed at the elegant family home of popular Australian racing driver, Lex Davison. Over dinner Lex recounted how he'd bought a warehouse for his shoe business and had been told by the contractor that the outside and inside measurements didn't match. They realised that a section of the warehouse had been walled off, so they punched a hole in the brickwork…and discovered two brand-new German 1922 Wanderer rolling chassis, complete except for the bodywork! Lex had an open body put on one and sold the other.

His first sight of Britain in 1958 came as something of a shock to 20-year-old Bruce. 'Everything was vastly different to the pictures I had conjured up, with so many people going everywhere so quickly. Long rows of houses followed each other down narrow streets in the suburbs. Sports cars were everywhere. If someone had an MG TC in Auckland, I usually knew him by name. The owner was an enthusiast and the car usually had a competition history. It was obviously very different in England…'

Jack Brabham met Bruce at the airport and drove him to his home at Dorking. The next day they drove to Surbiton, where Bruce had his first sight of the Cooper Car Company's office, with its distinctive curved frontage. John Cooper showed Bruce around the workshop and when he asked where his car was, John famously pointed to the rack of chassis tubes. 'I couldn't see any car in the pile of chassis tubes, but it slowly dawned on me. I had to build it. I felt very small.'

John Cooper had a robust sense of humour and, having suitably embarrassed his new young driver, he showed him a new, just-completed and freshly painted chassis — the makings of his car. While the car was being built, Bruce was to race the prototype coil-spring Formula 2 Cooper that Brabham had driven to victory at Goodwood the previous weekend. At least that was the plan until Charlie Cooper, John's father, heard about it, and loudly announced that he wasn't making his new racing cars available to any raw colonial who walked into his workshops. John disappeared upstairs to persuade his father to change his mind, and returned with the OK, on condition that Bruce insured the car. It cost £50, but as he received £60 starting money he was in profit before the car had turned a wheel.

The Cooper era in racing started with Charles Newton Cooper, who was born in Paris in October 1893. He was apprenticed to Napiers of Acton straight from school at the age of 15 and spent time working on S.F. Edge's racing Napier. After the First World War he started his own business reconditioning ex-army motorcycles and leased a builder's yard in Ewell Road, Surbiton, registering the property as Cooper's Garage (1920). He married in 1922 and his son John was born in 1923. In the 1930s, Charles competed in long-distance regularity trials, raced Zenith motorcycles and qualified for his pilot's licence. In 1933, the business moved to 243 Ewell Road and it was still there in 1958.

Naturally, John Cooper grew up in a motor-sporting environment and spent time at the nearby Brooklands track. In 1938 he started working with his father, but the Second World War interrupted his apprenticeship and it was 1945 before the father-and-son team got together again. They built a 500 cc car of their own for the newly formed '500 club', in which they used the independent suspension from wrecked Fiat 500s and a 500 cc JAP motorcycle engine in the back, just as Auto Union had done before the war. It would become the Cooper trademark. It took them a mere five weeks to go from concept to reality, with its first competition being a hill climb at Prescott in July 1946. Cooper cars would go on to dominate 500 cc racing with drivers like Stirling Moss and Peter Collins cutting their racing teeth in them. The last Cooper 500 was built in 1959, after 14 progressive different types had been designed.

Mike Hawthorn, driving a front-engined Cooper with a Bristol engine, emerged as a future champion and in 1955 the first Cooper was fitted with a four-cylinder Coventry Climax engine for 1100 cc sports car racing. This motor was originally developed to power a fire pump that could be carried by two men and it proved the perfect lightweight power unit for a small racing car. The Cooper father and son team persuaded the engineers at Coventry Climax to increase the engine's capacity first to 1500 cc for Formula 2 and then up to 2 litres. A further squeeze to 2.2 litres and finally the engine hit 2.5 litres making it suitable for the Grand Prix formula.

Stirling Moss won the first World Championship race in a Cooper-Climax when he drove Rob Walker's privately owned 1.9-litre car in the 1958 Argentine Grand Prix. His tyres were worn close to the canvas, but it was the first of many Cooper Grand Prix victories. Bruce McLaren could be forgiven for thinking that he had arrived in the right place at exactly the right time.

4 Works driver for Cooper

Aintree was something of a surprise for Bruce. He had expected some form of champagne venue, since the circuit was built within the Aintree steeplechase horse-racing track, with its top-hat-and-tails punter reputation. Instead, he found a dreary venue with high, dirty brick walls. The paddock was a revelation for the new boy. 'I felt like a fish out of water coming from circuits in New Zealand where I knew everyone, to Aintree where I didn't know a soul. Every second male sported a handlebar moustache and everyone seemed to have an Oxford accent. If you wanted to find anyone, the best bet was the bar. This shook me. Surely there was a race on and work to be done.'

Alcohol was, and still is, banned in the paddock at New Zealand motor racing circuits during events. Bruce didn't drink but the paddock bar opened his eyes to a different attitude. In the race he finished ninth. Not the result of a future champion, but it was a start. At 8 a.m. the following morning he was at the Cooper workshops, waiting for them to open so that he could begin building his new car.

When Colin Beanland arrived with Bruce's New Zealand Cooper and their tools, the pair moved into a room in the Royal Oak next door to the Cooper factory. Meanwhile, Jack Brabham had been working away in the background on Bruce's behalf. He'd arranged £75 starting money for the International Trophy race at Silverstone on 3 May…and had also put in a word for the young colonials, persuading the landlord of the Royal Oak that they would be reliable room-mates and boarders.

True to his promise, Colin bought a Mk 1 Zephyr to transport the fledgling team and the races came thick and fast. Bruce placed third at Silverstone in the new Formula 2, then shot down to Brands Hatch for a test day, where he broke the lap record. And then spun. 'Big Ginger' Devlin, chief mechanic at the Cooper workshop, had been standing with Colin at the time and he said, 'That mate of yours will either be bloody good or he'll kill himself.' Colin said nothing. The same thing had occurred to him...

During the first Brands Hatch race Bruce was startled to be passed by Ken Tyrrell, driving another Cooper. Tyrrell knew the tight little Kentish track like the back of his hand and was using lower gears and higher revs than McLaren. Bruce collected a second place and a win and Ken Tyrrell would say years later that when Bruce gathered the speed to pass him into Paddock Bend that day, he made the decision to quit being a driver and start his own racing team. 'I didn't even know who the bloke was and he went sailing past me!'

Bruce's first race on the Continent was at the old banked Montlhery circuit near Paris. The track took in one of the bankings plus a road section and there was plenty of advice from the old hands. 'People told me to hold the car high on the banking and dive off the end, but I preferred to let the car find its own line and banking height, so that wasn't affected by either up or down thrust. I finally rejected the advice of the "keep it high" school when I was shown the missing bricks at the top of the banking and the concrete plaque at the bottom, where someone had gone into orbit. I was to be reminded of this incident and poisoned against banked circuits a few months later at Avus.'

As the closing laps sped past, Bruce was in the lead, but then the oil pump hiccupped and he fell back on lower revs to finish third. His car had been taken to France by Harry Pearce in the Tommy Atkins team transporter along with the Atkins' Cooper, which was driven by Ian Burgess.

The drivers had come over together in Burgess' Ford Anglia and after the race they all went out for a bit of a celebration. The quiet little Kiwi who didn't drink was introduced to champagne. Pearce recalled that evening: 'It was Bruce's first European drive and after dinner we were all having a great time. On the way back to the hotel we jammed Bruce in a dustbin. Poor guy. We went back to rescue him but he'd already got himself out of it by rocking the bin till it fell over and he scrambled out.'

The next race was at Reims, the fast open circuit made up of main roads in the champagne country. It was Bruce's first experience of slipstreaming on the long straights of a circuit and to prepare the car they fitted higher compression pistons, disc brakes and a taller windscreen. The continental flair of European races was an eye-opener for the Kiwis. The racing cars were not transported to the track, they were driven on public roads, ducking in and out of the spectator traffic!

During practice for the Grand Prix, Bruce walked down to Gueux, the long, fast right-hander after the pits. 'Fangio was barrelling through on full noise with the 250F Maserati. He tweaked the tail out coming under the Dunlop Bridge and held the drift all the way through the curve. Mike Hawthorn was another spectacular performer in the Ferrari, but though he wasn't lifting his foot through the curve — and only a brave few were game to keep it down all the way — he was working hard at the wheel and did not seem as neat as Fangio.'

During the race, Fangio and Moss diced wheel to wheel, until Fangio's clutch pedal broke. Moss went on to come second to Hawthorn, who refused to lap Fangio after he re-entered the race. Sadly, the Gueux corner would take the life of Ferrari driver Luigi Musso during the race.

Bruce finished seventh behind Henry Taylor in another Cooper, but the highlight of the weekend was the post-race party at Brigitte's Bar, where all the drivers and mechanics gathered. Bruce and Colin had eyes like saucers watching their heroes, like Ferrari drivers Hawthorn and Collins, letting their hair down. There was a small garden at the back of the bar and a tree-climbing competition started. 'Mike was leaning against a tree trunk and looked up, thinking it had started to rain. The audience nearly went hysterical as someone announced from his perch that at last he had peed on Hawthorn from a great height!'

The German Grand Prix on the 14.2-mile Nürburgring was the race that made Bruce McLaren's name and it was a race in which he came close to not making the start. The race was to be run as a combined Formula 1 and Formula 2 event and the entry was over-subscribed. Even John Cooper was having trouble getting entries. He could only get one place in each category, Salvadori in the Formula 1 car and Brabham in the Formula 2. Cooper persuaded Bruce to try to get a place on the reserve list and when he managed this, Tommy Atkins offered him transporter space to take his car over. 'You'll get a start. Someone will shunt in practice for sure,' said Cooper with morbid certainty.

Once again Bruce made the road trip with Ian Burgess in his long-suffering Anglia, which he also drove to learn the circuit. The Nürburgring was built in the 1920s to solve the unemployment problem in the region and famous races had been won there during the 1930s when the Mercedes and Auto Unions battled. Bruce was approaching the 'Ring as just another circuit and another new challenge. 'I had spent hours studying maps of the circuit and couldn't wait to get to grips with it. According to my map there seemed to be only six obviously tricky corners and I fondly imagined I would soon pick up the rest. I hadn't taken into account that the circuit runs round a choice section of the Eifel Mountains and included many vertical hazards not indicated on my map. These made a simple curve, hidden by a hump on the approach, a trap that had to be carefully memorised to avoid breasting the rise at 100 mph getting ready for a right-hand sweep, when the track actually dropped away to the left.'

It was a steep learning curve that had been faced by generations of drivers who had never seen the track, never imagined the enormity of the challenge. The first neverending lap was terrifying. Ian drove Bruce round in the Anglia. 'I had many frights on that first lap, with Ian winding up the Anglia and approaching blind bends at a suicidal rate, only to have them open out in front of us as kinks in the forest. The dips and rises on that long main straight made the overhead bridge at the end seem about three feet above the track. I swallowed hard and closed my eyes…'

When Harry arrived with the transporter, Bruce took the wheel of the Anglia and treated the mechanics to a tour of the circuit. 'The 'Ring was pretty, late in the evening — the long black ribbon of road winding haphazardly through the trees, up hill and down dale, between rustic wooden fences. The long rays of the setting sun shone down through the valleys and glinted on the bonnets of the Ferraris and Porsches, as drivers familiarised themselves with the tricks of the long circuit. A blue Alfa Romeo whistled by — Behra. Then a Porsche Carrera screeched past on the limit into the Wipperman curves — Bonnier. I had covered the circuit eight times before going back to Adenau for dinner and lay awake a long time just thinking about it…'

Graham Hill, in his first season with Lotus, had arrived in his Speedwell-modified Austin A35 and a race was arranged between the Austin and the Anglia. Bruce was allowed a minute start because the Anglia was stock standard, and once out into the country he braked to a halt and tried to hide the car to watch the A35 wail by in vain pursuit, but Graham spotted the ruse and gave them 'the fingers' as he swept past.

Roy Salvadori and John Cooper arrived in a rental Volkswagen and Roy took Bruce, John and Ian for a few laps, describing all the accidents that had happened round the long difficult track. 'Roy described this butcher's tour tonelessly as he held big over-steering slides, while John, Ian and I clung to the seats and privately hoped he would stop next time round.'

By race day Bruce had done 16 practice laps in road cars and with his entry in the Formula 2 section accepted, he took Salvadori's advice and memorised the circuit in sections in preparation for the race. He warmed the Cooper up on the short section around the pits and then set off for his first lap of the main circuit. 'I was swooping down into the sharp right-hander before the Foxhole and I was really getting with it when I suddenly had the funny feeling that something was wrong. As I swung right, the feeling strengthened. There was a sudden shriek of tyres and puffs of rubber smoke and I jerked round to see a Vanwall front wheel almost in my cockpit. My biggest worry was that the wheel was still connected to the Vanwall and connected to the steering wheel of the Vanwall by one hand was an irate Stirling Moss. His other hand, in use as a fist, was being waved violently in my direction and continued to be, all the way down through the Foxhole until I lost sight of the Vanwall tail.'

Bruce made himself scarce in the pits, having been told by Harry that Stirling was looking for him, and that he didn't seem best pleased.

Hawthorn put his works Ferrari on pole position for the 15-lap race, with Vanwall drivers Tony Brooks and Stirling Moss alongside and Collins in the other Ferrari on the outside of the four-wide front row. Bruce was on row four, behind Jean Behra and Harry Schell in the works Formula 1 BRMs. It was his first real Grand Prix. John Cooper had told him to ignore the starter's flag and watch Schell's rear wheels instead. The advice worked. Bruce was fifth into the South Curve with only four Formula 1 cars ahead of him. Salvadori went by in the South Curve and on the first straight behind the pits, the Formula 1 cars started to stream by. When he reached the main straight Bruce could see the race forming in the distance. 'There was a lone green car [Moss in the Vanwall], two or three red Ferraris and Maseratis, a gaggle of green cars [Vanwalls, a BRM and a Cooper] and a BRM was pulling past me. I didn't know who it was, but it was a faster car to follow…'

Moss had taken the lead with Brooks behind him in the other Vanwall, but Hawthorn and Collins passed Brooks by the end of that opening lap. Moss went out on lap four with a magneto problem so Collins led Hawthorn in a Ferrari one-two. Brooks fought back, passing Hawthorn at the end of the tenth lap and Collins on the next, to take the Vanwall into the lead. Collins tried to stay with Brooks but the Ferrari ran wide at the Pflanzgarten, hooked a wheel in a ditch and the car somersaulted. Collins was thrown out into a tree and suffered severe head injuries. He was flown to hospital by helicopter but he did not survive. Hawthorn was lucky to avoid his teammate's crash but failed to complete another lap before retiring with transmission failure. Hawthorn and Collins were close friends as well as teammates.

Back in the race, Colin signalled to Bruce that he was second in the Formula 2 section behind Phil Hill's Ferrari and ahead of Edgar Barth in a Porsche. In a few laps Bruce had closed on Hill. It was Bruce's first Grand Prix and it was also Phil's debut race with Ferrari.

'I was soon on Phil's tail, but although the Ferrari brakes were fading badly, he wasn't giving in without a struggle. He was slamming the car round the circuit, bouncing off the earth verges, but I felt I could pass him and the stones that shot back only added to my determination. At the next corner I ducked through on the inside of the Ferrari and, with one eye on the mirrors, pressed on to widen the gap.'

He kept up the pressure and took the chequered flag to finished fifth overall among the Formula 1 cars and first in the Formula 2 category. As he crossed the line, slipped the Cooper into neutral and relaxed, he became aware that he had a problem. 'When I tried to uncoil my left hand from the steering wheel, I found that I couldn't. It was stiff with cramp from not being shifted during the race.'

Salvadori had come second to score the best finish for the Cooper team in a world championship Grand Prix. John was so delighted that he turned a somersault in the pit lane. 'Huschke von Hanstein, the Porsche team manager, walked up with a large cine camera under his arm and asked John to perform again. John told him he'd do another somersault when I crossed the line ahead of the Porsche. And he did.' There were three Coopers in the first five finishers. Maurice Trintignant was third in Rob Walker's 2.2-litre Cooper and Wolfgang von Trips was fourth in the Ferrari, just 10 seconds ahead of Bruce's car. Bruce shared the top step of the rostrum with Tony Brooks as winners of their respective categories. The British national anthem was played twice, once for Tony and once for Bruce. He had arrived.

The next major Formula 2 race was at Avus — the name stood for *Automobil Verkehrs und Ubungs-Strasse* — near Berlin in Germany, a course built in 1907 as a test track for the motor industry. The original layout of two lightly banked turns linked by a flat-out stretch of motorway, had been altered in 1937, a steeply banked, brick-surfaced 43-degree turn replacing the Nordkurve. After the war half the circuit ended up in Soviet East Germany, so a new unbanked southern loop was added and the circuit shortened to 5.5 miles.

In 1953 John Cooper had won the 500 cc race at Avus driving a special streamlined Cooper — after spinning and stalling in the first corner, then getting out and push-starting his car single-handedly!

Bruce had completed eleven Formula 2 races that summer and finished in every one, but the high-speed Avus circuit had him spooked. There seemed to be an accident every few laps. The cars were packed together in a flat-out slipstreaming group when Ian Burgess's Cooper spun out and somersaulted. Bruce was almost relieved when his engine let go on the back straight with a rod through the side of the block. Ian had broken several vertebrae and a leg so Bruce stayed the rest of the week to make sure he and his wife were organised in the hospital and then he drove the Anglia back to England.

The final Formula 2 race of the season was run with the Formula 1 cars in the Moroccan Grand Prix at Casablanca. Bruce could win the Formula 2 championship if he did well in Casablanca, but there were problems beyond his control. Brabham had been entered in a Formula 1 Cooper, but then he was switched to a Formula 2 entry. It was all political. Jack said he would have preferred to race the Formula 1 car, but John wanted to have two cars to secure the Formula 2 title and said that the decision had come from Esso.

The Formula 1 championship, which could be won by Moss or Hawthorn, hung on this race. Stirling had to win, set the fastest lap and have Mike finish lower than fourth. Moss soon established a good lead in the Vanwall after an early-race tussle with Ferrari's Phil Hill. Hawthorn was running third when Bruce was troubled with a clutch problem. He pitted, but nothing could be done so John sent him out to nurse the car to the finish.

'I was pounding down the back straight when Stuart Lewis-Evans' Vanwall passed. He had just pulled by me when there was a huge puff of smoke from the exhaust, the rear wheels locked and the car slewed sideways. I stood the Cooper almost on its nose in an attempt to stop and Stuart tried very hard to hold the Vanwall, but it spun into the sand and overturned in a clump of trees. A thick pall of smoke hung across the road on the next lap. Stuart died later of burns received in the crash.'

Moss won the Grand Prix but lost his best chance at the title when Hawthorn motored in second and clinched the championship by just one point. Brabham won the Formula 2 championship and Bruce was second, although a miscalculation in the final points led to a wire service story in New Zealand newspapers the next day stating that Bruce had won the title.

The European season was over but McLaren's racing career seemed to be in limbo. Bruce was contracted to race in the 1959 New Zealand Grand Prix in January as part of his Driver to Europe package and also had the option of going back to college in Auckland, but he felt he had proved his potential. He wanted to race. He didn't want to design bridges. He wanted to stay with Cooper and he wanted John to make him an offer he couldn't refuse. All John would say was, 'Don't worry, we'll look after you, boy.'

Not much to build a career around. In my experience, you start worrying when someone says, 'Don't worry…'

5 | Grand Prix driver

The 1959 New Zealand Grand Prix was literally a world championship event shipped south. Stirling Moss drove a 2-litre Rob Walker Cooper. Ron Flockhart had one of the shapely 2.5-litre P25 front-engined BRMs. Harry Schell and Carroll Shelby were in 250F Maseratis, entered by American millionaire Temple Buell. Jo Bonnier had his own 250F. Ross Jensen was the top local driver with a 250F that had an uncertain pedigree, most likely being a rehash of the car Prince Bira had driven to win the 1955 Grand Prix at Ardmore. Jack Brabham had his 2.2-litre Cooper and Bruce had his Cooper, which had been uprated in transmission at the end of the previous season and fitted with a 1960 cc 178-bhp Climax engine.

Flockhart put the BRM on pole for the Grand Prix, but stalled at the start. Moss had broken a half-shaft in his race heat and so started from the back of the grid. By the end of the first lap he was in the lead! Was it a measure of his pace under pressure or the quality of the opposition? Bruce mixed it with the Maseratis until he spun and lost the knob off his gear lever. Subsequently gear-changing was first uncomfortable and then painful, as his glove wore through and his palm became bloodied. Yet the Maseratis stumbled for a variety of reasons and despite a split header tank, Bruce finished third, a lap behind Moss and Brabham.

At Levin the following weekend Bruce won a couple of minor races and then at Wigram, Flockhart and Brabham set the pace in practice. In the race, Bruce finished third, having slowed due to soaring temperatures outside the car and inside the engine. The head gasket had failed.

Bruce won the national race around the streets of the sleepy little South Island town of Waimate on the way south to Teretonga, where once again Brabham and Flockhart were his main rivals. Here, Bruce took victory from the BRM, Brabham having spun late in the race. There was another win in a national race at Ohakea, the airfield circuit near Palmerston North in the North Island. Denis Hulme was a spectator at that race, having come with a view to buying Merv Neil's Formula 2 Cooper, which featured a Climax engine bored out to 2 litres. At the end of the 1958/59 season Bruce sold his Cooper to George Lawton and throughout the following season Denny and George sparred off, both exhibiting the talent that would earn them the 1960 Driver to Europe scholarship on a joint basis.

John Cooper had agreed to give Bruce a works contract for Formula 2 in 1960 and an Esso contract came with it, and although that was a year away, McLaren's mind was made up. He was going back to Surbiton. Phil Kerr was coming, too. Bruce had suggested to Jack Brabham that Phil had the management and accounting skills to help him establish his garage business and he then set about finding accommodation for the pair of them. By the time Phil arrived Bruce had bought Betty Brabham's Morris Minor 1000 to use as 'team transport', Colin Beanland having returned to Auckland after his season in Europe.

Things had changed on the Cooper team. Bruce's Formula 2 drive had turned into a number three drive in the Formula 1 team. Jack had a 2.5-litre Cooper-Climax and there were a pair of 2.2 Coopers for Masten Gregory and Bruce. Bruce's works mechanic was Mike Barney, a tall, quiet Englishman. There was another Mike mechanic on the team — Mike Grohman, who was nicknamed Noddy — so Mike Barney was always known as Big Mike.

Monaco was the first Grand Prix in the 1959 World Championship and Bruce and Phil drove down to it in the Morris Minor. A Morris Minor is regarded now as a modest classic car, but in 1959 Graham Hill, still three years away from his first World Championship, commuted to European races in a tuned Austin A35 the way today's Formula 1 drivers use their executive jets. Bruce's pace through a French village raised *gendarme* whistles. 'We decided it would not be diplomatic to see whether the policeman had been whistling at us,' Bruce recalled in a letter home. 'So we continued with the speedo needle bouncing off the ignition light. Suspicion that the speck magnifying itself in the mirror was a *gendarme* straddling a big BMW motorcycle was confirmed when he arrived alongside and flagged us to the kerb. We put on our best "Who, us officer?" expressions in French, though neither of us knew a word of the language — none that would have been useful in this situation anyway.

'He soon became exasperated with his foreign "catch" and he started writing a ticket for a heavy fine when howling tyres heralded another speedster through the village and an A35 went hurtling past — Graham Hill in a hurry. We managed to convince the cop that our few francs wouldn't cover his fine, so he reconsidered our offence in the light of Graham's performance and decided that we had only broken a fiver's worth of French law. We paid up smartly and hurried after the A35 on the way to Monaco...'

Monaco has always been the jewel in the World Championship crown, the race every driver most wanted to win and flaunt on his resume. The race was first run on the streets of the tiny principality in 1929, when the mysterious English ex-pat William Grover Williams won in a Bugatti. His life ended in the Second World War, when he was shot by the Gestapo for being a member of the French resistance. The original Monaco course was 1.95 miles long and has stayed around that distance over the years despite the changing surroundings, with high-rise apartments replacing old-world grace. If it was suggested as a race venue now, it would be rejected out of hand. With inadequate pits, few run-offs and virtually no safety measures, the only thing this street circuit has in its favour is history. And money. Even from the start, the race attracted the wealthy set and the parties on the yachts in the harbour are legendary.

It was at Monaco in 1959 that Bruce discovered the way the works team pecking order operated. 'I had been given a 2.5-litre car for Monaco and had prepared it myself. When I arrived at the garage, however, I found Jack's special seat in my car, which was polished up and ready to go. My seat was in another car. The first practice session was also my first run with a 2.5-litre motor and the improvement in performance over the 2.2 was startling. I found myself getting wheelspin all the way up the hill to the Casino. Jack stopped practising because of overheating problems and the next day I practised in my own car, now fitted with its 2.2-litre engine. In the third session Jack's engine was still overheating and his brakes were giving him trouble. Masten's 2.5-litre engine was running well, but the American felt Jack would fare better with the good engine and he insisted on a swap. This was done and Jack also borrowed my brakes, so he went to the start with the best bits of all the team cars. Jack had a car in A1 condition, Masten had one with a duff engine, while mine had a good 2.2 engine fitted with SU carburettors.' Jack put his car on the front row of the grid; Masten and Bruce ended up on row five, each with the same qualifying time.

In the race, Bruce found himself between the works BRMs, with Bonnier in front and Schell behind. That situation would not last. On lap nine, Schell tapped the tail of the Cooper and Bruce spun on to the footpath. The car felt odd, so Bruce stopped at the pits for a check and John sent him away to finish with a rear wheel knocked out of line. Jack won his first Grand Prix that afternoon, taking the lap record as well, but by the finish his gearbox was on its last legs, totally bereft of oil. Bruce came fifth, despite his problems.

Next up was the Formula 2 race at Pau, a street circuit not unlike that at Monte Carlo, but rated by Bruce as even tougher than Monaco. Once again Bruce and Phil drove down in the Morris Minor. Having driven Ken Tyrrell's Formula 2 Cooper earlier in the year at Goodwood, Bruce was going to repeat that at Pau. He finished second to local driver Maurice Trintignant, also in a Cooper. Bruce had a lot of respect for Tyrrell: 'I always rated Ken one of the best team managers in the business. He had the ability to size up a situation, technical or psychological, with remarkable common sense.'

After the race he saw a classic example of that technical nous when Tyrrell asked him how many revs he had used off the line. 'I hung my head and admitted that it had been quite a lot. "Five thousand," I said. "Five thousand?" spluttered Ken. "That's a lot? You should have screwed it up to *seven*!" He was right, of course. The 1500 cc Formula 2 engine revved safely around 7000, but the 2.5-litre was fussier and had to be treated more gently.'

Bruce had just experienced his first of the famous Tyrrell 'froth jobs'! However, Ken had taken a shine to the young New Zealander and took him to Zandvoort for the Dutch Grand Prix. Yet the organisers deemed him too inexperienced for their race, so he was relegated to the role of spectator, watching Bonnier score the first Grand Prix win for himself and for BRM. Jack and Masten were second and third.

His first experience of the 24-hour race at Le Mans was in a 2-litre Cooper Monaco with Jim Russell. They lost second gear early on and when Bruce handed over to Jim at 9.30 p.m. it was jumping out of top. Bruce suggested they take it easy and aim to finish, but Jim was all for pressing on and when he hit oil on the fast White House corner the Cooper crashed in flames. Jim was badly burned and was rushed to a local hospital. Dr Frank Faulkner, a British ex-pat paediatrician working in the USA, had allied himself to the Cooper team, and he advised that Jim should be flown to hospital in Britain as soon as possible. Bruce and Frank would go on to become close friends.

The Sunday of the French Grand Prix at Reims was a busy one for Bruce. He drove a 2.5-litre Cooper in the Grand Prix and, soon after that finished, he had to line up in the Formula 2 race, where he was driving Ken Tyrrell's car.

Cooper had built a special streamlined 'sports' body and fitted it to Brabham's chassis, but when he found that the nose was lifting at 190 mph and the handling was decidedly spooky in fast corners, the streamliner was abandoned and Jack returned, relieved, to the normal open-wheeler.

Race day was a scorcher. 'By noon the sun was beating down with such intensity that a spanner lying on the ground for ten minutes was almost too hot to handle.' Before the start the drivers doused themselves with buckets of water. John Cooper advised Bruce to stay out of the slipstreams to avoid overheating the car...and the driver. In the braking area at Thillois, the right-hander at the end of the long straight, the track surface melted and was torn apart by the flying race cars. 'The first few laps were murder. It was impossible to keep clear of the battering hail of pebbles from the lead cars if I was to stay anywhere in the hunt.'

Tony Brooks took an early lead in the works Ferrari and held it to the finish. Jack and Trintignant fought for second place. As Masten chased them on lap seven he was hit by a large stone and pitted, half-dazed, to retire.

'Halfway through the race I tucked in behind Gendebien's Ferrari in ninth place,' recalled Bruce. 'The heat was almost unbearable. My knuckles were being burnt by the hot blast of air coming over the screen. I tried licking them, but it didn't help. It was getting past the hot stage and I began to feel strangely cold. Going through the long fast curve after the pits behind the Ferrari was like walking in a furnace. The heat of the vicious Ferrari exhausts added to my discomfort. I could hardly breathe and was desperately trying to scoop air into the cockpit going down the straight. Jack had punched out his screen in an effort to increase ventilation and Phil Hill was almost standing up in the Ferrari seat on the straight.

'I had to stay on Gendebien's tail to hold my position, but I was taking a fearful battering from flying stones. The mixture of sweat and blood in my goggles was like pink champagne. I raised them and the mess sluiced down over my face.'

His goggles were almost completely shattered by 35 direct hits from flying stones. The lenses were splintered but still intact.

'The chequered flag was never more gratefully received. I climbed out of the cockpit, took off my helmet…and cried my eyes out. I don't know why, but I wept uncontrollably for several minutes. This was the first race Mum and Pop had seen in Europe and they were staggered to see it develop into a bloodbath.' He had finished fifth, just a length behind the Ferrari. Jack had managed third place.

The Formula 2 race started half an hour later and Ken told Bruce to stop if he started to tire. 'I felt on top of the world as we formed up on the grid, but in the opening laps I did things I wouldn't have entertained under normal conditions. I was hanging the tail out through the fast bends, almost as though I had been drunk and unaware of the consequences. Jack had already stopped. After a few more laps, I decided it would be a lot safer sitting on the pit counter, so I pulled in to join him.'

Moss won the Formula 2 race and passed out at the back of the pits after the presentation.

Life was busy for Bruce that summer. In the weekend between the French and British Grands Prix he raced the Tyrrell Formula 2 Cooper to third place at Rouen, his blistered fingers having been taped up at a hospital in Paris.

While Bruce carried his scars from France on his hands, his car still bore the marks of its stone battering come Aintree. Budgets in 1959 did not permit the strip-and-rebuild approach of today's Formula 1 teams.

'Big Mike' Barney was officially appointed Bruce's full-time mechanic at the British Grand Prix — they would work together for the rest of Bruce's life, Mike moving to the McLaren team from Cooper. Jack was fastest in practice and Bruce ended up on the third row, tied on time with Moss in the light green British Racing Partnership P25 front-engined BRM. Moss ran second for much of the race but Bruce took over that spot when Stirling had to pit twice, first for tyres and second for fuel. Bruce was driving the wheels off his Cooper trying to stay ahead of Stirling.

'After a few laps I began to think I might be making a clown of myself in front of Stirling. I saw the pastel BRM nose come alongside the cockpit going into the fast wiggle at Melling Crossing but left my braking a little later than usual and stayed in front. I could see people in the pits getting excited watching our dice. Stirling was braver than I through the flat-out right-hand sweep at Waterways and I tailed him into Anchor Crossing. I got back alongside when he missed a gear going through the tight Cottage loop and, wondering if Stirling was getting annoyed, glanced across.

'To my surprise, Stirling was thoroughly enjoying himself and gave me an encouraging thumbs-up sign. He was driving neatly as always and I tucked in to follow. Our pace hadn't slowed and I made several attempts at passing. Jack was cruising around, well in the lead, but Stirling and I had captured the crowd with our dice, which was lowering the circuit record on nearly every lap. It was finally credited to us both at 93.31 mph.'

They crossed the line side by side with the BRM just ahead in second place. Bruce was deservedly delighted with Stirling's approval. It was a far cry from the German Grand Prix the previous summer when Stirling had been shaking his fist!

The 1959 German Grand Prix was held on the super-fast Avus circuit, with its high, bricked banking. The only hope for the Coopers was to slipstream the Ferraris, which had a huge speed advantage, and Masten was in his element tucked in behind the red cars. 'The drag behind the Ferraris was terrific. Moving sharply across behind the faster car, you could actually feel the Cooper being jerked forward.'

Bruce described the race in a tape he sent back to Auckland. 'During the last couple of practice sessions at Avus, Ferrari got really cagey. If either

Masten, Jack or myself went out to try to tail a Ferrari, as soon as were in the slipstream, out would come the Ferrari team manager with the rampant horse on the flag, waving it vigorously in front of the driver, who would then have to pull over and let us go past down the straight, or pull in to the pit.

'This resulted in many a funny incident when a Ferrari would pull in to the pits, the Cooper would follow and the Ferrari manager, hoping the Cooper was stopping, would immediately wave the Ferrari out again…and the Cooper would promptly go out on the tail of the Ferrari. Masten and I complained that the Ferraris just wouldn't play but Jack had been lucky and had got a tow early on, before Ferrari realised what was happening.

'By 1 p.m. on race day the tyres were pumped up to 40–45 lb and we were gassed up with 16 gallons for the first of the two 150-mile heats. From the start we bumped and nudged wheels, desperate to get into the slipstream of the Ferraris up the next straight. Brabham, Gregory and Bonnier were successful, but the rest of us — Schell, Trintignant, myself and Graham Hill — were left in a little bunch by ourselves. It went on like this for 15 laps or so. Masten and Jack held on to the Ferraris and, in the early laps, Masten was really determined and passed them round the fast right-hander before the banking. The Ferraris couldn't quite take this flat, but Masten could. I suppose you could say that this circuit was made up of speed and guts and Masten had plenty of both.

'Going around the top of the banking was better if you were really in a hurry, as Masten definitely was. Gurney and Phil Hill were doing their best to keep him back. Actually, it was Masten's job to try to push Brooks's Ferrari and perhaps blow him up if possible. About once every lap or so we all changed positions between five and eight. Masten's race ended with a rod through the side, but he had certainly given it a game try.

'The Ferraris had been really trying and they soon started to close on us, having picked up a lap. It became a matter of whether we could get into their slipstream and be towed away, so there was quite a little fight between Schell, Trint and myself. Fortunately, the Ferraris weren't quite as quick out of the hairpin and by getting right on their tail, within a few feet or so, you could get dragged right along the straight. My car by itself could do 6300 rpm down the straight (that was about 170 mph), but behind the Ferraris I could do 6800 and at one stage I managed 7000 rpm, which was around 185 mph! It was certainly worth trying for a tow.

'I managed to hang on and in the last five laps I opened out about 20 seconds on the other group, which gave me fourth position in the first heat and put me on the front row of the grid for the start of the next heat, half an hour later. We only had time for a quick top-up with fuel, and a quick look around the car to make sure that everything was somewhere near right. With Jack and Masten out, we were able to concentrate the whole team effort on my car.

'I made a really good start in the second heat, smoking the tyres for 200 yards and I actually managed to lead halfway down the straight until very near the end, when two of the Ferraris came past, Schell tucked in behind Brooks. Then Hill and Gurney came past in their red cars so I slipped in behind them and got towed past Brooks!

'That left a group of three Ferraris and my Cooper, going away from the field. It looked as though we might be able to keep the Ferraris hurrying for the rest of this heat and Brooks might break, but it was eventually my car that broke. The drop-gears stripped and I cruised to the side of the track. It wasn't the best place to park, as I realised when I saw the three Ferraris coming round the very fast right-hander straight towards me. They were taking it just about flat-out — over 170 mph — in a drift. The three of them nose to tail certainly looked impressive. After that we considered hanging out the stars and stripes to spur on Gurney and Hill so they would wear Brooks out.'

The Cooper team's focus on Brooks was because he looked like being the driver most likely to upset Jack's chances of the championship. However, Jack was taking a bumpy ride towards the title, regardless.

With the Italian Grand Prix running just a fortnight after Portugal, the Cooper team loaded up everything they needed for both races so they wouldn't need to return to Surbiton between times. Brabham's bad luck started as soon as he arrived in Portugal. He nearly lost a toe dragging a boat up the beach and then had his wallet stolen by a pickpocket.

'The Portuguese Grand Prix was run on the Monsanto circuit outside Lisbon and it had cobbles in places! I was fourth behind Stirling, Jack and Masten when we started lapping the tail-enders. Stirling passed local driver Mario de Cabral in a Cooper-Maserati, and he pulled back in behind Moss, not realising that the two works Coopers were on Stirling's tail. Jack was pushed off the road at 120 mph, smashed into a power pole and somersaulted. Mercifully, Jack had been thrown out of the cockpit before the car junked itself.'

Bruce had only seen the wrecked car and was worried that Jack had been hurt. His drop-gears failed again and when he got to the pits he found that Jack was in hospital. 'We visited him and found that he had escaped with bruises, scratches…and very strong views about the inclusion of inexperienced drivers in *Grandes Epreuves*…'

Jack's car was a write-off and when the news reached Surbiton they started building up the spare chassis. Two engines and three gearboxes were flown back to Britain for rebuilds and John eventually set off for Monza with his Zodiac loaded and the car on a trailer behind.

Meanwhile, Masten also returned to the UK to take part in the TT at Goodwood. There he performed one of his celebrated exits over the back of a Tojiero-Jaguar after a brake pipe broke sending him straight on at Woodcote. He ended up in hospital with a broken leg, a broken collarbone and fractured ribs. Suddenly, Bruce was the fittest member of the Cooper team.

'This meant that I had two cars to sort out in practice for the Italian Grand Prix. I never fancy this situation, as inevitably one feels car 'A' would surely be better with 'B's' gearbox, or that 'B's' chassis with the engine, gearbox and brakes from 'A' might be a race-winner.'

At the start of the race Tony Brooks trundled away from the grid with a broken clutch in his Ferrari, leaving Brabham relieved to see the red car at the side of the track.

'Stirling took the leaders away with his Rob Walker Cooper, fitted with wire wheels at the rear in case a tyre change was necessary. Jack was happy to sit in fifth place and I stayed in his slipstream, having trouble with second gear on the slower sections. We were bombing down into the South Curve and I was easing my foot off the throttle when a rod went through the side of the engine with a colossal BANG! With no braking from the dead engine I went into the corner far too fast and, with no sane hope of making it, braked hard and skidded nose-first into the bank.'

Stirling won the race, Phil Hill was second for Ferrari and Jack was third. He still led the chase for the world championship. It all hinged on the final race of the series, the United States Grand Prix, to be held on the Sebring airfield circuit in Florida.

Jack had 31 points, Stirling 25.5 and Brooks 23. If Stirling won and took fastest lap, he would take the title. For Brooks to be champion, he not only had to win and take fastest lap but also needed Brabham and Moss to finish outside of the first three places. Amazingly, there was a three-month gap before the last race of the season. Everyone had to bide their time.

6 Grand Prix winner

The first United States Grand Prix held under World Championship regulations nearly didn't happen. It had been scheduled for early in the 1959 season as the series opener, but was postponed. There were suggestions that the race had in fact been cancelled, but it was eventually relocated as the season finale. It would become the deciding race in the championship.

The race was the brainchild of Alec Ulmann, a Russian-born promoter who saw his first motor-sport event in 1908, when Victor Hemery won the St Petersburg–Moscow race in a Benz. An entrepreneur, Ulmann dealt in war surplus aircraft parts in the late 1940s and his storage facilities included warehouses on the abandoned Hendrick airfield near the retirement township of Sebring in central Florida. The runways and perimeter roads could be turned into a 5.2-mile motor-racing circuit and Ulmann promoted a six-hour sports car race there in 1950, an event that became a 12-hour race in 1952. In 1953 Sebring hosted the first race in the new FIA World Manufacturer's championship, which was won by John Fitch and Phil Walters in an American Cunningham. Wayward cars had to cope with parked aircraft past their fight-by dates — not the usual type of off-circuit hazard.

Briggs Cunningham was a wealthy sportsman who raced yachts in the America's Cup and wanted to campaign American cars in international sports car racing. When Bruce McLaren first met Briggs the magnate was sweeping the floor of the hangar he had rented to the Cooper team for the 1959 Sebring race.

'Briggs, seemingly oblivious of all the excitement with television cameras and cables and lights, was sweeping the floor to give us the cleanest possible working conditions and keeping us supplied with hot coffee and chicken soup. His hospitality was almost unbelievable.'

Bruce was not originally entered for the US Grand Prix, with the works Cooper entries being allocated to Brabham and Gregory. However, Masten was still recovering from his sports car crash injuries so it was decided that as Bruce was on his way home to New Zealand anyway, he should stop off at Sebring. It proved an excellent decision. Masten failed the medical; Bruce got the start.

The main title contenders made the trip over for the Grand Prix and the field was filled out with a collection of American make-weights. Moss had a Rob Walker 2.5-litre Cooper, as did teammate Trintignant. Jack and Bruce had works 2.5-litre Coopers. Ferrari brought a total of four cars over — one each for Tony Brooks, Cliff Allison, Wolfgang von Trips and Phil Hill. Hill's car was painted in white and blue American colours, but it was still an early-model Dino with a twin-cam 2.4-litre V6 and De Dion rear suspension. The other three Ferraris had four-cam engines and all-independent suspension.

Team Lotus had front-engined Type 16 cars for Innes Ireland and Alan Stacey. There were 19 entries including Indianapolis winner Rodger Ward in Bob Wilkie's Leader Card Kurtis speedway midget, powered by a 1.75-litre four-cylinder Offenhauser engine. For the Grand Prix it had been fitted with lever-operated disc brakes all round, a two-speed gearbox and a twin-speed back axle, each with a separate lever. Ward was the reigning American champion and the front-engined speedway car carried race number 1. It was the first time the European Formula 1 cars had been seen in North America and Ward and his fans were confident of success. Until practice started...

John Cooper was amused at the Americans' ambitions and had taken a $20 bet that Rodger wouldn't get within 20 seconds of pole position. Stirling was fastest, with a lap of three minutes exactly. After a variety of problems in practice, Rodger's best was still only 3:43.8 and John won his wager.

The Cooper team was in a measure of disarray during practice. Bruce had the drop gears fail again and Jack had engine problems. It was decided that Jack would drive Bruce's car.

Jack recalled the race lead-up in his 2004 autobiography: 'He [Bruce] put in a couple of laps in what had been my car to see if he wanted to make any adjustments to it. Within half a lap the crown-wheel and pinion broke! I took out what had been his car and found it didn't handle at all well. We checked it that night and found the chassis was twisted. I played around with the suspension to compensate, but next time we ran it the brakes juddered violently. We then checked the gearbox and found its main-shaft was cracked so our spare gearbox had to be fitted. For us, Sebring just seemed to be going from bad to worse...'

Jack and Bruce worked with the mechanics until midnight before the race and Jack's mechanic, Tim Wall, worked through the rest of the night to make sure Bruce's car was ready for the race.

'Next morning I was at the garage early to run the car round the service roads to bed in tyres and brakes and to make sure the cylinder-head bothers were cured.' Bruce was ready for the race that would make his name.

Moss had the Cooper on pole, with Brabham in second and Harry Schell on the outside of the front row. However, Schell's time of 3:05.2 was a bone of some contention, which was still being gnawed on as the grid formed up. Schell had not been timed better than 3:11.2 by other team watches and the outside spot on the grid was reckoned to have been earned by Brooks in the Ferrari. But Harry had been born in Paris to American parents and it looked like being the best way — the *only* way — of placing an American prominently in the race, so Brooks was relegated to the inside of the second row beside Trintignant's Walker Cooper, but more importantly in the outcome of the race, directly in front of von Trips.

Row three was all Ferrari: Trips, Allison and Hill. Row four was made up of Innes Ireland (3:08.2) in the Lotus 16 and Bruce in Jack's hand-me-down Cooper (3:08.6).

'When the flag fell I made my best-ever start,' Bruce wrote in *From the Cockpit*. 'The car left the fourth row like a rocket and at the first corner, if memory serves me right, I went in side by side with Moss. Discretion being the better part of valour, I let Stirling through and followed him closely with Jack snapping at my exhaust.'

Early-race twitches undoubtedly played a part in Trips accidentally running into the tail of Brooks on the opening lap. Moss was in the lead and so had the best chance at the title, but Brooks was concerned about the possible damage to the back of his car and made a precautionary pit stop. The nose on Trips' Ferrari was stoved in, but the German continued. It seems in retrospect that Brooks' Catholicism could have cost him the championship. Recalling the event many years later, Tony said, 'I always felt it was morally wrong to take unnecessary risk with one's life because I believe that life is a gift from God and that suicide is morally unacceptable. I suppose there are those who would say that driving racing cars at all is an unnecessary risk, but I wouldn't agree with that. However, driving one which may be unsound or damaged, while not exactly suicide, is verging towards it...'

By the fifth lap Moss was nearly 10 seconds clear of Brabham. A lap later and Stirling was out, parked at the side of the track with a broken Colotti gearbox. Another championship lost.

'Jack's championship was now in the bag and he gave me a thumbs-up wave as we settled down to some careful but quick motoring,' recalled Bruce. 'In the closing laps a new challenge emerged as Trintignant started to close on Bruce at the rate of around a second a lap. Bruce maintained he couldn't have gone much faster although if Jack had upped the pace he could have towed Bruce clear. With two laps to go Bruce's pit board showed Trintignant six seconds behind. Just as Bruce began to wish Jack would speed up, Brabham suddenly slowed and waved Bruce past. 'I was staggered and looked across at him in utter dismay. I'd slowed right down, so I picked second gear, thinking that as Trint wasn't too far away, I'd better get on with it.'

Jack had lost the race but he had won the championship. He had run out of fuel though the reason for this would never be clear. Bruce reckoned Jack had made a last-minute change, going slightly smaller on choke-tube size. 'This made his engine run a little bit richer and the fact that he had been towing me in his slipstream helped to save my fuel…and exhaust his. Moss had gone down 2 millimetres on choke tubes in practice and found a considerable improvement. Jack had spotted this by looking at Moss's carbs and changed his accordingly. Probably Moss would have run out of fuel as well had he lasted the distance, as the tanks on both Coopers were presumably the same size.'

On the other hand, Jack reckoned that John Cooper had miscalculated the number of fuel churns put into his car before the start. Sir Jack told me recently: 'They argued for years over how many churns went into my car because I think John lost count and I went out with one churn too few…'

As Bruce took the chequered flag, Jack pushed his car towards the line. John Cooper did his victory somersault…and then realised that it was the wrong car! But it was a Cooper win nonetheless. It was not the plan, but they had won the race and the title. At 22, Bruce was the youngest-ever Grand Prix winner, a record he held until 2003 when Fernando Alonso won the Hungarian Grand Prix.

Trintignant shadowed the works car to the flag, taking second place just under a second behind Bruce, having set a new lap record at 101.13 mph in his hectic pursuit, three laps from the finish. Tony Brooks was third and

Jack salvaged fourth, collapsing as he pushed his car over the line.

It was the race that Brooks had had to win to take the title, but the manipulation of Schell's grid time had left Tony an inadvertent target for Trips on that fateful first lap. While I was writing this book I had a letter from Tony, recalling that day. 'It was Bruce's first Grand Prix win, which was marvellous…but why did he have to choose *this* one!'

Part of Bruce's victory spoils included a victory wreath of green leaves and golden kumquats…and a lengthy kiss from Miss Sebring Grand Prix. In a caravan behind the press stand John Cooper commiserated with Jack while the journalists clamoured for interviews: 'I'm sorry, Jack. It was full up you know, just like Bruce's car and he had four gallons left. You must have sprung a leak…' Then Cooper yelled for his winner. 'Where's Bruce? Where's the bloody Kiwi gone? Can't somebody get him away from Miss Sebring? Get him in here!'

Rene Dreyfus, winner of the 1930 Monaco Grand Prix, interviewed Jack for a French radio station. *'Parlez-vous Francais?'* Rene asked Jack. Jack, uncertain what he'd been asked in the heat of the moment, said, 'Thanks very much.' The interview continued in English…

John Cooper shouted once more. 'Someone tell Bruce to put that woman down and come over here!' Bruce finally arrived, shook Jack's hand and said, 'Great, Jack! Thanks for the tow….When you slowed down I wondered what was up. I thought maybe you were planning a grandstand finish with both of us going over the line together, but I had Trint on my tail. And no, I didn't think of getting out and giving you a push!'

7 Grand Prix winner — again!

Bruce flew back to New Zealand after his Sebring win, to find out that he was no longer classed as a Kiwi for his home Grand Prix at Ardmore on 9 January. He was an 'overseas driver'. 'Our negotiations are with the Cooper Car Company, not McLaren,' said Reg Grierson, chairman of the New Zealand Grand Prix Organisation's rules and race committee, in the *New Zealand Herald*. 'We have paid them £3000 to send two cars, which Jack Brabham and McLaren will drive. McLaren will not be driving as a New Zealander — he will be driving for an English entrant.' Pop McLaren was quoted as saying the race organisers evidently thought his son had a split personality… 'Bruce will receive £500 to race at Ardmore after Coopers take their share. That means he will have nothing left after he has paid his return air fare from England. It is obviously going to cost Bruce money to race here…'

Moss, Brabham and Bruce had 2.5-litre Coopers for the New Zealand races, David Piper had one of the elegant but fragile front-engined Lotus 16s and Ian Burgess a 2.2 Cooper. Jack had to start the Grand Prix from the back row after a fire during the race heat and it was Bruce who led the race from flag-fall, heading Moss in the Yeoman Credit Cooper. But Jack was soon through the field — Bruce led the first three laps before Stirling moved ahead and a lap later Brabham was in front! Moss and Brabham disputed the lead until Stirling's transmission broke. Jack and Bruce then took over the race and they finished one-two, with Bruce a mere 0.6 seconds behind Brabham.

A fortnight later at Wigram the 2.5-litre Climax engine in Bruce's car wrecked itself in practice, when a rod snapped and came through the side of the block. Malcolm Gill stepped in and loaned Bruce his aero-engined Lycoming Special. This was a famous New Zealand car, built in Auckland by Ralph Watson in 1954, powered by an air-cooled four-cylinder 4.7-litre engine turned upside down in the chassis, dry-sumped and fitted with fuel injection. Bruce had not driven the front-engined Special before the race started, but he soon came to grips with it.

'To be sitting bolt upright near the back wheels with the engine in the front was a novel change from the Coopers and an interesting experience. I only had to change gear a couple of times a lap. The torque from the flat-four engine from 1000 to just under 3000 rpm was fantastic and there weren't many cars to match me on acceleration.' The rev counter failed and the brakes faded during the race, but Bruce still finished fourth, close behind Burgess's Cooper. Jack won from Piper's Lotus. As a thank you for the loan of his car, Bruce sent Gill a set of disc brakes out from England for the Lycoming.

In the Ecclestone era of Formula 1, when cars and equipment are sent around the world in Boeings, it is difficult to imagine the problems involved with getting the Coopers back to Britain from Sebring and then out to Buenos Aires for the Argentine Grand Prix the following February. Andrew Ferguson, who handled the Cooper team's affairs before moving to Lotus, wrote of the problems. 'The ship carrying our cars back from Sebring was eventually delayed for over a week, the arrival coinciding with the London Dock dispute involving the gentlemen who were to unload the cars. The captain of the American freighter took matters into his own hands and made the perilous journey up-river to the dock-side on his own judgement. Unfortunately he chose the dock concerning itself with meat imports and another dispute arose. After countless telephone calls to labour-gang chiefs and Union officials, permission was received to unload the crates into barges and thence to the dock side. The cars were found, after tunnelling through four thousand tons of lard, and after another day of waiting the crates arrived at Surbiton in thick fog. The delays involved left us with only six days to prepare the cars and re-crate them for Argentina. The engines were sent to Coventry-Climax, stripped and rebuilt in commendably short time, cars re-assembled, re-crated and sent back to the docks.

'Again we struck trouble. On warming-up the ship's engines, one threw a rod and only continuous work by the Blue Star shipping people over three days, saved the situation. Departure time for the *Scottish Star* finally arrived and the ship sailed full steam for Buenos Aires. More engine trouble followed, the Argentine dockers went on strike and the ship was finally towed into dock by a vessel manned by the Argentine army. Final arrival at the track was just half an hour before the end of Grand Prix practice. Between times, the Argentine Post Office had also been on a five-week strike and all cables and letters with information regarding the Grand Prix had been lost. Argentine Airlines also went on strike and the team personnel eventually arrived by a variety of means.'

Bruce had his own travel problems getting from Auckland to Argentina. 'Having flown for nearly two days on a Super Constellation, I arrived in New York to find that my Comet flight south with an Argentine airline had been cancelled and I had just missed a PanAm Boeing. It took me half a day to get the Argentine airline to let me have my ticket and I finished up pounding down to Buenos Aires in a Douglas DC3, another vintage piston-engined aircraft. This took a further 36 hours and I arrived in the Argentine capital two days late…and a physical wreck. I slept for 20 hours.'

The chaos caused by the various strikes meant that Bruce could not find out where the Cooper team was staying. And the cars still had not arrived. 'By Friday night the boat still wasn't in port. It hadn't arrived by Saturday morning. By midday there was still no sign of it, not by 2 p.m. or even 3 p.m. John and the mechanics were out at the mouth of the River

Plate peering at the horizon and willing the boat to appear. It eventually did and they kept pace with it along the river road to the docks, watching the ship's cranes lifting the crated cars out of the holds. While the ship was still berthing the wharf cranes were swinging over to drop the crates on waiting trucks.

'By seven o'clock the still-crated cars were being unloaded at the circuit 20 miles away. There was frantic activity as they were rolled out, numbers went on, petrol in, water, the brake discs cleaned of grease and, with only a few minutes of light left, Jack and I set off on a dozen laps to find out which way the circuit went. On race morning there was a little more practice, but it was only a warm-up just before the race, so we could only scrub tyres, bed brakes and hope...'

In fact, Stirling Moss had loaned his Walker Cooper to Jack for a few laps while they'd waited for the works cars to arrive. Ferguson noted that Bruce had contented himself with a two-hour walk round the circuit...only to find out later that he had been walking around the motorcycle circuit!

An important works Cooper accessory was added to each car for this race — a Thermos of ice-cold orange juice, complete with long rubber feeding pipe, was tied to the bolts mounting the windscreen. It was 110°F as the cars lined up on the grid.

The biggest cloud on the Cooper horizon in South America was the new Lotus 18, a boxy, purposeful rear-engined design that replaced the front-engined Type 16s. Other threats included BRM, which had brought two front-engined cars for team leader Jo Bonnier, and either Graham Hill or Dan Gurney. The latter pair flipped a coin for the drive and Hill won; it was his first BRM drive. Also in the field were the Ferraris of Cliff Allison, Wolfgang von Trips and the veteran Froilan Gonzales, the Argentine driver who had won the first World Championship Grand Prix for Ferrari at Silverstone in 1951. This Grand Prix would be his last.

It initially looked as though the Coopers were being out-Coopered by

Colin Chapman: Innes Ireland qualified the new Lotus second to Stirling and led the race until he spun. Brabham retired with a broken gearbox, Moss followed with a broken wishbone and the BRMs did likewise with engine troubles, although Bonnier had been leading in the closing laps before his engine failed. Stirling took over Trintignant's Cooper when the French driver stopped, suffering from heat exhaustion.

Bruce, who had qualified in mid-grid mainly because of his lack of track knowledge, initially found it difficult to keep pace with local driver, sportsman and polo player, Carlos Menditeguy, in a Cooper-Maserati.

The blazing heat was affecting everyone in the race and Bruce was thankful for the iced orange juice in the Thermos until he became aware that, if he sipped too much at a time, he got 'high' and took risks beyond his normal reach. As the race unwound he realised that the drink tube had slipped from its anchorage, but as he groped around for it on the floor of the cockpit, desperate for another drink, he saw that the Cooper signal board showed FIRST and the team was waving him on. Allison's Ferrari was only eight seconds behind and this was encouragement enough to make him forget his orange juice fix and press on to open the leading gap to 26 seconds by the time the chequered flag came out. The shared Walker Cooper of Trintignant and Moss crossed the line in third.

On his slowing-down lap Bruce became aware that he had a painful blister on his right foot caused by the heat of the brake pedal and the need to press it so hard in the rough-surfaced braking areas. He also had blisters on the palms of his hands, caused by the vibration of the steering wheel.

'As I rolled the car into the pits, I thought I had found a riot. There were spectators fighting, police struggling with them, officials pushing, cameras shoved in my face, people screaming. I was dragged into the grandstand. I tried to walk but my feet weren't touching the ground — I was being propelled by three burly, sweating Argentinian policemen on each arm. Down in South America, they don't just show enthusiasm — they go mad!

'Soon it was all over bar the shouting and even that was dying away. We had been lucky and we knew it, but we had learnt two things: no matter how impossible things seem to be, keep trying...and that we had to get quickly down to work with our new Coopers. The BRMs had out-cornered us, Lotus had the edge on acceleration and the Ferraris weren't too far behind, but we had a championship start on them and we were going to try and use it to our advantage.'

Their South American Temporada sojourn ended with a chaotic race in Cordoba, run in even hotter conditions than the Grand Prix. Bruce sent a letter to Pop detailing the event. Transport yourself back to South America in 1960 and experience the chaos first-hand from the driver who had won the opening race in Buenos Aires:

'We're off to Cordoba, 500 miles away, and what a performance getting the cars on the transporter. A couple of "Arabs" turned up with these big trucks and that's all. No ropes, no chocks, nothing. They were just going to push the Coopers inside and close the doors. After smashing three phones, John Cooper eventually got through to the Automobile Club, but nobody spoke English. Another smashed phone. After about six hours, enough rope was found to tie our cars in, in a rough fashion and I believe they've just arrived. The truck with the BRMs hasn't, though. It has disappeared somewhere.

'This place [Cordoba] is even hotter than Buenos Aires. The circuit is apparently like a quarry road and spectator control is even worse than in Buenos Aires. John said, "One lap practice, one lap in the race...and we should have gone home three days ago anyway..." We had a reasonable flight down here, but only because Fangio was with us and acted as courier. Last night we had a barbecue at a villa in the country. It was wonderful, eating chicken in the balmy evening air...until we found out what we were eating! Don't ask. There must have been at least 200 guests. Today we are trying to get a hire car and go and find a swimming pool.

'In fact, we didn't go for a swim — we had a look at the circuit instead. John had complete failure of all his faculties, but Jack and I didn't think it was *too* bad. Practice was interesting. I only did a few laps but it was obvious a lot of cars would be broken. Fangio did a few laps, in the Formula 2 Porsche and then hopped into a Maser [250F Maserati]. For the first time ever, Brabbo was sorry he couldn't speak the language. Fangio lost the Maser in the biggest possible way, bent all the wheels and nearly hurt himself. Jack just couldn't do a thing about it — if only he could have spoken the language to commiserate with Fangio. Gonzales was there, thrashing around in his Chevy-engined Ferrari Special, but it wasn't going at all well and he was just there to watch.

'Sunday was hotter than ever. We had tubes carrying air into the cockpits and scoops for our feet, but still we were getting hot and it was just plain unpleasant. The start was pure comic relief. Three minutes, 2 minutes, 1 minute, 30 seconds…flag up and down all in the space of a minute at the outside! I got a good start and arrived at the first corner with Jack. I'd been on the second row due to only a few laps of practice. On the first lap round John Cooper thought the rest of the field had stopped. Jack and I had such a lead and then for about 12 laps we really got down to it. Then the rot set in. It got so hot that my carburation went right off — too rich — then I realised I had forgotten to put my gloves on to save my hands. Then when I entered a corner a bit off line after lapping Harry Schell I used a very non-standard part of the circuit and shifted a straw bale in the process. The bottom pipe of the oil radiator was broken by the nose moving back a little bit, and when the engine started to overheat I was very glad to stop at the pits. Gurney in the BRM was starting to motor by now and was getting very close to Jack…and then Jack stopped with the fuel pump vapour locked and the tanks were too hot to touch. Bonnier stopped — no brakes. Gurney stopped — gear lever broken off! And just as John had prophesied early in the morning, Trintignant came in an easy winner.

'It was an object lesson, really. Still, it wasn't a world championship race and as I got a couple of trophies for making fastest lap, I was very happy. We also felt that it was good practice for Monaco and the cars weren't as slow as we had feared. The rear-engined Lotus broke transmission parts both in practice and in the race. Now comes the drama to get the cars back to the UK. The transporters were promised faithfully for 7 p.m. Sunday evening and still weren't there at 11 a.m. the following morning. Our plane to Buenos Aires was three hours late. Still, it's too hot to worry...'

Bruce went back to Surbiton in March as the leader of the 1960 World Championship and looking forward to the new 'lowline' Cooper that had been designed by Owen 'The Beard' Maddock. Owen operated alone in the drawing office, assisted on occasion by Bruce. 'I drew wishbone assemblies, suspension units and components, so that manufacture could start as soon as possible,' noted Bruce.

Cooper Car Company design blueprints carrying the 'B. McL' initials still exist. In fact it was Bruce who made up both prototype frames; mechanics Mike Grohman and Mike Barney completed the two cars between them.

After the team's endless troubles with gearboxes, Maddock had spent five months designing a completely new five-speed box to be built by Jack Knight's transmission company at Battersea. Stirling Moss had despaired of the Cooper gearbox breakages and had switched to the Italian Colotti transmission for the Rob Walker Cooper...and had even *more* problems!

There was an unscheduled delay when Maddock was involved in an air crash — or as Andrew Ferguson described it, 'At the most crucial time, Owen elected to spread himself over the Hythe-Lympne road in a failed take-off attempt in a glider, and at one stage the situation with the new Cooper seemed decidedly awkward...'

Bruce and Jack were directly involved in the building of the new cars. 'Jack would spend a few hours each day perusing the new drawings and putting forward ideas, while John Cooper, his pockets full of scraps of paper with figures and sketches heavily underlined, was phoning or calling on all the engineering and component manufacturers who were supplying and helping us.'

Charlie Cooper must have felt that his team was being taken away from him, as he issued a patriarchal decree that the new cars must be designed so that the original Cooper leaf springs could be re-fitted if — and the way he said it, he meant *when* — the 'new-fangled' coil springs did not work.

'We quickly assured him that this had been kept in mind all the time.'

Charles insisted that only one car be built, but the drivers were aware that the first car would be ready only just in time for the International Trophy race at Silverstone anyway, and then Monaco would be immediately upon them. As insurance, Bruce built a second car for himself in secret!

The new Coopers would dominate the 1960 World Championship, yet they were built by the drivers and just two mechanics. Forty-five years later the modern McLaren organisation employs 900 souls with the object of fielding two cars in Grand Prix racing. It is fitting, then, that the mighty McLaren empire is headed today by Ron Dennis, who started his racing career as a mechanic with the Cooper team.

8 The summer of '60

The first of the new 'lowline' Coopers was taken to Silverstone for secret tests and Jack and Bruce came back well pleased with the potential, both having knocked six seconds off their best lap times round the airfield circuit! A week later they were back at Silverstone, this time with the press invited, and they ran 90 trouble-free laps. They looked like sure-fire winners of the non-title International Trophy.

Practice, though, did not bode well for Bruce. It was teeming with rain. It was also Friday the thirteenth. And he had left his good-luck greenstone Maori tiki at home. Ireland, Surtees and Stacey all had minor accidents in the rain. Bruce's new car had still not arrived, so he did a few cautious laps in his 1959 car. In the last ten minutes of practice the rain eased. Harry Schell, driving a Yeoman Credit Cooper, was trying hard when the car got away from him at Abbey Curve, the fastest corner on the circuit, crashed heavily and 'Arree was killed. The remainder of the session was cancelled as a mark of respect for the popular driver.

Bruce's new car finally arrived late on the night before the race, so he took it easy off the start but then had to stop mid race to cure a throttle problem. The Lotus writing was well and truly on the wall when Innes won in the new Lotus 18 and set the fastest lap. Jack came second. To add insult to injury as far as Charles Cooper was concerned, Rob Walker bought one of the new Lotuses for Stirling Moss, who promptly popped it on pole for the Monaco Grand Prix.

At Monaco only 16 cars were allowed to start and more than 20 had entered so qualifying was a bit of a pressure cooker. Both Coopers were adjusted for the street circuit — the seat-backs were raised and moved forward three inches and the steering wheel was moved forward.

Bruce battled with reluctant carburation on the first day and worked on the fuel system overnight to such effect that he came out of the Gasworks hairpin with the wheels spinning and slid sideways into a kerb, breaking a wheel. He eventually got down to a time that would have put him sixth on the grid but the timekeepers had missed it. Saturday evening practice suddenly gathered importance. In fact, it was Bruce who brought the session to a halt — and almost cancelled his chances of getting into the race — when his gearbox oil bung dropped off and spread oil all round the track.

'Not only did we stop practice — we stopped French television as well! The cameras were trained on activities in our pit and a telephoto lens zoomed in, bringing viewers face to face with John, who was red in the face and telling the mechanic in words loud and clear what a quaint thing it was, not to wire the gearbox plug and what an unusual sort of chappy he found the mechanic to be. Only he didn't say "quaint" and he didn't say "unusual" and he didn't say "chappy". French viewers had their English vocabularies enlarged by three words that afternoon…'

A total of 19 cars had qualified under 1:40.0 and Trintignant, Gregory, Halford, Surtees, Ireland and Stacey still had to make the grid. Bruce once more managed 1:39.1 and incredibly the timekeepers missed it *again!* The announcer said that Bruce was sixteenth fastest on 1:39.2 and that Trintignant had done 1:39.1. Thinking he was safely qualified, Bruce had had his car fuelled up to test its race handling. Suddenly he had to charge out again with the worst of all options to try to make the grid. He recorded 1:39.0 as the flag came out and was classified as twentieth. It looked like being a long Sunday for Bruce…until the timekeepers managed to discover one of his 1:38.6 laps and he was promoted to eleventh.

But the drama didn't stop there. There was a problem with the braking system on Bruce's car that only manifested itself at the last moment. 'By now we had the car on the grid, but the nose was off, the tail was off, the gearbox was in pieces and the brakes were stuck on. John and Charles were demoralised, but I didn't mind too much. Sometimes a last-minute panic is a good thing. I knew our boys would get it sorted and it was just the frame of mind in which to start a race.'

Moss led from pole for the first 30 laps, but then it started to rain and Jack moved ahead…until he spun backwards into a kerb, broke the rear anti-roll bar and twisted the chassis. Meanwhile, Bruce had worked his way up to third place after a wheel-banging dice with Phil Hill's Ferrari, but then his Cooper also spun just beyond Ste Devote, ending up facing the wrong way on the footpath where Jack was surveying his bent car. Jack supervised Bruce's re-entry into the race and then decided that he might as well rejoin too, since there were so few cars running. Bruce spun again when his goggles misted up. 'I was having trouble with my goggles and could see only with my right eye, as the other lens was completely steamed up. By then it was really slippery. Twice I came to a stop on the hairpins, completely sideways with full opposite lock on to try and stop the car spinning. I once scared Phil Hill by blasting out of the tunnel at 110 mph on the footpath! Come to think of it, I don't suppose Phil was the only one frightened. I seem to remember three marshals leaping the sea wall to dodge the Cooper. One magazine report said I left the tunnel backwards — but this wasn't quite true…it was only sideways!'

Stirling won the race, the first Grand Prix victory for Lotus. Bruce finished second and still led the World Championship from Moss and Cliff Allison, who'd suffered a huge accident in his Ferrari during practice that put him out for the rest of the season.

The Dutch Grand Prix at Zandvoort followed a week after Monaco, which meant three Formula 1 races on three successive weekends and after Monaco the Cooper team had a very bent car to fix.

The mechanics had a race of their own between Monaco and Zandvoort. The trailer unhitched itself somewhere in France and it was several miles before they realised it was no longer following the transporter. Fortunately, the rig had stayed upright and the car was undamaged. When Jack's Cooper finally reached Surbiton Mike Grohman worked round the clock to right it, but the comedy of errors continued when heavy holiday weekend freight plane bookings meant that Mike and the Zodiac had to go to Ostend on one flight and the racing car and trailer on another flight an hour later. 'Mike boarded the Ostend flight and was rather surprised to arrive at Calais,' Andrew Ferguson noted in the team report. 'Luckily he decided to return to Southend rather than drive to Ostend and wait for the trailer's arrival. On return to Southend he found that the trailer had been pushed into the car park and completely forgotten. After hectic panic, both car and trailer were reloaded and deposited at Southend. Mike was at Zandvoort by 9.30 a.m. on the Saturday, just half an hour before the first practice session began.'

A year earlier Bruce had been denied entry at Zandvoort because he was an unknown. In 1960 he came to Holland as the leader of the World Championship!

Jack started from the centre of the front row with Lotuses either side, Stirling on pole in the Walker car and Innes third fastest in the works car. Jim Clark made his Formula 1 debut with Lotus and qualified eleventh, two places behind Bruce. In the race, Bruce had climbed to third when a universal cross-joint broke. Jim retired with transmission trouble. Jack, leading Stirling, clipped a kerb, dislodging a kerbstone that flew back and hit the Moss Lotus, bursting a front tyre. 'He seemed to think I'd done it on purpose,' Jack said later. Brabham went on to win his first Grand Prix of the season and move into third place in the title hunt, with 8 points. Bruce (14 points) still led from Moss on 11.

The next race was on the fast, open Spa-Francorchamps road course in Belgium, where average lap speeds hit 130 mph.

This was a black weekend for Formula 1, and it started during practice. Bruce was coming down from La Source Hairpin before the pits and spotted Stirling heading out for some more practice laps. 'I jumped at the opportunity to follow him and learn more about the circuit. I sat in behind as he accelerated up the hill, up through the woods to the long left-hander before the plunge down to Burnenville corner. He left me going down the hill and opened a gap of a hundred yards or so. We swung into the long right-hand curve made blind by farm houses immediately beside the road. I had a strange feeling something was wrong and backed off a fraction. Just as well. I was shattered to see Moss's Lotus spinning wildly on the road in front of me. It hit the left side of the road, rocketing across to the right and bounced wildly in the air. There was so much dust that I lost sight of the car. I was hard on the brakes and slid to a stop as the Lotus came to rest.

'At first I thought Stirling was still in the cockpit and, well aware of the ghastly risk of fire, raced back to the wrecked car. To my amazement it was empty! Stirling was lying in a patch of soft bracken where the car hit the left-hand side of the road. He was having trouble getting his breath, so I loosened his helmet and overalls. Stirling was asked for artificial respiration, but with the thought of possible internal injuries, I persuaded him to lie back and keep his mouth open until his breath came back. I felt sure he was only winded. The only thing I had forgotten was that he had false teeth and might have swallowed them. Fortunately he didn't.

'Within a couple of minutes we had virtually the entire field of 15 cars lined up on the side of the road, each driver having recognised the broken blue Lotus. We were worried at first as we had no idea how bad Stirling was, but we found blankets and pillows and were able to make him comfortable and warm. He was conscious and talking, concerned about what he might have broken.

'We assured him his arms and legs were all there and he looked just fine. But why wasn't there an ambulance? We had been waiting ten minutes and it was a further ten before the ambulances finally arrived.' Stirling had broken his back, both legs and his pelvis. But not his spirit. Incredibly, he was back racing just two months later.

At Spa, disaster followed disaster. When he stopped at the site of Stirling's accident, Michael Taylor had been despatched to the pits to fetch aid, but before he got there, the steering failed on his Lotus and it plunged off into the trees. At the pits, no one knew Taylor had crashed; they just assumed he was among the drivers stopped at Stirling's crash. Taylor was badly injured and never raced again.

In the race, things got worse. Bruce had qualified back on the fifth row, but Jack was on pole and led from the start. Early in the race Chris Bristow's Cooper went out of control at around 140 mph at the corner where Moss had crashed the day before. 'As I flashed past I knew it was a Yeoman Credit car, which meant it was either Brooks or Bristow and I knew it was bad. In fact, I knew it was as bad as it could be. As I went past an ambulance man pulled a blanket over the driver,' recalled Bruce.

'Within a quarter of an hour there were two huge black lines 200 yards further down the track leading off into a bushy area on the right. On the next lap the whole area was a bonfire...'

As the race wore on Bruce was caught in a battle with Graham Hill's BRM and Gendebien's Cooper when a piece of rubber matting glued to the undertray of the cockpit came adrift and worked its way in among the pedals. Bruce had no choice but to slow down, retrieve the matting and throw it out. It meant he lost touch with the other two — but Spa took care of them both. The Belgian Gendebien retired with a broken gearbox, and Hill with piston failure.

Bruce finished second to Jack, and both drivers were concerned to find out who had crashed. 'This was one of the worst things about Alan Stacey's accident. We had no idea who it was. For all I knew at the time, it might have been Jack, and vice versa. A priest who was first on the scene said he found the remains of a bird splattered over Alan's goggles. Something like this is easier to reconcile, on the basis adopted by the Battle of Britain pilots. If your number was up, that was it and there was little you could do about it. It's just a pity that the penalty for a misjudgement or a mistake on the part of any member of the team — whether a designer who draws a faulty part, a mechanic who assembles it poorly, or a driver who overdoes it or drops concentration — can be so final.'

Bruce still led the championship as the teams headed into champagne country for the French Grand Prix at Reims. As additional encouragement for pace, the organisers were offering 100 bottles of champagne to the fastest man on each practice day. Brabham's Cooper was in flying form and he had 200 bottles after the first two days. He was all for cranking up the speed on the Saturday, but John Cooper decided they were amply loaded with bubbly and they should save their pace for the race.

Team Lotus made history of a kind by fielding an all-Scottish team: Innes Ireland, Jim Clark and Ron Flockhart. Lance Reventlow had a pair of the striking-looking front-engined Scarabs for Richie Ginther and Chuck Daigh, but they wrecked the engines in practice so the cars were shipped back to California.

Jack had a race-long slipstreaming battle with Phil Hill's big front-engined Ferrari and came out the winner, while Bruce finished third after another long race with Gendebien that saw his temperatures climbing off the clock. Cooper cars took all four top spots and Jack's race average speed of 135.05 mph was faster than the previous lap record!

Andrew Ferguson noted that for the summer of 1960 the team had ten 2.5-litre FPF four-cylinder Coventry-Climax engines at their disposal, five of which were as used in 1959. Their practice was to return two engines for servicing after each race, and take four engines to the race.

'At this time the Cooper flag was flying high. It seemed as though there wasn't another car to compete with them. By driving my car steadily I could guarantee to finish in the first three and Jack, driving hard, could lead the race from start to finish.' It would be the last summer of such domination for the Coopers.

Jack and Bruce went to the British Grand Prix at Silverstone as joint leaders in the championship, with 24 points apiece.

Bruce qualified third fastest, led early on when the indefatigable Stirling Moss dropped the starter's flag, and finished fourth, a lap down. Graham Hill was the surprise of the race in his BRM, stalling it at the start and getting away dead last. During the race he drove like a man possessed and not only caught Brabham for the lead, but passed him with a third of the race to run. Unfazed, Jack pressed on and when the BRM spun into an earth bank at Copse, Jack was once again the winner.

Stirling Moss had made an amazing recovery after his Spa crash and was back in the Walker Lotus at Oporto for the Portuguese Grand Prix, qualifying fourth. The Oporto circuit was made up of public roads that included such local features as cobblestones and tramlines. John Surtees supplied his own piece of Portuguese excitement when, in only his third Grand Prix, he put his works Lotus on pole! John led the race for 25 laps and set a new lap record, but then the Lotus' fuel tank split and Surtees' soaked right boot slipped off the brake pedal and he slammed into a kerb, wrecking the radiator. Jack and Dan Gurney then fought over the lead until Brabham's Cooper suddenly tracked on to the tramlines and took him straight down an escape road! He came back into the race in eighth place just behind Bruce, who waved him through and followed him up through the field, helped by retirements of the front runners. 'We eventually scored our second one-two of the season and Jack's fifth Grand Prix win in succession. Jack was now unassailable on points and had clinched his second successive world title.' In fact, he *was* assailable, but only by Bruce in second place…and Bruce *knew* his place! The Cooper Car Company had also clinched the Manufacturer's Championship.

The British teams boycotted the Italian Grand Prix, which was being run on the banked track as well as the road course. 'This steeply banked oval circuit, used mainly for record-breaking attempts, had become bumpy and was dangerous not only if a driver lost control over the bumps, but also because banking of this nature imposes a far greater load on the suspension. All sorts of mechanical components could either give trouble or fail completely. The road racing circuit, set in the grounds of the Autodrome, is perfectly satisfactory, but the organisers wanted to combine the two. British constructors felt this to be dangerous and, in the hopes that the banking might not be used, met and decided they would not appear at the Italian Grand Prix. Things became a bit political, with considerable lack of understanding or co-operation between organisers and constructors. So far as Coopers were concerned, the race was immaterial — the championship was in the bag and there was little point in racing on what we felt was a dangerous track...'

Phil Hill scored his first Grand Prix victory at Monza, heading a Ferrari triple, with Richie Ginther and Willy Mairesse second and third, respectively. This took Phil to third in the championship. It was the first Grand Prix to be won by an American driver since Jimmy Murphy won the French Grand Prix for Duesenberg in 1921 and the last Grand Prix win for a front-engined car.

The final title race of the season was the US Grand Prix, held on the sports car course in Riverside, California. It was a well-kept secret. One promoter had placed a huge order of colour supplements featuring the 1960 Grand Prix cars of Cooper, Lotus, BRM and Ferrari — they arrived the day after the race.

It must have been a pale event. Moss won from pole in the Walker Lotus, Innes Ireland was second in the works Lotus and Bruce was third in the Cooper, but the event is not even mentioned in his autobiography, although the party at Lance Reventlow's home warranted three paragraphs!

'The Reventlow party was the highlight of the week. A couple of buses collected us from our hotels and delivered us to his sumptuous Beverly Hills home. Lance's wife, Jill St John, was the perfect hostess and for about half an hour the British Grand Prix contingent and a few dozen American journalists stood chatting formally about the weather and motor racing and taking care not to drop cigar ash on the rugs. But only for 30 minutes.

'Malayan boys were handing round apparently innocuous rum-based drinks with large lumps of pineapple on a stick. These went down particularly well and all seemed to take effect at once.

'Just then dozens of Jill's starlet friends made an entrance and the party woke up. Before you could say "Stirling Moss", Innes Ireland was down to his underpants, splashing into the indoor swimming pool, while Jill handed around towels for those who cared to join him. We all thoroughly enjoyed ourselves and many of the Britishers were found to be not so stuffy after all…'

The season had ended and Brabham was the back-to-back world champion, Bruce was second on points and Moss third. Bruce had ten years to live and much more to achieve.

9 The emerging McLaren

The season of 1961 was one that anyone without a Ferrari drive would prefer to forget. The governing body had announced in 1958 that the Formula 1 rating would drop to 1500 cc for 1961, but it seemed that the British teams thought this would go away if they ignored it. They had been comfortable and successful with 2.5 litres. Reducing the limit to what had been Formula 2 was regarded as ridiculous and retrograde. However, although Ferrari had run his big front-engined Dinos in 1960, he had also been fettling for the new formula, running a rear-engined prototype in Formula 2 during the latter part of the 1960 season. This car, in its Formula 1 guise, would totally dominate in 1961. Stirling Moss would win at Monaco and on the Nürburgring, two tracks where skill could still overcome horsepower, but otherwise the summer was a red-car whitewash. As Jack Brabham wrote in his autobiography, 'Entering 1961 we were all looking down the gun barrel and the finger on the trigger was Enzo Ferrari's.'

For Bruce, 1961 marked the beginning of his own aspirations to run a team. Cooper's early-season effort focused on Brabham's Indianapolis car, so Tommy Atkins offered Bruce a sports car drive in a Cooper Monaco. Bruce suggested they might be better to invest in a Cooper single-seater which could run in the 2.5-litre intercontinental races and — with an engine-switch — in Formula 2 and non-championship Formula 1 races, which the Cooper factory were ignoring. The times were changing. It was Jack's last season with Cooper before leaving to form his own team, and

∧
Fine-tuning the Cooper-Climax during practice for the 1963 Monaco Grand Prix.

> Cooper team mates,
Tony Maggs and Bruce.

O be it known hereby that Bruce McLaren and his Merrie Men: Young Eoin of Surrey, the Lord Mayer, Sir Walter Willmott and Alexander the Great, Knights of Night, prescribe the presence of the damsels and gentlemen preferred hereunder.

at ye Castle-Warming

The Warden, 20 Corkran Road, Surbiton
on Bank Holiday, August 3rd, which perchance befalls
at night after the Guards Tourney at Brands Hatch

Balderdash Slinging, Goblet-Tilting and Wenching will commence at 8-30 pm
to abet celebration/commiseration of the afternoon's competition

Iron gauntlets, broadswords and lances must be parked outside the portcullis

No swimming in the moat
No serfing

Raiment:
Bold Knights—Suits of Armour (No monocoques)
Fair Ladies—The Lady of Coventry was the Climax of style

∧
The invitation to the 'castle warming', held after the Guards Trophy at Brands Hatch in 1964.

∧
Bruce gets a victory kiss from Patty after winning the 1964 New Zealand Grand Prix.

PATTY MCLAREN COLLECTION

∧
Bruce, Patty and daughter Amanda in the BRM pit at Pukekohe in 1964.   PATTY MCLAREN COLLECTION

∧
Bruce discusses his second-place finish in the 1964 Italian Grand Prix at Monza with John
Cooper (right).   EOIN YOUNG COLLECTION

∧
Water-skiing was Bruce's other speed-oriented passion.   EOIN YOUNG COLLECTION

∧
Bruce (Cooper-Oldsmobile) leads Jim Clark (Lotus 30) in the 1964 Tourist Trophy race.

∧
Bruce takes journalist Denis Jenkinson for a CanAm ride at Goodwood, 1964 while Eoin
Young, Tyler Alexander and Wal Willmott look on.

∧
All-Kiwi chat: Denny Hulme, Chris Amon and Bruce get together at Silverstone, 1965.

∧
The McLaren Racing workshop in David Road, Colnbrook, 1965.

∧
Bruce McLaren and Phil Hill take part in a publicity shot at Wigram, 1965.

∧
Tyler Alexander (right) goes through some last-minute points with Bruce, tucked in his own M4
Formula 2 McLaren.

∧
Bruce, leading the 1966 sports car race at Silverstone.

∧
Robin Herd, seen here with Bruce in 1967, brought aeronautical technology to the McLaren race designs.

the Atkins car gave Bruce the chance to try his own ideas on development. As senior team driver, Jack had the final say on car set-up and Bruce did not always agree with him. The Atkins offer was a perfect opportunity for him to tailor a car to his own preference.

First though, he went back home again for the New Zealand races. The team had works Coopers for Jack and Bruce and, for the first time, John Cooper came on the tour as manager. There was a strong international field for the Grand Prix at Ardmore, including Stirling Moss, Graham Hill, Dan Gurney, Jim Clark, John Surtees and Ron Flockhart.

'John Cooper must have been tired of people asking whether the cars would be running to team orders. Most New Zealanders believed I had to finish second. My argument was that I couldn't head Jack anyway, but this was always greeted with a sympathetic smile and a wise nod. John silenced the queries by telling a reporter I was free to beat Jack if I wanted. This was splashed across the front pages, to everyone's delight. Except mine, as Jack was now more determined than ever to win...'

They finished one-two — Jack and Bruce — nose to tail in the Grand Prix. The Wigram race was a shortened wash-out, notable for a number of lurid high-speed aquaplaning spins. Jack won again and Bruce was a distant, damp and muddy fourth.

The next race on Bruce's schedule was at Sebring, where he was going to drive for the Briggs Cunningham team. In 1960, Cunningham had offered Bruce a drive in the prototype E-Type Jaguar at Laguna Seca, which was accepted. Briggs did nothing by halves. When Bruce got to the paddock and asked for the Cunningham team he was told to look for the biggest transporter and semi-trailer there. 'Sure enough, there was a huge mobile workshop and, parked alongside it, a car transporter with a couple of Maseratis, a gaggle of Formula Junior cars and a big white Jaguar.'

The team was run by 70-year-old Italian engineer Alfred Momo, who had worked for Cunningham in New York for 15 years. His accent, though, was still redolent of the Mediterranean and Bruce had trouble understanding him. He had no such difficulty with the car, however.

'The car had a solid feel about it. I started the engine, blipped it a few times and the whole car resounded and rang with the drum of the exhaust as though it were all one solid, bell-like unit. It felt good. You could spin the wheels nearly everywhere and controllability proved to be one of the car's better points. It was the sort of car you could get very sideways on, and still have it in control.'

That year, 40 entries contested the 22 spots on the grid. Bruce made the field in 19th place and impressed the team, who had thought he would fail to qualify. He finished fifth, a feat that earned him a regular place in the Cunningham team. Something else important happened that weekend in Monterey.

'I talked to an American of about my own age at the airport on the way back to England the following day. He had been driving a Porsche and seemed to have fared reasonably well. We became firm friends on the flight to New York and agreed to get together next time we were both at the same motor race. His name was Roger Penske.'

Bruce was fascinated with Roger's professional approach to everything he did. 'Do you know, he actually polishes the *backs* of his shoes…' Those were days when colonials abroad, if they polished their shoes at all, settled for scuffing the toecaps on the opposite trouser leg.

For 1961, Bruce drove for Cunningham in the 12-hour endurance race, for which he was entered in a rear-engined V12 Type 63 Maserati Birdcage.

'The term "birdcage" derived from the frame of the car, consisting of hundreds of pieces of small-diameter tube forming a sort of trellis-work chassis. It was certainly a unique form of construction and the story went that, when it was first built, a canary was released in the centre of the frame and anywhere it could escape, another tube was welded in! It looked and sounded fantastic. You couldn't call it attractive — forceful, perhaps — and we soon discovered it went round corners like its appearance…somewhat unusual.'

This was Bruce's first experience of being part of a big team. The Cooper Formula 1 team mainly consisted of John, Jack, Bruce and two or three mechanics and the mechanics usually worked all the hours God gave on a race weekend, so the three principals frequently ate together in the evening.

'One of the best things about a relatively large team was the way Briggs acted, not only as team manager but a sort of uncle. We all ate together, a large table being kept for the team each evening at the Harder Hall hotel, normally a golf resort. I was to share with Walt Hansgen in the new rear-engined car, while John Fitch and Dick Thompson were in a front-engined Birdcage and Briggs and Bill Kimberley were sharing a 2-litre front-engined Birdcage. We all tried not to be late for meals and waited until Briggs joined us before eating. Over dinner we were able to discuss team tactics and any questions we had to raise. There were also the private briefings. Alfred Momo would often arrange meetings with all the drivers and a couple of Italian Maserati engineers, with himself and Briggs presiding, for a quick run-down on the day's instructions. There was no excuse for anyone not knowing what was going on and what he should be doing.'

Bruce was proud of the fact that he was the only non-American in this very American team. He was mildly irritated when Briggs gave him a lecture about not scorching away at the start, and that the object was to finish the race. 'I was tempted to tell him that I'd been driving Grand Prix cars for several years, that it was my job and that I knew all about this…but the big thing in long-distance sports car racing is to finish.'

Before the 12-hour race, Bruce drove a works Austin Healey Sprite and thoroughly enjoyed the race. 'Down the straight Stirling and I were virtually able to talk to each other. He would push back his window and mouth, "How many revs are you getting?" I'd hold up five fingers, then six, to indicate 5600 rpm. He would glance at his rev counter and indicate five-five, or five-four...'

In the main event Bruce and Walt took the fight to the Ferrari works team. They ran as high as third on occasion, but the end was nigh. Smoke from a terminal engine oil leak told them and their crew that their race was run.

Back in England, Phil Kerr had bought an apartment that allowed him and Bruce the comparative luxury of a bedroom each, a lounge, a bathroom that they didn't have to share with everyone else in the building and a kitchen big enough that you didn't have to go outside to turn round. Patty had come over to England in 1960 and had stayed for the 1960–61 winter sharing a flat with a girlfriend.

Phil remembered those bachelor days: 'Bruce never became domesticated and never showed any likelihood of becoming that way. Housework was beyond him and although we were supposed to take it in turns to keep the flat tidy, I always seemed to have to do it. On a weekend when Bruce was away racing, I would get the place all sorted out spick and span, but within five minutes of his return the whole place would be a shambles. He would walk in the front door and there would be a trail of clothes and suitcases and shoes and packages of things he'd bought while he was away. This trail would go across the lounge and into his bedroom, where he would open his suitcase. Then there would be a trail of clothes from his bedroom to the bathroom. It was a turmoil and yet he always seemed to be quite oblivious to it all...

'He once made a rare foray to the laundrette with a bag of washing that included his favourite short-sleeved blue sports shirt, which he always wore when racing. It had almost become a mascot. As far as Bruce was concerned, the laundry machine was foolproof providing you remembered to put in the washing, the soap powder...and the sixpence. It wasn't until he got back to the flat and started to empty out the laundry bag that he realised all his white underpants, vests, shirts and sweaters were a delicate shade of light blue.

'When he saw what had happened, he just couldn't stop laughing. He sat down and laughed until the tears were rolling down his cheeks and his sides ached. He just hooted and rolled about like he couldn't bear it. That's what life tended to be like in the flat…'

In 1961 Bruce replaced the Morris Minor 1000 that he'd been using for his Grand Prix commuting with a 3.8 Jaguar, which he intended to ship out to his father at the end of the season. 'I bought it new from the factory with high compression, a high ratio rear axle, racing suspension and high-geared steering. The high-geared steering was the one mistake I made with the 3.8. It was just too heavy to be pleasant on the road and it made the car "darty", but it was great fun if you wanted to do a couple of laps round Goodwood between testing sessions. It was one of the most reliable cars I've ever owned, in direct contrast to the E-Type that came next. It was one of the first Es and when it was brand new it was a positive joy, but I made the mistake of fitting a rear end that was too high. I opted for the 2.9 Le Mans axle ratio, because I figured that with this sort of car, you could cruise quite happily at 120 mph, but when I tried doing that across Europe I found that I didn't really want to go that fast after all…'

Michael MacDowell worked with Jaguar in the service department. 'I was also involved in supporting Jaguar customers in motor sport,' said Michael, 'primarily the 3.8 Mk 2 saloon cars in touring events. The E-Type Jaguar was launched in March 1961 and I was immediately involved in its competition debut that season. A limited number of people, selected by Racing Manager, Lofty England, were offered the chance to own early-delivery cars and Bruce was one of them. These "special" customers received their cars direct from the service department at Coventry and it was my job to keep in touch with these people on a regular basis and collate information on their early experiences with this outstanding new model, which had attracted enormous public interest. Bruce also raced an E-Type for Peter Berry's team, so I had feedback from Bruce, not only as a private owner of a road car, but also as a top Grand Prix driver in a competition car.

'Those early cars had a lot of problems and bearing in mind that the competition cars were standard production models, these faults were magnified greatly under racing conditions. Brakes, and especially the servo unit, coolant loss and subsequent overheating, rubber suspension and steering rack bushes, were just a few of the items needing urgent attention.

'Bruce was always practical and supportive and seemed to genuinely enjoy racing the car. This was surprising for someone used to the precise handling of a single-seater, where there were no compromises. The E-Type must have felt "soggy" and unresponsive to a racing driver with his experience, but he extolled its virtues of a superb engine with a lot of low-speed torque and he simply drove it within its chassis limitations and made concise practical suggestions on how to overcome the problems. I quickly realised that Bruce was a fine engineer as well as an excellent driver with an ability to report accurately on the car's track behaviour. His ready wit also made my job so much more pleasurable — not everyone was so easy to deal with at that time!'

Unofficial advisor to Jaguar aside, Bruce's real job was driving a Formula 1 car and the season opened in May at Monte Carlo. Moss had stripped the side panels from his nimble Rob Walker Lotus 18 to help keep him cool and it obviously worked as he won from pole position, setting a new record race speed. Bruce started from the middle of the third row, his qualifying time equalling that of Phil Hill and Wolfgang von Trips' Ferraris. He finished sixth for a title point.

At Zandvoort, Ferrari's power advantage made itself felt when Phil Hill, von Trips and Ginther filled the front row. Moss had the fastest non-red car and sat beside Graham Hill's BRM on the second row. Bruce was back on the fifth row and struggled home twelfth in a race won by von Trips in the Ferrari. The race made the record books because it was the only Grand Prix where every starter finished and no car made a pit stop. It was von Trips' first Grand Prix win and the first for a German driver since 1939.

On the fast Spa course Ferraris filled the front row of the grid and took the first four places in the race. Bruce qualified back on row six and went out on lap 30 with a fuel pick-up problem.

That summer, Ferrari dominated much as they have in the 21st century. Yet in 1961 there was always a question of which Ferrari driver would win. And in no race was this more so than the French Grand Prix at Reims. An older-model Ferrari had been made available to Olivier Gendebien for the Belgian Grand Prix and he had led early on with it. For the French Grand Prix this car was given to the young Italian rookie, Giancarlo Baghetti, who had already won the non-title Formula 1 races at Syracuse and Naples. Once again Ferraris filled the front row. Bruce was on the third row, Baghetti back on the fifth row. The red works cars stormed away in the early stages but von Trips was forced to stop when a flying stone holed his radiator. Then Hill spun and lost a lap while he struggled to push-start his stalled car. Ginther retired with an overheating problem, which left Baghetti to battle the works Porsches of Gurney and Bonnier. In a slipstreaming battle to the flag, the young Italian won by just a tenth of a second from Gurney and so drove into the record books by claiming victory in his first Grand Prix drive. Bruce was fifth — by his standards, another poor result. He dismissed the first part of the 1961 season in a brief one-paragraph mention in *From the Cockpit*.

Four cars tied for fastest practice lap at Aintree — Bonnier's Porsche and the Ferraris of von Trips, Ginther and Hill — and Ferraris took the first three places in the rain-drenched race: von Trips, Hill and Ginther. Bruce was eighth.

Next up was the German Grand Prix on the Nürburgring, which saw the debut of the Coventry-Climax V8 in the back of Brabham's Cooper. Bruce remembered his first acquaintance with the shrill V8. 'It screamed into life with a piercing howl and sounded wonderful, a noise that was to become part of motor racing and put British manufacturers back on the map. Long, gradually outward-tapering exhaust pipes gave the engine a strange high-pitched note.' Brabham tested the new car first and Bruce waited to be allowed a couple of laps at the end of the day. 'After the four-cylinder engine, the V8 was very smooth. On opening the throttle on the four-cylinder, one felt something of a kick — not so much as on the 2.5-litre cars, but a reasonable sort of "kick in the back". This sensation changed with the V8. It became more of a smooth push and there was virtually no vibration.'

Phil Hill's pole position time was some 6 seconds faster than Brabham in the new Cooper, Moss (Lotus) and Bonnier (Porsche) were also on the front row, but it was Moss who would score his second win of the season, thanks to the circuit allowing skill to overcome horsepower.

Brabham's race on the 'Ring lasted less than a mile with the new engine. It was raining and for some reason Dunlop had only D12 Dunlop rain tyres available for the World Champion's front wheels. With more grip on the front than the rear, he plunged off the track and through a hedge, almost within sight of the pits. Bruce finished sixth.

Once more the Italian Grand Prix at Monza was held on a circuit that combined a banked section and a road course. BRM debuted their new V8 engine in a car that amazed Bruce because it looked so small. 'It seems hard to believe that a year or so later, the same car, although a World Championship winner, was one of the biggest and heaviest in the field.'

After the years of protest at the use of the banking, it was a tragic irony that the accident that killed title leader Wolfgang von Trips and 14 spectators, should happen on the road course part of the circuit. Jim Clark's

Lotus and von Trips' Ferrari had tangled in a slipstreaming tussle that saw the Ferrari spin out of control, tossing von Trips from the car before it ploughed into the perimeter fencing. The accident was unannounced and the race proceeded, drivers and crew unaware of the tragedy.

Bruce seemed to have been racing all summer with Dan Gurney's Porsche and again at Monza he and the lanky Californian slipstreamed each other to the finish. Bruce finished third behind Hill and Gurney, so was the first British car across the line.

Phil Hill's victory clinched him the World Championship, but it was something of an inherited title following von Trips' death. In the follow-up to the tragedy, Enzo Ferrari decided not to send any cars to the final race, the US Grand Prix at Watkins Glen, thereby robbing Phil of the chance to race in front of his home crowd.

The absence of the red cars gifted the race to the British teams and while Moss and Brabham led the first part of the race, both retired and it was left to Innes Ireland to score the first World Championship Grand Prix victory for Team Lotus. It was also Ireland's last drive for Team Lotus. He was dropped from the team in favour of Jim Clark and was forever bitter at what he regarded as this shameful treatment meted out by team boss, Colin Chapman.

Californian drivers had finished first (Phil Hill), third (Dan Gurney) and fifth (Richie Ginther) in the World Championship. Gurney had scored three second placings for Porsche against the might of Ferrari. Stirling Moss had finished joint third with Gurney and he had won two of the eight Grands Prix, the same number as both Phil Hill and von Trips. However, Stirling was a win-or-bust total racer and had only one minor placing — fourth at Zandvoort — to add to his pair of wins.

His Formula 1 season over, Bruce McLaren entered the motor racing business on his own account, having bought Tommy Atkins' Intercontinental Cooper to race in New Zealand and Australia. He had arranged to have

Atkins' mechanic, Harry Pearce, and he had also bought the special, stretched 2.7-litre four-cylinder Coventry-Climax engine that Brabham had used at Indianapolis. But when an order for a new Cooper Monaco was cancelled, Bruce saw the chance to run it in the dollar-rich Californian sports car races. The only snag was finding the money. Bruce had spent £10,000 on the single-seater project so couldn't afford the Monaco, but fortunately sold the idea to Peter Berry, who had raced Jaguar touring cars during the summer. They had got on well. It was difficult *not* to get on well with Bruce. The plan was to send the single-seater direct to Auckland and to put the 2.7 'Indy' motor into the Monaco chassis, race it at Riverside and Laguna Seca, then fly it on to Auckland.

Tests at Silverstone showed the new Monaco sports racer to be a second faster than Moss had been in his Lotus 19, so Bruce felt confident as the car and spares were flown to Los Angeles. Bruce's Cooper mechanic, Mike Barney, was loaned to the Berry equipe and flew to California with Bruce. Arrangements had been made for the car to be cleared through Customs and delivered to Riverside, but it didn't quite work out like that. The car had disappeared. Bruce checked with Reventlow's Scarab team manager, Warren Olsen, who had been looking after Bruce's arrangements and he suggested they check with Customs at Los Angeles airport.

'It was good advice. Mike and I arrived at the Customs area to find an official sitting on the ground surrounded by hundreds of bits and pieces of specialised racing equipment — bearings, bolts, bushes, pipes, cylinders, pistons — all unwrapped and lying on the ground as though a naughty child had been delving into the spares box.'

The Customs man asked Bruce if he knew anything about these parts. 'Yes. I'm going to drive it when you get it all together for me!' Officialdom surrendered, the car and the spares were cleared and they were soon in the paddock at Riverside, a circuit that has today disappeared in the relentless expansion of Los Angeles.

Brabham was their main opposition and Bruce knew that Jack had the 'other' 2.7 Indianapolis engine, the motor that had been Jack's spare for the '500'. As the race got underway Stirling led, but had to drop out, the brakes of his Lotus baked. Bruce and Jack both cooled off their pace in order to save the racing for the last few laps. But just as their tussle began, Bruce's Cooper started snapping into vicious slides and he realised his water temperature was off the clock.

'My choice was to ease up or blow up, so I backed off. Jack went past and in another lap the chequered flag was out. Jack had won the race, $4000 and a Pontiac Grand Prix sedan. With the bonuses added, he had probably won around £7000, but I had some small compensation in collecting lap money for leading 75 of the 200 laps.'

A pit-lane autopsy revealed the cylinder head sealing rings had failed; the slides were caused by water gathering in the undertray and sloshing on to the back tyres in the corners.

The race at Laguna Seca a week later was no better, Bruce retiring early with piston failure.

'After Laguna Seca, I flew to New Zealand to get married. Patty and I, after a two-year engagement, were wed at St Paul's church in Christchurch and we flew to Fiji and Tahiti for a two-week honeymoon, with not a motor racing circuit within 3000 miles.'

The Grand Prix at Ardmore was won in startling form by Stirling Moss in Rob Walker's Lotus, who confessed later that on several occasions he thought his number was up as he went into a sideways slide. The race was stopped early. The newspaper headlined his win 'BOSS MOSS' and that covered it well. Bruce finished third behind Surtees. At Levin the following weekend the rain turned up again, with town and track flooded. It was Brabham's turn to get ahead and dodge the spray and spinning cars behind him. The chequered flag was waved after only eight laps, Jack leading from Moss and Bruce.

'Stirling was livid after the race, saying that if the organisers intended stopping the race after only eight laps, they should never have started it. Jack, smiling broadly, reminded Stirling that he had never objected to the Ardmore race being curtailed when he was a lap in front…'

In contrast, the Wigram race was a scorcher. Bruce started from pole but spun and finished fourth behind Moss, Brabham and Surtees. His first three races had yielded poor placings, but Teretonga was different. The race was only 75 miles and most of the corners were left-handers so Harry Pearce removed the right-hand fuel tank from the car. Bruce beat Moss in the first heat, started the race from pole and won. Moss was second, and Brabham — almost lapped — was third.

The next race was the Australian Grand Prix on the Warwick Farm circuit close to Sydney. The event was run by the very British Geoff Sykes, who had been hired away from the British Automobile Racing Club. Bruce's Cooper did not arrive until the morning of final practice, which gave Brabham and Moss, who had sent spare cars direct to Sydney before the race at Teretonga, an advantage.

In the race Moss and Brabham battled for the lead until Jack's gearbox broke after 20 laps, which enabled Bruce to finish second, 20 seconds down, but with the lap record to his credit. The following race, at Lakeside near Brisbane, was so hot they had to use ice to cool the fuel. Drivers packed ice into their pockets before the start and Angus Hyslop stopped his Cooper on the warm-up lap to dive into the lake! Problems with the Colotti gearbox sidelined Bruce and Brabham went on to win.

In the two-week break before the next race at the new Sandown circuit in Melbourne, Bruce flew back to the UK to test the new Formula 1 and Formula Junior Coopers. He'd told John Cooper and Ken Tyrrell that he was prepared to fly back and test every day for a week, but that if either of the cars was not ready and the trip was wasted, they would have to pay his air fare.

On arriving in London Bruce went almost immediately to the British Racing and Sports Car Club dinner-dance at the Park Lane Hotel. He was catching up with the UK racing gossip when he was amazed to be called to the telephone. 'With an ability that seems to exist only with American telephone operators, they had traced me from Sydney to Surbiton and from Surbiton to the Park Lane Hotel. It was Frank Faulkner. He said Briggs Cunningham was flying over to Monza in three days to test the Type 64 Maserati sports car and a Cooper Monaco which was being fitted with a 3.8-litre four-cylinder Maserati engine at the Modena factory. Frank wondered if I would fly down and try the cars, also whether I would be available to drive one of them at Sebring a week after the Sandown Park race at Melbourne. Sydney to London, London to Milan, Milan back to London, London to Melbourne and Melbourne to Sebring — all in a fortnight!'

Briggs Cunningham was impressed with Bruce McLaren's abilities which had seen him rise to the position of team leader following the departure of Jack Brabham. Thinking about it now, Bruce was obviously an ideal driver for Briggs, a sort of surrogate son, a young, well-behaved gentleman, a good ambassador for the sport, and a brilliant racing engineer as well as a racing driver.

The British weather put paid to the Cooper testing, heavy snowfalls meaning that Bruce could fly down to Milan for the Monza testing with a clear conscience. First up Bruce tried the Type 64 rear-engined Maserati, but he was quicker with the Cooper Monaco, which he thought may not have been in the script as far as the Maserati engineers were concerned. The cars were also tested on the Modena circuit around the airfield in the centre of the town and Bruce lopped 1.5 seconds off the lap record in a Formula Junior Stanguellini, much to the delight of Signor Stanguellini.

Dr Guiseppe Farina and Luigi Villoresi turned up at the Modena tests, and Villoresi talked his way into the Maserati sports car then stormed off without goggles because they wouldn't fit over his spectacles. Bruce was aware of the reputations of the two old Italian racers — Farina had won the first World Championship when the title was created in 1950 and Villoresi had won the 1949 Dutch Grand Prix — but Roger Penske, who had flown over with Briggs, wasn't. 'Who is this guy, Villoresi, anyway?' he asked.

Bruce was expanding his plans. Back in Surbiton, before he flew out to Australia for the final races of the series at Sandown Park, he asked Tommy Atkins if he would employ a young New Zealand mechanic, Wally Willmott, who was working with Harry Pearce in the series. 'The thing that impressed me [about Wally] was that he worked as though he wanted to do a good job.' I had known Wally back in Timaru, where he had raced a Mk 9 500 cc Cooper and had also worked on Angus Hyslop's Cooper on the Tasman Series.

Then it was my turn. Before the race in Melbourne, Bruce took me aside and asked if I would get in touch with him back in Surrey, because he wanted to talk to me. I had been in Europe during 1961 on my colonial 'OE' (Overseas Experience), I had travelled around the European Formula Junior series with Denny Hulme, I had flown out from Luton to Tasmania on a delivery flight for Jack Brabham's Cessna 180, and I was covering the international racing series with a view to staying in Tasmania as the motoring writer for the Hobart *Mercury*. I suggested that if we were to talk, we should do it there in Melbourne. Bruce asked if I would like to join him and work as his secretary. I asked what a secretary to a racing driver did, and he said he wasn't sure but some of the other drivers had secretaries and I could be his. We would make up the terms of employment as we went along. Before the final race in the Antipodean series, he had, one way or another, hired his first two employees.

With this rattling round my head, I watched the race in a bit of a daze: Jack, Bruce and John Surtees raced wheel to wheel the whole way, the three of them finishing virtually brakeless, with Brabham ahead. Their pace had been so torrid that they had lapped Moss before half distance.

I had agreed a careful deal with Bruce that saw him pay for my air ticket back to Britain via Sebring, the cost to be deducted from my salary, so that I worked for that summer of 1962 for £12 a week. It was to be a gem of a job that set me up for a career in motor racing writing and public relations.

10 Monaco winner in '62

The summer of '62 was another pivotal season in Grand Prix racing. Stirling Moss crashed out of his career at Goodwood and Ferrari eclipsed their domination of the year before. The new BRM V8 emerged as the car to beat and Graham Hill, who hadn't won a Formula 1 race before the Easter Monday Goodwood event, went on to win the world title. Bruce thought it may have been Graham's unusual line through St Mary's that triggered Stirling's crash, an accident that has remained unsolved.

'On the third lap when I was following Graham round Fordwater I was within inches of his tailpipes. He pulled over to the right to brake in a straight line for the right-hander at St Mary's and I thought for a split second he was giving me a chance to get by, as I normally stay out to the left and brake in a slight curve for this corner. In fact he [Graham] was taking a slightly different line for St Mary's. Perhaps Stirling found himself in a similar position, started to go outside Graham, and then realised his mistake…

'The trouble with an accident like this, however, is that definite conclusions afterwards are almost impossible. Even reliable eye-witness reports vary. The evidence left in the wreckage of the car is also liable to be inconclusive. Earlier in the race Stirling had made a pit stop. When the bonnet was clipped down and he started the engine, the throttle stuck open and the bonnet had to be removed again to free it. The throttle linkage on the Climax V8s at that time was complicated and a little messy. Had the throttle stuck open at that particular part of the circuit, the car would have gone straight off, or if anything broke in the steering, which is not impossible, a similar accident would have been inevitable.'

Bruce and Patty had flown back to Britain via Sebring, where he'd started the weekend with a win albeit a reluctant one. Briggs Cunningham had bought three Abarths on his European shopping spree, and Bruce had been persuaded to race one the day before the 12-hour race, in which he was sharing the Maserati-engined Cooper Monaco with Roger Penske.

'The Abarth was fast, the 1000 cc twin-cam engine having bags of power for its size, but the engine hung way out behind the rear axle and it was a case of the tail wagging the dog.' Bruce was not at all keen on driving, but he emerged the winner of the three-hour race after a tussle with Hansgen in another Cunningham-entered Abarth and Moss in a Healey Sprite.

In the main event, the Cooper Monaco was quick, but it seemed to spend more time in the pits than on the track, first with brake pad problems, then with electrical problems that stemmed from generator damage sustained when the Cooper had been flicked into the hay bales by a spinning Corvette. Bruce and Roger eventually finished fifth.

However, Bruce felt the Monaco had huge potential and back in England, he enthused to John Cooper about running it in races like Le Mans and the Nürburgring 1000 kilometres. John was interested, but his father, Charles, was not. 'The fact that Jack was now building his own car had made Charles feel that drivers employed by him should be kept purely as drivers and not involved in development, or more particularly, design. In my opinion, I felt it was unfair for Charles to feel they had taught Jack all he knew. It is similarly unreasonable for anyone to suggest that without Brabham, Coopers would never have developed their successful Grand Prix cars. John and Jack had been a terrific combination, one complementing the other, but it appeared things would now be a little different.'

At Goodwood on that fateful Easter weekend, Bruce won the race for four-cylinder cars and for the main race put the four-banger on the front row of the grid beside Moss and Hill's V8s. He finished second at Goodwood, repeated that at Aintree, following Jim Clark's Lotus home, and at Silverstone he finished on the tail of Innes Ireland in the factory V6 Ferrari.

It's possible the Ferrari that Innes drove had actually been intended for Stirling, before his accident cancelled all such arrangements. Bruce felt at the time that Enzo Ferrari had been trying to get a second opinion on the car, that he needed a comparison to Phil Hill. 'Ferrari found out what any of us would have been able to tell him—that Phil Hill was as good a driver as he could get. Phil can boast the determination and ability to match anyone, but he has had to handle some poor cars.'

He went on to expound his theory on ability, which makes interesting comparison with the Ferrari/Schumacher situation of today. 'Motor racing isn't only drivers *or* cars, it's car-driver combinations. More than that, it's car-driver-team combinations and driving a racing car on or over the limit is a special art. Nerve has nothing to do with it.'

And while that aspect of motor sport is little changed, compare Bruce's recollections of his team with that of the modern McLaren team, which boasts a staff of 900. 'The Cooper factory in Surbiton is a small one, and all work on the Formula 1 cars is done in a workshop down a narrow lane, not far from the main works. Three mechanics and two body-builders make up the team, assisted by John Cooper, Tony Maggs and myself, so we're anything but overstaffed...'

The first round of the 1962 World Championship season was the Dutch Grand Prix at Zandvoort and Bruce's new V8-engined Cooper was launched before practice began. The chassis was much simpler and lighter and for the first time both oil and water were piped through the chassis tubes. The start of the season also saw Porsche unveil their new flat-8 for Dan Gurney and Jo Bonnier, but this, and Bruce's Cooper, were totally overshadowed by the new monocoque Lotus 25. This was the future of Formula 1 design and Jim Clark would make it a winner. Bruce was impressed with the small shape of the Lotus. 'Colin Chapman has given special attention to slimming the body down to a minimum and Jimmy has to twist sideways to get into the cockpit. Once in there he is almost out of sight — but this does not stop him motoring quickly…'

The Lotus may have stolen the limelight in Holland, but Bruce liked the noise his new Cooper made. 'A distinctive feature of the new Cooper was the howl from the downward-swept exhaust pipes, which converged from the tangle cross-over system that Coventry-Climax had devised for us.'

Bruce qualified on the second row beside his old teammate Brabham, who was racing a customer Lotus while he waited for his own car to be completed. Bruce had had problems with the new gearbox in the Cooper and on the warm-up lap fourth gear failed, but he was able to drive around the problem and had made it up to second place when the quill shaft in his gearbox failed. Race one, retired, lap 15. Graham Hill went on to win his first World Championship Grand Prix, in a season that would see him win four Grands Prix and the title. Trevor Taylor came second in his first race in a Lotus-Climax V8. Clark, who had led initially, also suffered gearbox problems and trailed in ninth. The Ferraris that had dominated the previous summer were soundly beaten by the new generation of cars from the British teams.

Bruce's next race was a real contrast. He drove a five-year-old Aston Martin DBR1 for John Ogier's Essex Racing team in the Nürburgring 1000-kilometre race and, as was the fashion of the day, Patty and Bruce drove to Germany in their E-Type Jaguar in convoy with Lotus teammates Jim Clark and Trevor Taylor in Jim's Lotus Elite, and Tony Maggs in his Ogle Mini Cooper. The Lotus pair were to race the radical new Lotus 23, fitted with the first twin-cam Ford 1.5-litre engine. Clark opened up a giant lead on the opening lap, but a leaking exhaust eventually ended his drive. Bruce had been philosophical about the chances of the elderly Aston, but he was pleasantly surprised.

'It wasn't long before the modern metal went thundering past me in the opening laps and I settled down in eighth place, lapping at an agreed speed and waiting for the opposition to eliminate themselves, as they obligingly proceeded to do. Two Ferraris finished up in trees and the starter failed on another, bringing the Aston up to fifth, but according to the complicated classification system, we were actually second behind Phil Hill and Gendebien in the winning Ferrari.'

In Monaco for the next Formula 1 race John Cooper had decided to play safe after the gearbox problems they'd experienced in Holland, and had reduced the 'box from six speeds to four. 'With its short straights, climbs, swoops and tight corners, Monaco is sheer murder on gearboxes and rather than overtax the 'box (and the driver) we decided it would be better to go into a corner with only three gear-changes rather than five. Wonderful — I'd just saved myself 600 gear-changes in the race!'

It was the twentieth running of the famous street race and once again entry was restricted to 16 cars. Works teams automatically had two entries; the remainder had to qualify. However, the British teams did not yet have their full complement of V8 engines; the number one driver had a new V8 but the number two was still saddled with an older four-cylinder. It had been suggested in some quarters that the older works cars should qualify with the rest, but that was ignored so eleven qualifiers set out to fight for six places on the grid. The BRMs and Lolas were wearing shortened snub noses, perhaps anticipating the mayhem that erupted at the start.

Practice started on Thursday and Clark's Lotus and Graham Hill's BRM set the pace. It rained on Friday and the positions didn't change. On Saturday the Côte d'Azur sunshine returned. Although the positions still didn't change, the times plummeted. Clark was on pole with 1:35.4 and though this gave him the inside running down to the right-hand hairpin it was not necessarily the best side of the grid, considering that the Gazometre Hairpin (today absorbed in the reshaped Rascasse) was only 300 yards away. Hill's BRM (1:35.8) was in the middle and Bruce's Cooper (1:36.4) was on the outside, which meant he probably had the best line into the first corner. Belgian driver 'Wild Willy' Mairesse confounded form in the 'extra' Ferrari on the second row, with a time equal to that of McLaren. The 'official' Ferrari works entries — Phil Hill and Lorenzo Bandini — were back on the fourth row of the 3-2-3 grid. In fact, Gurney's Porsche had also tied on the same time as McLaren and Mairesse. Ginther was on the fifth row with the works BRM. The starter was Louis Chiron, who had won the Monaco Grand Prix in a Bugatti in 1931 and as late as 1950 had finished third in a Maserati behind Fangio and Ascari. He'd gone on to achieve fame as race director and starter, but he made his own rules. His usual procedure was to raise the flag with 30 seconds to go and start a careful countdown, but in 1962 the flag came down before the count and caught the front row by surprise. Mairesse shouldered his way between Clark and Hill, stormed down into the Gazometre Hairpin, overdid it and half spun in Clark's path. Jim had to stop, but Bruce and Graham threaded through.

Behind them was chaos. The throttle on Ginther's BRM had jammed wide open coming off the grid and the diminutive American ploughed through the group of cars braking at the blocked first corner. He clouted the Lotuses of Taylor, Trintignant and Ireland and Gurney's Porsche and wrecked his own car. A rear wheel ripped off, bounced over the barrier and fatally injured an official.

Gregor Grant captured the chaos in his *Autosport* report: 'Cars collided and hit straw bales in all directions. A wheel flew off the BRM and knocked down a race official; Trintignant charged the bales, and Gurney's Porsche was struck by at least two cars. Someone ran into the back of Ireland's Lotus and the nose of Trevor Taylor's Lotus was torn off. The race was over for Trintignant, Gurney and Ginther. Taylor stopped briefly at his pit and chucked away the smashed nosepiece. Poor Ireland's car looked as if the termites had got at the rear end and a leaking petrol tank had to be dealt with before he rejoined the race, several laps in arrears.'

For Bruce, though, the race was unfolding in a much more positive manner. 'Lady Luck must have squeezed in beside me at the start, I think, for apart from trouble selecting gear a couple of times and a bit of cramp in my right leg from heavy braking in the small cockpit, I had no worries at all. Jimmy had started the race with a 'V7' Lotus but when the oiled plug had cleared itself, he climbed through the field, setting a new lap record on the way, until he got between my Cooper and Graham Hill's BRM which was leading. I passed Jim on the side of the track on lap 55 with clutch failure and with only seven laps to go, Hill's BRM stopped in a cloud of blue smoke and a pool of oil. That left me out in front with a 20-second lead over Phil in the Ferrari, who tried his hardest to catch me and came within 1.3 second of doing so, but I wasn't taking any chances of losing the Cooper on the oily surface in the closing laps.

'With three laps left Mike Barney and John Cooper began feverishly hanging signals on the pit board. They had been timing the gap between my Cooper and the Ferrari on one side of the pits and hurriedly putting the numbers on the board for me to read as I went past on the other. They were working fast and on one lap they dropped the numbers. As I accelerated past, John was frantically trying to pick them up and hold them on the board. I had time to chuckle.

'Phil was still five seconds away. I didn't think he could pick that up in two laps and by holding my pace I was sure he would be a couple of seconds away at the finish. Even if he were on my tail, there was nowhere to pass on that last half-lap. Especially if I didn't want to let him! As I braked into the chicane for the last time, I couldn't see the Ferrari in my mirror, but on entering the left-hander at Tabac there was a red dot about 200 yards behind. I had won.'

The final laps were electrifying, even though Bruce made them sound calm and controlled.

'Phil Hill treated the crowd to a wonderful demonstration of Grand Prix driving,' wrote Paul Frere in *Automobile Year*. 'Lap by lap he cut down McLaren's lead until there was but three seconds between them — and one lap to go. The excitement was intense. McLaren kept calm even though Hill was gaining on that very last lap. As they tore towards the chequered flag the Cooper kept ahead and the New Zealander beat the American by 1.3 seconds — after 190 miles of hard motor racing!' Only six cars were running at the finish.

I was now officially on the McLaren payroll as his first employee and I drove to the races in Bruce's Mini Cooper while he drove his E-Type. He loved that Jaguar and it certainly looked like a Grand Prix driver's sleek conveyance, but it was a very early model and it was desperately unreliable.

Emboldened by the success of my boss and perhaps further buoyed by a glass or two of the victory champagne, I asked a good-looking American girl in the bar of the Hotel d'Europe if she would care for drinks and dinner, and doubtless mentioned a few times that I worked for the winner of the race. She told me to f**k off.

From Monaco we moved to Spa. The two road circuits were poles apart. Where the streets of the Principality are incredibly tight, the sweeps of the then 8.76-mile Spa-Francorchamps road course were super-fast. Spa underlined the difference in pace between the 1500 cc formula and the previous 2500 cc cars. Jack Brabham's lap record of 3:51.9 set in the 1960 race with a 2.5-litre Cooper still stood. Graham Hill's pole lap in the BRM V8 in 1962 was 3:57.0. Bruce was beside him on the front row in the Cooper on 3:58.8 and Trevor Taylor in the 'old' Lotus 24, who had never raced at Spa before, was third fastest on 3:59.3. He had been fastest on the first day of practice! Where was Jim Clark? His Climax V8 engine had failed on the first day and he had to wait for a fresh one to be sent over. It only just arrived in time for the race. Jim's best lap in his teammate's

Type 24 — with its old-fashioned 'chassis' — was only good enough for the middle of the fifth row of the grid.

Race day was different. Hill stormed off into the lead, Bruce slipstreaming behind him, but it wasn't long before Taylor and local driver Mairesse in the Ferrari came through, nose to tail and side by side, as the lead BRM faltered with ignition trouble. Bruce's memory of Mairesse a fortnight earlier at Monaco made him cautious. 'If there was going to be an accident I had no intention of being in it, so I sat back a safe 20 feet. Jimmy was motoring as though he meant business and had passed the three of us for a lead he never lost, but my race ended when a big-end bearing let go.'

The engine failure had probably done Bruce a favour. He watched Taylor and Mairesse locked in high-speed battle as he walked back to the pits, wondering at Trevor's pace for a driver who had never raced on the spookily fast circuit before. Taylor wasn't giving an inch to the Belgian driver, who was eager to impress his home crowd. With seven laps left, Bruce saw a column of smoke a mile away rising across the circuit. The wild pair had tangled, causing the Lotus to fell a telegraph pole and leaving the Ferrari upside down on fire. Incredibly, Mairesse escaped with minor burns and bruises and Taylor's only injury was a graze on his wrist caused when he snagged his watch-strap during his hasty exit from his wrecked Lotus.

Meanwhile, Jim Clark took a run-away win at a race average speed of 131.9 mph. He shattered the lap record too, his best lap being 1.4 seconds faster than Hill's pole time! It was Jim's seventeenth Grand Prix and his first win. The Clark legend had begun.

Le Mans was the next race on Bruce's calendar. He drove the 4-litre front-engined Cunningham Maserati he had tested earlier in the year, but failed to finish, a piston failing when Hansgen was at the wheel in the pre-dawn hours.

The Reims Grand Prix held by the Automobile Club du Champagne was the following weekend, a non-championship race scheduled confusingly just a week before the French Grand Prix proper at Rouen. Experience had taught the Cooper team that race pace was more important than practice times so they left Team Lotus to do the champagne laps and instead took the Coopers back to the garage in town to prepare them for the race.

'Reims is always hard on cars, with the engine screaming on full throttle for nearly four miles out of five and two slow hairpins to give the brakes and gearbox a good workout. Slipstreaming was what Reims was all about.'

Bruce put the car on the second row of the grid, just behind Jimmy on pole, and he felt ideally placed because he could latch on to the fastest Lotus. But it didn't work out like that.

'The more carefully you lay plans, the more easily they go wrong. Jimmy made a bad start. I couldn't believe it. Assuming he would make a good one and to ensure I would be right on his tail, I had jumped the start a fraction. With the Lotus almost at a standstill in front of me and my back tyres smoking, I had the busiest of moments trying to swing out past Jimmy and howl off with the pack.'

I wish I had kept a copy of the Reims newspaper from the following morning. The enterprising photographer had been above the grid and his front-page shot showed Bruce almost sideways on the second row, tyres smoking as he tried to dodge the Lotus! He rescued the situation and was able to chase Surtees in the leading Lola on that opening lap.

It got better. 'When Jimmy went by as we accelerated up the long hill before the downhill run where we reach nearly 160 mph (tame after the old 2.5-litre cars at 180 mph), I ducked in behind him. Within a lap he had drawn well clear of the pack, but one thing was upsetting both our calculations — John Surtees was a couple of hundred yards ahead of us with his Lola and he was pulling out half a second or so every lap, on his own with no one to slipstream.'

It got worse. Jimmy's hand went up and he disappeared into the pits with a burst header tank so Bruce was left alone, losing time to Surtees and the Lola. He knew that the chasing trio of Hill's BRM, Brabham's Lotus and Ireland's UDT-Lotus would drag themselves up to him by slipstreaming and when they arrived they set about an exciting flat-out run with positions changing all round the track. This is when the new six-speed Cooper gearbox showed its advantage.

'While the others changed into top in their five-speed boxes, I could hang on to my fifth gear, which gave me a definite pull to the top of the rise on the straight. My V8 Climax was running sweetly and I hadn't revved over 8500 rpm. Three or four times we passed the pits side-by-side before barrelling into the long, fast right-hander. At least twice Graham and I went into this corner abreast. I thought he would back off for an instant and tuck in behind, but he stayed on the outside all the way round. Graham was certainly putting a lot of faith in my judgement...'

Surtees retired after 26 laps, which meant the group was racing for the lead. Bruce decided to experiment with his braking distances in case it came to a last-lap shoot-out, but this came unstuck on lap 33. 'Going into the Muizon hairpin on the back of the circuit I left it really late, squeezing the brake pedal hard, but when I arrived at the part of the track where I normally locked over into the corner I was still a fraction too fast. I squeezed the pedal harder and the right front wheel locked with a puff of smoke from the tyre. Rather than risk a spin by trying to get round, I put the wheel straight again and shot down the escape road. Fortunately there was another way around the back of the corner, which was simply a rounded-off section of a road junction. This was a handy unorthodox dodge if one was in trouble — which I was! — but Graham and Jack had picked up a hundred-yard lead. Next time past the pits I could see the despondency among the Cooper crew...'

Bruce was determined to make amends for his mistake. 'With only five laps left, I pulled out all the stops. It was worth extending things a bit and I started using an extra 300 revs, taking the engine up to 8800 rpm between gear changes. Within a lap I was back on the tail of Graham and Jack and soon I was in front. With those few extra revs I could pull out a second a lap and I cruised across the finishing line with a five-second lead.'

Denis Jenkinson, as usual, had his own take on the race, which he had decided was devalued by the non-appearance of Ferrari or Porsche. In those closing laps, he wrote in *Motor Sport*, 'It was all very exciting but somehow could not be taken too seriously as all the cars were green and the three drivers were nice friendly lads, enjoying themselves but with nothing to stimulate them into doing anything heroic or desperate, such as we saw in 1961 when Bonnier, Gurney and Baghetti were in a similar situation with the end of the race in sight. The three "chums" were not hanging about, for McLaren clocked 2:24.8 on lap 44, an average of 206.397 kph (approximately 128 mph) and this got the other two out of his slipstream. On lap 47 Graham Hill did 2:24.0, the fastest lap of the race and on lap 48 the issue was settled, for McLaren led Hill by 5 seconds and Brabham by 9 seconds.'

Bruce had beaten two drivers who would in time win five world titles between them.

'That night there was plenty of champagne and a noisy dinner at the Cafe de la Paix with a battle of bread rolls and sugar lumps between the Cooper and Brabham tables. The next morning John Cooper found the works Mini van on the footpath between two trees and it took the help of several puzzled Frenchmen to rescue it.'

I think it was that restaurant that saw the Cooper team dining on one side of an elegant glass partition and the equally noisy Brabham crew on the other. When a huge platter of *pomme frites* arrived, John Cooper grabbed it from the waiter, climbed on his chair and emptied it over the table on the other side. It took some time for Jack's wife to get the chips out of her hair…and see the funny side of it.

This was before the big money arrived in Formula 1 and racing became professional and serious. No wonder I look back on the '60s as the Good Old Days. They were. The after-race dinners at the Hotel de la Ville at Monza became legend, ending in pitched bread-roll battles between the Cooper and Lotus teams, all of whom were staying in the hotel. It seems hard to believe now, but when the meal was finished and a suitable amount of Italian *vino* had been supped, the big heavy tables were tipped up to form barricades and the waiters watched as the mad *Inglese* hurled bread rolls at each other. Occasionally they would arrive with more rolls as ammunition and final ordnance was a bread roll dunked in wine for weight, flight and impressive result. John Cooper and Colin Chapman, who had usually been fighting alongside their mechanics, happily settled any clean-up charges the following morning on departure. It may read like an early version of soccer hooliganism but the owner of the hotel was always on hand as the bills were paid on the Monday morning, assuring the team owners that their rooms would be waiting next year...

The French Grand Prix at Rouen in 1962 was a turbulent affair. Porsche had passed on Spa but were back for Rouen, presumably having solved their problems. Enzo Ferrari, by contrast, had staged one of his temporary withdrawals and the World Champion, Phil Hill, arrived in France as a spectator. These were the days of flexible grids, before Bernie Ecclestone arrived on the scene and guaranteed grids for race organisers.

Rouen was a new course for most of the drivers. The 3.9-mile Les Essarts course had been last used for Grand Prix cars in 1957, when Fangio won in a 250F Maserati at an average speed of 100.02 mph, his race captured in a classic *Motor Sport* photograph of him drifting downhill through the curves after the pits.

In 1962, Jim Clark took pole position with a time of 2:14.8 in his 1.5-litre lightweight Lotus. Hill's BRM was second and Bruce, still on form, started third. McLaren's race almost ended when his fourth gear failed going into the uphill hairpin and he spun, clouting the kerb and breaking the chassis. Yet Bruce thought that, given the attrition rate, it might be worth pressing on and doing his best with the car's weird handling. It paid off, as he lasted the distance to finish fourth. Dan Gurney was delighted to score the first Grand Prix victory for Porsche…and for himself. It was this race that the *gendarmes*, for some dense French reason, stood together arm in arm and blocked the pit entry at the end of the race. Surtees' Lola came limping down to pull in and quit, only to be forced to swerve back on track. Trintignant in turn had to swerve to miss him only to be literally run over by Trevor Taylor's Lotus, which was finishing the race at speed. Once more Trevor escaped unscathed from what looked like a nasty accident, both cars losing wheels.

The British Grand Prix at Aintree marked the first of Bruce's 'From the Cockpit' columns in *Autosport*. It was a moment in history — the first time a racing driver actually wrote for the readers. The columns became hugely popular.

On Bruce's page in that issue of August, 1962, there was a photograph of Patty McLaren, Paula Cooper, Bev Jane and Gail, Tony Maggs' fiancée, all perched on the pit bench tending stopwatches and lap charts. There was also a photo of a grinning Jim Clark, with his flat cap worn rakishly backwards. The all-important opening paragraph read: 'Liverpudlians say that if you can see the end of the Aintree grandstands from the pits, it'll be raining in half an hour, and if you can't see the stand, it's raining already. However, on the day of the British Grand Prix this wasn't quite true and though the rain was not far away, the circuit was dry for the race.'

We were able to take the reader right on to the grid — a sort of precursor to Martin Brundle's televised grid stroll of today. 'An incident on the grid ten minutes before the start raised a laugh. For ease of entry the Porsche steering wheel is detachable, rather like a knock-on wire wheel. Dan Gurney's steering wheel and its big three-eared wing nut were sitting on the nose of the Porsche and for devilment Jimmy Clark "borrowed" the wheel and nut and vanished into the grid crowd. He threw me the wheel nut and passed the wheel to someone else and before long no one — least of all Dan — knew where the Porsche tiller was. Poor Dan was in quite a state, but when the five-minute board went up we took pity on him and returned his steering gear.'

There had been a Cooper panic at midnight before the first day of Aintree practice when the engine on the transporter blew itself to pieces on the M1 motorway. 'The transporter was towed to the all-night service station and a phone call woke the Cooper household in Surbiton at 5 a.m. A horde of Mini vans and trailers put on a "Gulliver and the Lilliputians" act to get my car and equipment to Aintree for the first practice session. The C.T. Atkins mechanics were woken and their transporter borrowed to ferry the other works V8, the spare four-cylinder car and the spares to the circuit.'

There wasn't much about Bruce's race participation in that first column. In fact, we seem to have forgotten to mention that he finished third. He had equalled Hill's BRM qualifying time to sit beside him on the second row. Clark cleared off and won as he pleased from Surtees' Lola and Bruce's Cooper.

That first column ended with the story of the drivers visiting Blackpool the day after the race. 'On the way back from an afternoon spent scanning the bleak "Riviera" scene of bingo halls, Blackpool rock and the anatomical horrors in the wax works, the James Clark Lotus Elite was flagged down by a police car for allegedly touching 31 mph in a restricted area. After a lecture on the evils of speed, the constable proudly finished berating his choice "catch" by saying, "You young fellows with fast sports cars don't appreciate the dangers of speed…" '

The German Grand Prix on the Nürburgring got off to a poor start for Graham Hill, who crashed out during practice when he ran over a big television movie camera lying in the middle of the track. It had been fixed to de Beaufort's Porsche but had fallen when the mountings fractured. Bruce was right behind the BRM. 'I was swooping down into the Fuchsrohre when a cloud of dust spelt trouble and I jammed on the brakes, stopping a little further up the hill to glimpse Graham and the BRM virtually out of sight behind a belt of trees. The car left the road and went ricocheting down a ditch for about 200 yards, getting farther and farther into the scrub. If I'd been any closer to Graham, I probably would have missed the warning cloud of dust, hit the oil and joined him in the ditch.'

Race day was desperate. It started with fog and rain and got worse when Bruce realised that his helmet bag had been stolen and he had to borrow kit from the other drivers. Fellow Kiwi Tony Shelly loaned him a helmet. Bruce had also lost his wallet, which contained all his racing documents. It was returned some months later, having obviously been thrown into a river. It had been sent to the German race organisers, who mailed it on to Bruce. He finished a very damp fifth in the race, which was won by Graham Hill, in a reversal of his pre-race fortunes.

After von Trips' fatal accident the year before, the Italian GP at Monza used the road course only, abandoning the banked section of the circuit, and for Bruce — who started from the second row — it was a slipstreaming extravaganza. 'For me the race was one long battle — or rather a series of battles. First it was Dan Gurney in the Porsche, and although we tried to tow ourselves nearer to the leading trio of Hill and Ginther in the BRMs and Surtees in the Lola, we made no impression. We were soon engulfed in a bellowing mob of Ferraris and Lotuses, headed by Innes Ireland in his UDT-Lotus, but he was a lap down after a pit stop and was aiding his teammate Masten Gregory. Dan and I couldn't beat them, so we joined them. What a session! Motoring at such close quarters called for continual alertness. Being sandblasted by the flying grit, and the nonstop exhaust racket made my position rather uncomfortable, compounded by the fact that I had forgotten to fit my earplugs and I was nearly deafened.

'At times I glanced around to find a Ferrari roaring up alongside me, while Dan's Porsche was ducking out of my slipstream on the other side. The following lap I would be tucked in behind Tony Maggs' Cooper and the next it would be Bonnier's Porsche. On one occasion passing the pits I glanced at the signal board, scanned my instruments, then looked into my left-hand mirror for Dan as I eased to the right to let him through. He wasn't there! The only place he could have been was on my right, and he was. Poor Dan. I nearly had him in the wall...'

Ferrari had entered *five* cars for their home race at Monza but despite this and their domination of the previous year, they were eclipsed by two BRMs and a Cooper. On the final lap Hill and Ginther were well out in front; Willy Mairesse, recovered from his Spa shunt, came through to take third place from Bruce. But Bruce had it all worked out and slipstreamed the Ferrari over that last lap, took the lead into the last corner and held it to the flag.

Jim Clark had started from pole but had retired with a broken gearbox and so earned no points. This meant that Bruce's third place lifted him to second in the World Championship. Graham Hill had 36 points, Bruce 22, Jim 21 and John Surtees 19. 'Coming home in the plane we were working out the possible scoring combinations from the two races left in the series, and I found that even if I win both races and Graham doesn't place in either event, he will still beat me by one point.' Only the best five results could be counted, so the title would be fought out between Clark and Hill. As it happened, Bruce took third at Watkins Glen, which left everything for the final race of the season, the South African Grand Prix at East London. This was being run incredibly late — 29 December — so we filled in the time racing in America and Australia.

These races really marked the start of the McLaren team. Bruce had bought a Cooper Formula 1 chassis from Tommy Atkins and had Harry

Pearce and Wally Willmott fit it with a 2.5-litre Climax engine for testing before its debut in the Australian Grand Prix in November. A cutting from a New Zealand newspaper about Bruce's fledgling team announced that we were all Kiwis and all under 25. I was 23, Wally was 21. 'As secretary, Young has to handle a lot of fan mail, which McLaren receives from all parts of the world. He has to keep 500 to 600 autographs of McLaren at all times.' And they were all signed by Bruce. I wish I had kept a few. They sell for £200–£300 each now. Those were the days when, if you wrote to a driver, you knew that the signed photograph you received in reply was guaranteed to have a genuine signature. This is no longer so certain; I know for a fact that Ayrton Senna used to hire a journalist to sign his mountain of fan-mail postcards on his behalf.

The newspaper feature continued: 'Young also handles travel bookings for the team, along with his public relations duties as McLaren's manager. Wally Willmott has probably had one of the most meteoric rises of any Grand Prix mechanic. He served his apprenticeship in Timaru and often raced a Cooper 500 in South Island club events. He went to Australia at the beginning of this year [1962] for a fortnight's holiday. Willmott had never seen the engine of a 2.5-litre Cooper-Climax before, but some emergency work was needed on Angus Hyslop's car before a race. Willmott surprised everybody by stripping the engine and gearbox and fitting new pistons all in one night and had the Cooper going perfectly in the morning. McLaren was impressed with the young mechanic's knowledge and ability and, as a result, McLaren was able to get Willmott a job with C.T. (Tommy) Atkins' garage in England.'

The new Cooper Monaco sports car had been sent to California for the races at Riverside and Laguna Seca, and Bruce and Patty had flown to Watkins Glen for the US Grand Prix, then on to California. The TWA flight from New York to Los Angeles was hilarious. There were five of us — Bruce and Patty, John Cooper, Mike Barney and me — and three other passengers in the economy end of a Boeing 707. That was it — eight passengers in the entire economy section. The twist was all the dance rage in Britain and the flight hostesses insisted that we teach them. It was a flight to remember. When we left the plane our flight bags were crammed with drinks miniatures. Apparently each flight had a set allocation of booze and somehow we hadn't managed to drink ours. One of the girls was a race fan and we invited her to Riverside. She said she would be driving a blue Chevy, so we left tickets at the gate with instructions that they were for the girl with the blue Chevy. Halfway through race morning a message arrived at the pit from the gatekeeper. I went out to find a tearful lady, unable to get her tickets. I asked where her Chevy was. Oh. She'd forgotten about bringing the Chevy. She was driving her Cadillac convertible instead...

The Cooper Monaco had trouble getting through scrutineering at Riverside because it didn't have safety belts. John tried to explain that drivers in Europe were men who scorned such namby-pamby safety extras, saying everyone knew that it was safer to be thrown out in an accident. It made no difference. No safety belts, no race. John solved the problem as only he could. Or would. He grabbed a pair of cutters, hacked the seatbelts out of the hire car, and *wired* them to the lower chassis rails of the cockpit. So, seatbelts in place, the car passed scrutineering...

In the event Roger Penske won both races — and all the prize money — in his pretty, lightweight sports car that was based on a Formula 1 Cooper that Walt Hansgen had crashed at Watkins Glen in 1961. Bruce later bought this car and, fitted with an Oldsmobile V8, it became the basis of the McLaren supremacy in sports car racing. Which begs the questions (a) why did John Cooper not copy Penske's idea since it was, after all, based on one of his Cooper Formula 1 cars, and (b) why did Penske not do what Bruce would eventually do, and replace the 2.7 Coventry-Climax engine with an American V8? No one knows.

Roger's victory was a definite plus for Bruce. Before the race at Riverside,

Bruce and Roger had made a deal that whoever won would treat the other to a spree in Las Vegas. 'The prospect of buying the key to Las Vegas for Roger and Lisa was never a problem for me as I was never in sight of the lead and with his stack of dollars, I shouldn't think it will worry Roger a great deal…' Penske covered his hospitality costs by winning large on the gaming tables.

The team flew down to Mexico City for a non-championship race, which got off to a terrible start when Ricardo Rodriguez was killed in practice. It was his home circuit and was later named after him. Ricardo had raced all season as a works Ferrari driver, but when the team did not enter the race in Mexico, he arranged to drive Rob Walker's Lotus-Climax V8. 'Ricardo was a friend to us all. With his charm and manner off the circuit he was well liked by all who had known him. His ability on the circuit made us respect him. At only 20 years of age, he had more racing miles and racing wins than most men twice his age.'

It was the first time the other drivers had seen the circuit, which race organisers hoped would run a championship race next year. Bruce was intrigued. 'At the end of the main straight there is a corner that seems to have "now solve this one!" written all over it. It's a decreasing radius corner; in other words the turn gradually gets tighter the farther you go around it, then it turns sharp left! It's the sort of corner Stirling would have revelled in…' It's interesting that Moss had been out of racing all season, yet his was still the name that Bruce used to benchmark his description of the corner.

Roger Penske had entered the Mexican race in a UDT-Lotus and to prove his point, if proof were needed that he had racing talent, he qualified fifth just behind Bruce in the works Cooper, and ahead of Brabham, Ireland, Salvadori, Gregory et al.

The start was a shambolic mix of delays, overheating cars, smoke and flames. When the flag dropped, little changed. Jim Clark had his flat battery replaced on the grid, then caught the field and took the lead…until he was black-flagged for a push-start. Showing his talent for strategy Colin Chapman brought Trevor Taylor in from third place, Jim jumped in the car, got back in the race — still in third place — and went on to win! Bruce retired with an engine breakage, but they all had good memories of the Mexican event, despite the shambles.

'On the rostrum, Jim was awarded the applause he deserved and both Jim and Jack paid fitting tribute to the very female film star handing out the trophies, but not in so many words, if you see what I mean. I hope next year's race is for the World Championship so that we will all have to go back,' he wrote.

A fortnight later the team was on the West Coast of Australia preparing both the new Cooper for the Grand Prix and a Mini Cooper that local agents BMC had asked Bruce to race in a separate event. The Mini Cooper was Bruce's favourite and he and Wally had already prepared a hot one and shipped it to New Zealand for the series there. The Mini Cooper in Perth was not tuned to the state of the car then on the water to Auckland, but it was still a novelty and we enjoyed ourselves at night, taunting lads in their Holdens at the traffic lights and then smoking them off.

Bruce delighted the Mini Cooper agents and amazed the crowd by finishing a cheeky sixth behind an E-Type Jaguar, a Ford Galaxie, a Lotus Elite and a couple of hot Holdens.

Bruce's Australian Grand Prix started with a theft — someone stole the team's racing tool box from the boot of the hire car while it was parked at the motel. After a police search and radio newsflashes the tools were mysteriously returned, left under a tree in a local park. Then Bruce had an 'off' in practice that smashed the car's nose, but overnight panel-beating had the car repaired. Brabham had flown his car out for the race too, and he and Bruce were easily the fastest on the 2-mile Caversham circuit. Jack had engine problems, though, blowing two in practice and only starting the race courtesy of Bruce loaning him the team's spare 2.5-litre Climax.

There were times in the race when Bruce may have wondered at his own generosity, as the extra revs permissible with the smaller motor, along with Brabham's eagerness to win his 'home' Grand Prix, meant that Jack was in a commanding position. It didn't last.

'Jack disappeared from the lap chart in a rather violent manner. I over-cooked things and spun with just 10 laps to go and as I went gyrating into the scrub I was conjuring up thoughts of having to say, "Well, if I hadn't spun..." but fortunately I finished on the track pointing the right way and grabbed low gear to take off just before Jack arrived on the scene. He must have got a little over-anxious when he saw how much the gap had narrowed, but unfortunately — fortunately for me — he tangled with a slower car and smashed in the nose of the Brabham against a line of markers.'

My main memory of Caversham concerns the Aussie flies. They were *awful!* Always on your face. You didn't dare open your mouth or they'd be in. We either had to wear an anti-insect spray that was just about as unpleasant as the flies, or some sort of mask like the Lone Ranger. It was nice to get back to New Zealand for some fly-free time at home.

There wasn't much rest for Bruce, though, as he had to fly to South Africa before Christmas, stopping first at Tony Maggs' home in Pretoria before tackling the 800-mile drive to East London, the historic sea-side home of the Grand Prix in South Africa. Bruce had been looking forward to surfing and sun, but he took ill on the long trip down and spent three days in bed with a bad bout of influenza, rising from his sick-bed just in time for the first practice session. The Cooper team trialled a V-shaped radiator in an effort to gain an advantage on the long straights, but it looked awful, performed worse and it was rejected. In the days before wind-tunnels and computer-aided design, it wasn't uncommon for 'streamlining' to actually increase the drag.

Both the race and the world title were fought out between Jim Clark and Graham Hill and it didn't look good for Graham. 'Jimmy was running fuel injection on the Lotus and was having a bit of bother with misfiring, but it was still performing pretty well. Graham told a tale of roaring healthily down the straight in the BRM...and being passed by Clark, running on seven cylinders! He was most upset.'

Both drivers had three *Grande Epreuve* wins to their credit, but Hill's two additional second places gave him a higher total on the 'best five' basis. The fact remained that if Clark won the race, he would take the title. But if Clark finished in any position other than first, Hill could retire from the race and still be World Champion in 1962.

The cars were weighed before the race: Jim's Lotus was right on the limit at 990 lb, Graham's BRM was beefy at 1115 lb and the fuel-injected Cooper was even heavier at 1140 lb.

'Before the race we had to "run the gauntlet" of the parade lap in sports cars. It was all right until we got to the section reserved for coloured spectators. They were all highly excited and keen to touch the drivers. Have you ever been "touched" at 40 mph? Most of us shrunk down in the cars, but we were still battered and bruised. Richie Ginther said he was waiting for one with an axe!'

Clark sat on pole, three-tenths faster than Graham's BRM, and when the flag dropped the Flying Scot simply drove away from the field. Bruce started on row four alongside Ginther's BRM. Clark's domination lasted for 62 of the 82 laps. 'Jimmy pulled into the pits. His car had been spraying oil out for a few laps and was at the stage where there couldn't have been much oil left in the tank. The mechanics hurriedly searched for the leak, but in Formula 1 you couldn't add oil, so that was very definitely that. Colin Chapman and Jimmy, not to mention the rest of the Lotus boys, must have been on the verge of tears. A bolt locating a jack-shaft bearing had screwed itself out — why don't bolts ever screw their way in?'

As a result of Jim's misfortune Graham led the race and was guaranteed the title whatever happened. Bruce was second; his South African teammate

Tony Maggs was third and probably anxious to be second. Jack Brabham was in fourth and definitely wanted to be third. 'Towards the end of the race Tony closed up on me and we diced backwards and forwards for a while and Jack began to apply the pressure, but the chequered flag caught him before he caught us. On the victory lap it started raining…'

After the title celebrations it was time to get back on a plane and fly across the world for the 1963 New Zealand Grand Prix at the brand-new Pukekohe circuit. 'Graham, Tony and Gail Maggs, John Surtees, Jack, Innes, Reg Parnell, a few of the mechanics and myself set off on the long trip halfway across the world, but we were held up in Karachi waiting for a jet that had been snowed-in at Heathrow. Most of us had yellow fever vaccinations, but those who didn't, Graham among them, were confined under quarantine in the airport jail! How would you feel as newly crowned World Champion, one minute sitting in the first-class section of a Boeing 707 drinking champagne and singing 'Auld Lang Syne' on New Year's Eve, the next being virtually in jail. Every plane that took off from Karachi backed up to this shack first, vibrating the ants out of the rafters… We were eventually bundled on another plane bound for Sydney and a group of very weary travellers eventually stepped off in Auckland, on the eve of first practice for the Grand Prix.'

So much for the glamour of international Grand Prix racing…

11 The racing summer of '63

Bruce started the 1963 season on a high, taking pole position for the New Zealand Grand Prix on the new 3.65 km Pukekohe circuit near Auckland, built in and around a horse race track along Aintree lines. He'd made headlines by running faster in practice than Brabham, Surtees, Maggs and the new World Champion, Graham Hill. It was a fantastic start to the eight-race series, four of which would be run in New Zealand and four in Australia.

Bruce's pole position lap of 1:26.8 was comfortably faster than Surtees who was second fastest (1:28.2) in his 2.7-litre Lola Climax. However, Bruce bogged the start and Surtees led away, but only for the first eight laps with the crowd behind him, Bruce took the lead but lost it when his engine started to misfire. 'It wasn't too bad at first, but it gradually got worse, and I had a strong suspicion that it might be ignition trouble. I thought the magneto switch might have been making contact with something it shouldn't have, which would have made the engine start to miss, so I pulled the wires off the switch, but this made no difference to the off-beat of the engine. By this time my speed along the back straight had dropped from over 150 mph to about 130 mph, so I decided to stop at the pits in the hope that my mechanics might be able to cure the trouble in time for me to set off after John again. Discounting the magneto switch, spark plugs seemed to be the next most likely source of a sour engine. The boys checked all the leads and waved me off again just as Graham went by into second place in his four-wheel drive Ferguson. I pulled by him on that lap, but the engine was still not behaving so I let him go and called back to the pits.'

Harry and Wally changed the spark plugs in record time but they discovered that the magneto was well and truly roasted from the heat of the day and the exhaust. To compound things, the fuel tank had a small stress crack and was leaking. Bruce had to sit and watch Surtees win in the Lola. He wasn't alone. Brabham had retired with a blown head gasket and Maggs with bent valves. Graham also had problems but at least he was mobile. On the second lap his clutch had failed, leaving him to make clutchless changes. Two laps later first gear failed, but Graham pressed on gallantly, only to be robbed of second place almost within sight of the flag when the transmission finally gave up. Graham had also been suffering from the heat of the summer sun as well as the front engine, saying it was like 'racing a bloody oven!' He ended the day by walking back to the pits.

Though the team had thoroughly checked the magneto it failed again at Levin the following weekend when they tried to start up for the qualifying heat. A new 'mag' was quickly fitted but then a clutch problem appeared. 'Harry and Wally set some sort of record pulling off the Colotti gearbox, finding and fixing the trouble and bolting everything back together again, but by this time the race heat was over.'

Missing the heat meant that Bruce was well back on the grid and had to fight his way up through the pack on the tight circuit. He got up to second place on the tail of Brabham's new turquoise car, but that was as good as it got. He spun into a pile of marker tyres, smashed the nose in and altered the camber of a front wheel. 'So for the second time in a week I was a spectator before the race was half over and didn't feel particularly interested in the fact that Jack had won his first international race in a car with his name on the nose.'

At Wigram the three fastest qualifiers — Brabham, Surtees and McLaren — all gambled on using Dunlop D12 rain tyres, knowing that they could be in trouble if they ran hard for the whole race in the baking sun. The D9 'dry' tyres were a safer bet, but they were slower too; if one person was going to fit D12s, the others had to as well.

Surtees made the best start but had Bruce on his tail. On the second lap a collision between Jim Palmer's little Lotus and Lionel Bulcraig in the big front-engined Aston Martin left oil all over the circuit. Surtees went one side of it and Bruce went the other, diving into the lead. By twenty laps into the race the order was McLaren-Surtees-Brabham. 'I'd been keeping a close watch on the red nose of the Surtees Lola in my mirrors and I noticed that he appeared to be in a haze of oil smoke. But if it was his oil smoke, the haze should have been behind him, not in front, and I realised that it was *my* car laying the smoke screen,' recalled Bruce.

At half distance Surtees came into the pits with gearbox problems and Bruce took the lead, paying close attention to his oil pressure and wondering how close Brabham was. Next thing he found out! 'I was about to lock over into the hairpin and the Brabham arrived beside me with tyres smoking. I'd forgotten he had been right on John's tail, and now Jack was in front of me…the number of miles I've raced behind Jack! Now we really started to fly, using all the track out of the corners and then some. We had wheels on the grass and we must have been using up the rear tyres at an alarming rate.'

If Bruce had a minor problem with a smoking exhaust, Jack suddenly had a major one and had to pit to take on more oil. Jack and Bruce had different types of piston in their 2.7-litre Climax engines. Jack's pistons were a type that didn't break but used a lot of oil because they had only two rings. The McLaren pistons had three rings and didn't use very much oil, but they did break occasionally. And in this race, two of the piston ring lands *had* broken, but Jack's pit stop gave Bruce an 80-second cushion with 25 laps to go. It was a cushion that Jack did his best to deflate. Bruce drove as slowly as he dared, expecting his oil pressure to drop to zero at any time. Jack pushed hard to close the gap, but he had an absolutely bald rear tyre. Similarly, Bruce's right rear tyre had only half a millimetre of rubber left and he was well aware that if they had kept up their mid-race pace they would have both punctured. Bruce hung on to win, but at the end there were only two quarts of oil in his oil tank, which normally held three-and-a-half gallons. But a win was a win.

Innes Ireland had been driving Graham Hill's Ferguson, and it expired on the fast airfield circuit in a cloud of steam, a blown head gasket ending his race 15 laps from the finish. 'The gauges that weren't reading 212 degrees were reading zero,' said Innes afterwards.

The Ferguson was better suited to the Teretonga circuit and the following weekend Bruce and Innes had a battle in the first race heat. 'The Ferguson really goes off the line like a shell and to hear Innes describing all four wheels biting and scrabbling is quite amusing. It is the only one of the present-day racing cars in which the driver sits almost upright, and we have a strong suspicion that if the seat was reclined to the flat-on-your-back position of our other cars, the acceleration off the line would shoot Innes out straight over the tail!'

Bruce made a good start in the race but botched a change to second, which left him mid-field going into the first long loop. Surtees led the opening lap and then spun, giving Brabham the lead. Bruce caught up to his old teammate and when he made an uncharacteristic mistake — 'I suddenly realised I'd left the gate open,' Jack said after the race — Bruce went through and held the lead to the line.

There was a fortnight break before the first Australian race at Sydney's Warwick Farm, but the time was necessary to get the cars and equipment across the Tasman Sea by ship. Brabham had sold his car to Australian journalist/racer, David McKay, and he had a brand-new vehicle sent out by sea from the UK. The boat had to make a detour to aid a vessel in distress so when it finally arrived in Melbourne an impatient Brabham was waiting on the dock, while everyone else prepared to start practice in Sydney. 'Jack found that his car was buried beneath the huge crates containing Donald

Campbell's *Bluebird* land speed record car and tons of spares. The Brabham patience must have run very thin on the wharf and I doubt if he shared in the general consternation when *Bluebird* almost rolled into the sea while it was being unloaded.'

The usual new-car teething troubles meant Jack started from the back of the grid, so the other competitors crossed him off their problem list. Surtees qualified on pole in his Lola, Bruce alongside him. The Sydney sun beat down as they took the grid and the team packed dry ice round the Cooper's fuel tank. Bruce emptied a watering can into his seat and stuffed his pockets with ice. He moved into second place on the second lap. And then spun. Surtees built up a big lead and then *he* spun. 'He recovered immediately, but the Lola was in the Brabham sights — this is the same Brabham we were ignoring! — and the race was all over bar the shouting. There was plenty of that. Jack, using more grass than road, closed in and passed the Lola, carrying on to win his first-ever Australian Grand Prix in his own Brabham, a car that had still been on the drawing board 12 months previously. I finished third. Jack unwisely called at our motel on his way home and my crew showed their appreciation by tossing him fully dressed into the swimming pool. He was probably expecting it...'

Water-skiing was the sporty fashion for the drivers in the 1960s and the opportunity to perfect their style and skill was one of the reasons the Down Under races were so popular among the drivers. Bruce and Patty drove to Surfers Paradise for some skiing with Bob and Beverley Jane, before the race at Lakeside near Brisbane. Disaster struck on the river. 'Bob's speedboat, with Patty, Beverley, myself and a driver aboard, capsized in freak conditions while Bob was skiing behind and threw us all into the water.'

Patty was a strong swimmer, but she was run over by the propeller, which smashed one ankle and lacerated the other. The boat righted itself and started to circle the struggling group in the water, dragging a rope behind that started to wind itself round Beverley. The boat was eventually brought under control and they made a dash to the shore where an ambulance was waiting. The bones in Patty's left ankle and heel were badly smashed and she had a lengthy and painful time ahead in a thigh-high plaster cast.

Warwick Farm had been a scorcher, but Lakeside was deluged by a thunderstorm on race day. Bruce spun early in the race but recovered. 'I set off again as fast as I dared, but a few laps later I scudded straight off the track on a huge pool of water that had formed on the pit straight. I must have been doing 110 mph when I hit the water, but fortunately the car wasn't damaged and came to rest a few feet from one of the lakes.' Bruce watched Surtees win unchallenged, the rain having sent 11 of the 15 starters spinning off the circuit.

Surtees had signed with Ferrari for 1963, which meant he had to fly back to Italy after his wet win at Lakeside. Brabham had returned to Surrey after his Warwick Farm win but was back for the next race in the series at Longford in Tasmania.

The 4.5-mile Longford circuit demands description. It is run on public roads just outside Launceston, giving it a definite flavour of Reims. The average lap speed was nearly 115 mph when we went there in 1963. One long, rollicking straight put top speed up around 170 mph and the other straight was good for 160 mph. There was a very solid-looking viaduct, a slightly rustic, long, bumpy wooden bridge, a railway crossing and a 90-degree right-hander with a country pub on the apex where the locals leant on the bar and watched the cars flashing past the windows. Permanent pits and a timing tower were also redolent of Reims. Bruce reckoned it to be one of the best of the few genuine road circuits then in use.

Practice was held on Friday, with qualifying heats on Saturday, Sunday left free for lunch parties — or repairs — and the main race on Monday. Bruce was fastest in practice, stalled at the start of the first qualifying race — 'I was very relieved when everyone managed to scrape past without coming over the top or taking one of my rear wheels with them' — recovered, took the lead but then suffered a burst drive-shaft yoke. Brabham missed this first race entirely as a result of engine troubles, leaving popular Australian gentleman-racer Lex Davison to win in his Cooper.

Bruce's crew organised for a new drive-shaft yoke to be fabricated locally on the Sunday so he was all ready for race day. The length of the main straight meant that accurate judgement of gear ratios was essential. On Saturday there had been a 10 mph head-wind, but on the Monday the wind had switched direction and there was a 10 mph breeze up their tails. Mercifully, the team decided to change the ratios on Bruce's Cooper, because they discovered a cracked ballrace just two hours before the start. In the race proper Jack and Bruce fought out the lead for the first 15 laps, but then Jack's engine blew in spectacular fashion leaving Bruce to win by some 80 seconds in the end. 'I felt sorry for Jack because I know what it is like to have worked so hard on the car and then not finish.'

Bob Jane in a Jaguar won the touring car race in fine style from Lex Davison in a big Ford Galaxie and everyone joined forces over dinner, awash with presentation champagne. I think this may have been the occasion when the hotel manager insisted on charging corkage in the dining room. He was a fairly pompous piece of work and when Bob told him that they had risked life and limb to win the champagne and that he should loosen up, the manager drew himself to his full height and said, 'Young man, I'm old enough to be your father.' To which Bob replied in devastating style: 'You're not *smart* enough to be *my* father…'

There was more champagne (100 bottles) up for grabs for pole position at Sandown Park, the final race in the series. Jack and Bruce were virtually tied for the fastest lap, but it was Bruce who earned the nod from the timekeepers — and the bubbly. The race was again held on a Monday and it began with a little light skirmishing between the old Cooper teammates. 'For the first few laps Jack and I swapped places for the fun of it to see who could run away from whom, but we were rapidly convinced that we were stuck with each other. Jack was pretty keen on winning this race and so was I. In practice we hadn't been much under 1:11.0, but in the last third of the race we didn't get above 1:09.0! We passed and re-passed each other a dozen times at least. Normally, you look after your own engine fairly carefully, but Jack was using as many revs as I was — I know, because we were changing gear at the same time and I had an overdraft of 500 revs...but what the hell — it was the last race of the series. With a lap and a half to go, I didn't think I could have got past the Brabham when suddenly a big-end bolt let go in his engine, and spectators were still returning pieces of engine to Jack hours after the race.'

Of the nine races on the Down Under series that started with the Grand Prix at Perth, Bruce had won five. He conceded that Brabham's engine problems had helped his cause, but expounded the obvious that to win a race you had to finish it. 'And to do this one needs a fast, reliable, well-prepared car and a competent crew. For that 1963 season "Down Under" I had both.'

During the series Harry Pearce and Wally Willmott had towed the Cooper all over Australia on a trailer hitched to an Austin Freeway. This was a modest, middle-size saloon, its main quality being that it was free, on loan from BMC. Harry hated it. I remember when we had loaded the car on the trailer after the first race of the Australian series at Warwick Farm. The back seat had been removed and was stacked with spares. The boot was filled to capacity and beyond and the spare Climax engine stood tall and proud. It became apparent that the boot lid would not *quite* shut over the cam covers. 'I'll shut the bloody thing,' Harry announced testily, and with that he slammed the lid down. A twin line of little round dimples appeared in the boot lid, miraculously matching the lines of bolt-heads on the cam covers.

After the final race Bruce sold his Cooper to Lex Davison, then flew back to Britain for the start of the new season. As usual he went via Sebring, less than seven days after Sandown, to drive Briggs Cunningham's new lightweight E-Type in the 12-hour race. He and Walt Hansgen finished eighth overall with Surtees taking overall victory in the factory Ferrari. Bruce didn't much care for the race at Sebring. 'Sebring is entirely different to Le Mans. There are so many corners and if you're not concentrating on going fast, you're concentrating on nursing the car, particularly the brakes. In the coupes there is a lot of noise, so you get a crashing headache out of it and in the open cars, by the end of 12 hours you often get a lot of fumes, brake-pad dust, and smoke being sucked back through the cockpit, as was the case with the Surtees Ferrari.

'John, I gather, after winning the race was really ill. I can understand this. You can't eat properly for the 12 hours. With the heat you get terribly thirsty. You drink too many Cokes and orange juices and the more you drink, the thirstier you get. Not speaking from experience, but I guess it's a bit like being hung over and exhausted at the same time...'

After the sunshine of the Antipodes, the cold and rain that greeted Bruce in the UK came as an unpleasant surprise. Fortunately, John Wyer had asked Bruce to drive one of his works Aston Martins for the test weekend at Le Mans, then held several months before the actual race. Bruce obliged, flying over with Wyer, Innes Ireland and American driver Bill Kimberly in the company executive plane. They landed at Le Mans at 5.55 p.m. and the ground transport — a Lagonda shooting brake and a DB4 Aston Martin — arrived at 6.03 p.m., the drivers apologising for being late. Wyer's team management efficiency was legendary. His nickname — never to his face — was 'Death Ray' and woe betide a driver who damaged a car or made a racing mistake.

This was Bruce's first visit to Wyer's team headquarters, located behind the Hotel de France in the little village of La Chartre sur-le-Loir, some 20 miles from the Le Mans circuit. 'Later that evening a transporter pulled up in the little village square and while half the townsfolk looked on, three dull-green and purposeful Aston Martins were rolled down on to the cobbles. Breakfast was at 7.30 a.m. the next morning (no one was more than a minute late) and at precisely 8.15 a.m. the three works Astons wakened the countryside for miles around as they set off for *Le Circuit* in line astern, bellowing and coughing in the cold and misty morning air.'

Wyer was delighted with Bruce's technical input to the car's set-up. Used to being fully involved with the Formula 1 cars, Bruce was in his element with the Astons. The previous summer he'd raced a 3.8 Jaguar for a private team in a touring car race in Britain and had been amazed at the reaction when he'd asked for the rollbar to be changed. Everyone had looked doubtfully at each other. The next morning Bruce asked if the rollbar had been changed and they confessed that it hadn't. They had called the factory and had been told no changes were to be made. The car was a *Jaguar*, and Bruce thought they regarded any suggestion of changing it as a measure of impertinence.

'Aston Martin, I think, feel as I do, that a racing car chassis is like a piano. You can make something that looks right with all the wires the right length, the right size and pretty close to the right settings, but until it is tuned it won't play so well. The Aston was a delight, particularly on the fast corners, and late that afternoon we managed to record some times that were substantially better than the best GTO Ferrari times. At a team drivers' meeting before dinner on the Saturday night, Jo Schlesser, Lucien Bianchi, Bill Kimberley and I marked circuit maps with our gear change and braking points and noted the rpm attained on each straight and through White House corner. From these, the tech men were able to check back on the sheets for the 1962 car and so analyse their improvements.'

Bruce returned to England in time for the Easter Goodwood meeting, for which his new Cooper was available. Cooper had the first of the new Coventry-Climax V8s, with a shorter stroke and revised fuel injection. The car was slimmer, as the chassis had been narrowed slightly. Size and weight had also been saved by having a special petrol tank built in the shape of a seat. The suspension was still wishbone all round, but the wishbone angles were slightly altered to stop the nose of the car diving under braking. The nose was slimmer and the tail little more than a curved cover over the engine, ending in a turn-up above the gearbox. In the new unpainted car Bruce qualified second to Graham Hill's BRM, led the opening lap and eventually finished second behind Ireland, driving the apple-green UDT Lotus-BRM.

Goodwood also saw the debut of young Chris Amon, 19, who drove Reg Parnell's Lola. His fifth place and polished, understated performance drew favourable comment. In due course Chris would become a works McLaren driver, share the 1966 Le Mans win for Ford with Bruce, and then go on to lead the Ferrari and Matra teams.

Denny Hulme was another Kiwi to make his mark in 1963, driving the works Formula Junior car for Brabham in a deal that would see him win the 1967 World Championship in a Brabham and then switch to the McLaren team in 1968. Bruce wrote: 'He is now being trained in the Brabham tradition by building, working on and developing his own car. He looks after the car and tunes it in the Brabham racing shop under Jack's watchful eye, and his fine drive in the rain at Aintree was the result — his first really big win for some time, and a most convincing one, at that.'

Bruce finished a dispirited fifth at Aintree, worried that the new car wasn't handling as it should. His worries multiplied when John Cooper crashed on the Kingston bypass in his twin-engined prototype Mini and was badly injured when the car somersaulted. John missed several races that season while he recuperated and Ken Tyrrell stepped in to look after the Formula 1 team. However, by the International Trophy race at Silverstone, Bruce was happier with the new car and put it on the front row of the grid. Although he led the opening laps of the race, Jim Clark eventually came through to win, with Bruce taking second.

At Monaco, common sense had finally prevailed and the start had been moved to what had been the back of the pits so the Gazometre Hairpin was no longer the first corner. The qualifying system had also been changed, from two works car per team to World Champions or previous winners, so Bruce qualified automatically, courtesy of his win the previous summer. He started well back on the fourth row beside Mairesse in the Ferrari. Clark and Hill were on the front row and it was Hill who led away, but after half an hour the order was Clark-Hill-Ginther-Surtees-McLaren. By half distance only eight cars were left running. Gearbox problems stopped most of the Lotuses, including Clark's car which selected two gears at once on the 78th lap. Hill and Ginther raced on to a BRM one-two, with Bruce third.

The new team ATS appeared for the first time at Spa, their car designed and built by a group who had quit the Ferrari team. ATS was headed by Carlo Chiti, with Phil Hill, disillusioned with the Ferrari politics, as its driver. The car looked a trifle gawky. Someone remarked on this to Dan Gurney, who sided with his fellow Californian. 'Don't worry,' said Dan. 'If it wins this weekend, it'll be the best-looking car here…'

The fast Spa circuit was awash on race day. Hill's BRM sat on pole, McLaren and Maggs shared the second row in the Coopers, and having had a succession of practice problems, Jim Clark was back on row three. Not that it made any difference. He was in the lead as the field climbed up the hill from the swoop of the first corner at Eau Rouge.

'The rain teemed down and soon there was evidence on the track where several cars had spun. It was just a matter of plodding on and hoping the race would soon finish. Clark was flying out ahead as usual and lapped the entire field during the race. In the closing laps, my pit crew emerged from shelter and began to signal enthusiastically that I was catching the man in front. Ahead, I could see two columns of spray. I knew one was Jimmy who had just lapped me, so I presumed the other sheet of water hid second-place man Dan Gurney in the Brabham. I pressed on as hard as I dared and overhauled both cars to move into second place. Dan was half-blinded in the spray with a broken lens in his goggles. I was damply delighted with my last-minute placing, as it meant I led the World Championship by one point from Graham, Jimmy and Richie.'

Jimmy had won the Belgian Grand Prix at Spa two years in succession. Only two drivers had scored the Belgian double before: Ascari in 1952–53 and Fangio in 1954–55. Clark was in good company.

Bruce's time at the top of the title ladder was brief as the Clark winning machine got into its stride: 'When I was dislodged from the top of the championship by Jimmy, I seemed to keep on falling.' The jinx that haunted him that season started at Zandvoort. Bruce had started from the front row of the grid, but as he chased down Clark the Cooper jammed itself in fifth gear and the race was over.

Things didn't improve at Le Mans, despite the positive feelings that had emerged at testing. Four hours into the race proper, the engine of the DB4GT Aston Martin failed. 'I was roaring down the Mulsanne Straight on full glorious song in the big car when a sudden loud clatter from the engine, accompanied by a tingling sensation at the top of my spine, told me that my rear wheels were covered in oil and I was still doing the best part of 175mph.' He made it through the fast kink in the straight and stopped on the grass before the hairpin, but the oil on the track had sparked an accident that involved several cars.

At Reims, scene of the 1963 World Championship French Grand Prix, Bruce had just moved into third place after Brabham had pitted to re-attach a high-tension lead, when the 'black box' in the Cooper burned out.

In the British Grand Prix at Silverstone Bruce and teammate Maggs both put their Coopers on the second row of the grid, but Bruce lasted only seven laps before his engine failed. 'The song from my Climax V8 was abruptly strangled. Initially, it seemed as though it was a petrol or ignition failure, but a quick glance in the mirror showed enough smoke coming out the back to screen a small-sized army.'

Bruce had taken time out in practice to observe cars going through Club corner. 'At Silverstone you concentrate on shaving the brick walls on the inside, not just an inch or two away, and you hold the car in a drift that if it were any faster would take you into a bank or on to the grass. If you are any slower you know that you are not going to be up with those first three or four. You know perfectly well you are trying just as hard as you possibly can, and I know when I've done a few laps like this, I come in and think to myself, well, if anyone tries harder than that, good luck to them. But you haven't thought about the people who have been watching. At least I haven't anyway, but at Club corner the role was reversed and I was watching — it was really exciting!

'Jimmy came in too fast and left his braking so late that I leapt back four feet, convinced that he wouldn't make the corner, but he went through, working and concentrating hard. I'm sure his front wheel just rubbed the wall. I barely dared to watch him come out the other end. And then Graham came through with the BRM steering wheel moving almost quicker than you could see, and the front wheels arcing to and fro, just holding the car on that very fine balance between a ten-tenths corner achieved and a backwards-off-the-road incident.'

In his entire career, Bruce only had two accidents that hurt him. Neither of them was his fault and the last one killed him. The first was in the 1963 German Grand Prix. He had qualified on the second row and made a strong start, but on the fourth lap he crashed heavily and woke up in nearby Adenau hospital. 'Apparently, instead of turning right into the slow right-hander at the top of the Foxhole, my car turned left. Whether I turned it left or it turned left of its own accord, I wish I knew. I was a little sceptical when Stirling Moss woke up from his Goodwood accident and said, "If you told me I'd been hit by a bus, old man, I'd have believed you!" I thought he must have had some recollection of at least the initial stages of getting involved in his accident. Now I know how blank that space can be. I had been unconscious for about an hour. It seems that the mind conveniently whitewashes anything that it would be better not to remember.

'My legs were pretty sore and I assumed that I must have been ejected from the Cooper cockpit at some stage and scraped a bit of skin off here and there, but I was worried that perhaps the other characters in the hospital room with me — one of them with a very black eye, one with a foot in plaster, and another who didn't look so good either — were something to do with my accident and it was with some apprehension that I started questioning the welcome steady stream of visitors who came to ask *me* what had happened…'

A check of the wreckage back in Surbiton showed that the right rear wishbone had broken and the car had turned suddenly left at 100 mph.

I waited for two days until Bruce was released from hospital with his right leg encased in a full-length plaster cast, then drove him home in a press road-test Sunbeam Rapier. The only way he could fit in was stretched across the back seat. The cast was removed at Kingston hospital, where they confirmed nothing was broken and he was ready to race for Aston Martin in the Tourist Trophy race at Goodwood a fortnight later. Once more, fortune failed to smile, and the engine expired.

'After my crash at the 'Ring I had thought hard about my future. I had once promised myself to give up racing after my first big shunt, but I realise now that would have been the worst possible thing I could have done. It's essential to go straight out again and have a go, if you are ever going to look yourself in the eye again.'

Incredibly, the organisers of the Italian Grand Prix at Monza wanted to combine the banked section and road circuit once again, but Bruce was one of those instrumental in ensuring this didn't go ahead. During practice, a rear wheel bearing disintegrated on the bumpy banking and threw the

Cooper into a violent spin, one of three cars crashed on day one.

Chris Amon was not so lucky, crashing on the second day of practice, sending his Lola into the trees at the Lesmo corners. He suffered four fractured ribs.

Jimmy won Monza and clinched the World Championship but Bruce was just happy to finish third. At a function the following week, Graham Hill, invited to say a couple of words about losing the title, was fairly succinct: 'Sod it!'

Bruce's 1963 season melted away after that, with mechanical breakages at Watkins Glen and Mexico. By this time, though, Bruce was already thinking about running his own two-car team in the newly formed Tasman Series in New Zealand and Australia.

12 The McLaren team takes shape

Bruce had been very much aware of the feeling within the Cooper organisation when Jack Brabham announced in 1961 that he was leaving to set up his own Formula 1 team. Charlie Cooper felt strongly that they had been betrayed, that they had taught Jack all he knew and now he was taking their secrets with him. The problem was that there were not many secrets of success left at Cooper after their glory summers of 1959 and 1960. Formula 1 marched onwards and Bruce knew that his future lay in following Jack and establishing a team of his own. But in 1963 he couldn't afford to make the move, neither financially nor for the sake of his career. The answer was for him to form his own team within the Cooper team, to build a car of his own for the Tasman series in 1964 while maintaining his Formula 1 works drive.

The new 'Tasman Formula' was limited to 2.5-litre engines running on pump fuel, with races a maximum of 100 miles. Bruce decided the best car for this would be one based on the Formula 1 Cooper but smaller and lighter, with the space frame wrapped in a stressed steel skin for torsional rigidity. Eight gallons of fuel were carried in the seat tank, supplemented by three-and-a-half gallons in two tanks either side of the driver's legs. The Tasman Cooper was only 25 inches wide at the cockpit, compared with 31 inches in the Formula 1 car. The main chassis tubes doubled as oil and water pipes. Cooper works mechanic Wally Willmott completed the car while Bruce was racing in North America. The plan was to run two cars, with talented young American Timmy Mayer driving the second. Mayer had raced a Formula Junior Cooper in the USA in 1962, won with Roger Penske's Cooper Monaco in sports car races, drove a third works Cooper in the 1962 US Grand Prix and raced a Tyrrell Formula Junior Cooper in 1963. It was the classic route to a Formula 1 Cooper works drive and would be capped nicely by a drive in the Tasman Series. Mayer was handsome, erudite and great company. He had studied English Literature at Yale and started racing with an Austin Healey in 1959. Timmy and his wife Garrell fitted perfectly into the new McLaren team. His older brother Teddy was a lawyer and had taken time off to manage Timmy's racing.

We asked Michael Turner, the top motor racing artist of the day, to design a team badge based loosely on the British Racing Drivers' Club shield but with a Kiwi motif. This was used on the cars and team letterheads. Philip Turner, sports editor of *The Motor*, described the badge as 'a Kiwi being run over by a Cooper'.

To clear the air about the basis for his team Bruce wrote the following in his *Autosport* column: 'These are the facts: Bruce McLaren Motor Racing Ltd have entered and are racing these cars, but design and construction was by Coopers of Surbiton in the normal fine manner. I was just a customer at this stage. I have been thrilled with the performance of my car during testing and Timmy Mayer has recently been trying out the car he will drive. After four laps at Goodwood he returned 1:22.5 and after 10 laps he had knocked his time down to 1:20.2 — well under the Formula 1 lap record and terrific motoring with a brand-new car. My best lap was 1:18.9 so we are looking forward to the first race in New Zealand.'

Ever since his first laps of the garden in the Ulster Austin it had been Bruce's ambition to win his home Grand Prix. He had won Grands Prix in the USA, Argentina, Monaco, Reims and Australia, but he had yet to get his name on the New Zealand Grand Prix trophy.

The first race of the Tasman Series was at Levin and the main opposition came from Denny Hulme in a new works Brabham. He won as he pleased, laughing afterwards that the Brabham was just like a big Formula Junior car. Bruce didn't think it was quite so amusing, knowing that the opposition would be stronger the following weekend at the Grand Prix. Jack Brabham had arrived and so had Australian Frank Matich, also with a new Tasman Brabham. Jack and Bruce won their respective race heats, but in the Grand Prix it was Timmy who made the best of the start, leading until Brabham took over at the end of the straight. Brabham, Mayer, Matich and Hulme drove wheel to wheel in the opening laps but it wasn't long before 'the old firm' — Brabham and McLaren — drew out a lead, with Matich giving chase and clear notice of his pace potential. Bruce found that his new slimline Cooper had a slight edge over the Brabham at top speed and he gradually opened up a lead. At half-distance Matich made his exit in a cloud of smoke, having set the fastest lap before the demise of his Coventry-Climax motor.

The Grand Prix was gifted to Bruce when Brabham tangled with Tony Shelly's Lotus while lapping him. Hulme and Mayer finished second and third. 'When Jack crashed he left me with a lead of nearly half a minute, but Denny was only 4.5 seconds behind at the finish. I'd really been pussy-footing it, to make sure of the race I'd been trying for eight years to win!'

The race on the Wigram air base saw Brabham with a new Repco-built short-stroke version of the Climax FPF, featuring twin-plug heads. On the other hand, the Coopers of Bruce and Timmy both suffered from sticking throttles. The Brabhams of Jack and Denny set the pace in the race and as Bruce put in a challenge his throttle stuck again. He speared off into the hay bales, losing 20 seconds before getting back into the race.

'Going into the new loop in the opening laps, I realised that I was sailing in with an uncomfortable number of revs on the clock and there wasn't much I could do about it except steer — and pray that I didn't hit anything hard. I aimed for a gap in the hay bales and punched my way through at probably 30 mph, swung hurriedly round and set off after the two Brabhams.'

The incident probably helped to fuel Bruce's desire to win and he closed back up to Hulme, passed him, and then drove in Brabham's slipstream until Jack was wrong-footed by a car they were lapping. Bruce nipped through and won his second Tasman race in a row. Timmy was less lucky, having suffered further throttle-sticking problems with his car.

'I'm ashamed that we should have had these bothers on our cars,' wrote Bruce, 'as particular attention had been paid to arranging a throttle set-up that was smooth, progressive and strong. It was only on this particular circuit with two corners where the throttle was only open a fraction that the problem showed up…'

A win at Teretonga made it three in a row for Bruce. Brabham had gone back to Britain, leaving Hulme to fly the flag on new Goodyears and he flew it to some effect, pulling ahead at a second a lap in the hot conditions until he spun out, leaving the race to the McLaren team.

Hulme's performance in the series moved Bruce to remark in *Autosport* that, 'Denny has always been one of our biggest worries. He has certainly learnt a lot from Formula Junior racing and it surely won't be too long before we see him with a regular Formula 1 drive.' Hulme more than fulfilled this prediction — he was World Champion in 1967.

The Australian half of the Tasman series was a disaster for the pair of slimline McLaren Coopers. Bruce's new short-stroke Climax engine blew up in the Australian Grand Prix at Sandown Park while he was running second to Jack. At Warwick Farm, Matich set pole position and led on his home circuit until he spun, leaving Brabham and McLaren to come home first and second, with Mayer third. At Lakeside, Matich led again, but this time his engine failed. Mayer led briefly before his engine also blew; Bruce motored home third.

The final race in the series was in Tasmania, just one week after the Brisbane-based Lakeside event. On Sunday night we set off on a 1500-mile blast south in a pair of Ford Falcon station wagons, each towing a Cooper on a trailer, and loaded with spares. I rode with Wally Willmott, and Tyler Alexander and Teddy Mayer drove together. One man slept while the other drove; we stopped only for fuel and it still took us till dawn on Tuesday to reach our destination.

Bruce had already clinched the Tasman title and we were all looking forward to completing the final race and heading home to England for the new Formula 1 season.

The Longford circuit in Tasmania demanded courage. Timmy had been getting more competitive with each race and there was an unspoken suggestion that Bruce might help him to win the final race in the series. He was super-confident that weekend.

In his book *Longford — Fast Track Back*, Barry Green wrote of the first practice session: 'The T62 Cooper of Timmy Mayer was one of the first out, on one of those days weather-wise when it felt good to be alive. Screwing all that he could from the slim Tasman special, Mayer was on a flier; pole position vividly in the hairs of his 20/20 focus.

'Just precisely what happened next we will never know — maybe a crosswind got under the nose of the Cooper, as it so often did at Longford. Maybe. But from someone who has approached the 90-degree Pub Corner with that same intent — [Tasmanian driver] John Youl — this is perhaps how the cards fell. "Union Street had a dangerous hump — time and time again I thought I would get over that without braking, but I never did." Mayer, as many suspected then, as now, might have landed with the brakes on after getting the car airborne over the hump at something approaching 120 mph.

'According to a report in Saturday's *Hobart Mercury*, based on eyewitness accounts, the Cooper touched down "...on the road at an angle...(then) cannoned into a 15-foot plane tree on the right-hand side of the circuit, splitting it from top to bottom. Mayer was hurled 50 yards, landing on his back on the far side of the road. The car disintegrated and the petrol tank was found nearly 150 yards from the scene." The crash occurred on the 17th lap and was broadcast to the crowd with shattering impact by the announcer, who was not aware that Mayer's 23-year-old wife, Garrell, and his 28-year-old brother, Edward, were on the course. Mayer was driving brilliantly and had just been timed by his wife at two seconds off the course record when the crowd of 500 at the pits heard the announcer's horrified voice say: "Car number 11, Tim Mayer's car, has crashed — it is a terrific crash…" Tyler reached up and cut the wire to the loudspeaker above the McLaren pit.'

Bruce wrote of the crash: 'It would appear that Tim lost control of the car at a spot where the cars touch down again, having left the road over an undulation. It is necessary to brake immediately for a slowish right-hander at that point, and it is possible that Tim's car landed slightly off line, and braking would have been very difficult. It was a situation that would have been harmless on an aerodrome circuit, but in this case the Cooper hit one of a number of stout trees lining the road at very high speed and the car broke in two. Tim was killed instantly with a broken neck.'

Bruce withdrew from the Saturday heats as a mark of respect and later wrote in a postscript to *From the Cockpit* words that have been repeated whenever a driver has been killed: 'The news that he had died instantly was a terrible shock to all of us, but who is to say that he had not seen more, done more and learned more in his twenty-six years than many people do in a lifetime? To do something well is so worthwhile that to die trying to do it better cannot be foolhardy. It would be a waste of life to do nothing with one's ability, for I feel that life is measured in achievement, not in years alone.'

Having opted out of the qualifying heats Bruce had to start the main event on Monday from the back of the grid. 'I'd wondered how I would feel getting back into the cockpit on the Monday afternoon, but when the flag dropped I realised immediately that I was keen to go motor racing. More than anything I wanted to catch Graham and Jack. In the five years I have been Grand Prix racing I've seen quite a few accidents, but this one was different — Tim was my teammate. On the other hand, Tim would have had a darn good go at winning and I felt like that too. It seems that we race because we want to, and we want to because we enjoy it.'

Jack led from Graham until his transmission failed, which left Graham to take the lead and win the race. Bruce managed second but also had the satisfaction of setting fastest race lap at 113.05 mph.

Once more those Formula 1 teams who had indulged in a southern summer had to face the prospect of returning to a northern winter. It snowed the day we arrived back in Britain and the first Formula 1 race of the season at Snetterton was run in Arctic conditions. 'I won't attempt to describe the horror of trying to start a temperamental Formula 1 V8 engine in almost zero temperatures when the rain is going down the injection bell-mouths, down your neck and in your boots, not to mention the mud and slush that is showered back from the spinning wheels of the tow car.'

Bruce enjoyed describing what motor sport was really like in his columns. Ferrari did not send a car to the next race, a non-title event at Goodwood, but John Surtees was there as a reluctant spectator. 'There can't be anything worse than watching something that you really should be in amongst. It's like watching someone eating a steak when you're hungry. I can imagine John getting quite fed up explaining why the new Ferrari wasn't at Goodwood and, if I know John's temperament, it must have been particularly frustrating for him to sit there passively and watch such a close race.' Of the new BRM, Bruce wrote: 'With the tail section off, the BRM is almost poetry executed in metal. The entire rear shape of the car is absolutely full of engine, transmission and suspension. There would barely be room to hide an eggcup within the outline, so tightly and compactly is everything designed. The workmanship is superb.'

Bruce drove the Goodwood race in his 1963 car, but failed to see the finish line after getting into a tangle with Innes Ireland who spun in front of the Cooper late in the race.

The McLaren Racing team began for real in the weeks that followed. The Cooper-Zerex that Roger Penske had raced to such good effect in American sports car racing and in the 1963 Guards Trophy at Brands Hatch had been bought from John Mecom's team in Texas together with an F85 aluminium V8 engine. Teddy Mayer had arranged the purchase and Tyler towed the car to New York for air-freighting to London.

The car was late arriving — it landed on 1 April! — and the tiny team had just one day to fit a bespoke aluminium regulation luggage trunk, proper lights, a windscreen wiper and all the other pinpricking requirements of the FIA regulations. Wally and Tyler fitted a 2.7-litre Coventry-Climax four-cylinder engine and rebuilt the transmission, cramming a week's work into 24 hours. Bruce didn't seem at all surprised when an oil pipe came loose on the gearbox during their first practice session at Oulton Park. Seven laps into the race, the bearings ran and Bruce's race was over. The next race was just a week away, this time at Aintree, so the mechanics had the luxury of time — seven days instead of one. At least they knew what the car was capable of and Bruce proved it in practice at Aintree when he put it on pole and went on to win the sports car race. The new Lotus 30 had appeared too late at practice, so Jim Clark had started from the back of the grid. What may have been a black cloud on the McLaren sports car racing horizon actually turned out to be one of Colin Chapman's rare flawed designs, flattered only by Clark's skill in the silk purse department.

By Aintree Bruce's new Formula 1 Cooper — with its stressed skins welded around the tube frame as a sort of poor man's monocoque — was ready for racing and proved competitive until the water temperature went off the clock. Phil Hill had been signed as number two at Cooper, following Tim's death. Phil had won the World Championship for Ferrari in 1961, but his fortunes had faded along with those of the Scuderia and after an uneasy season with ATS in 1963, he'd signed to join Bruce at Cooper. They were also teammates on the Ford GT endurance racing project.

My part of the McLaren project was to find workshop premises some-where not too far from Surbiton, where Bruce and Patty were living. This was not the work of a moment, for small workshops in the Surrey area were much sought-after. The best thing about the place I found was the minimal rent. It was *awful*. It was half a high-roof shed, shared with a mighty road grader and as far from today's clinical racing workshops as it is possible to imagine. The earth floor was dirty, ingrained with oil from tired, leaky road machines. Late most afternoons the grader would rumble in and shake clouds of dust around as the driver switched it off. But Wally and Tyler were working to a tight deadline so they simply had to try to ignore the work conditions and get on with it.

The next race for McLaren's team was at Silverstone, but an engine failure in testing before this meant the intrepid pair had to build one good engine from two broken power units in double-quick time. Bruce repaid their efforts with a win. Life was a blur for Bruce at this time of the year. He dashed from testing the new Ford GT round the banking at the Motor Industry Research track in the Midlands, down to Goodwood to sort out the new Formula 1 Cooper, then raced both the Formula 1 car and the sports car at Aintree, and finally rushed to Liverpool's Speke airport with Phil Hill and Dick Attwood to catch a Ford plane to France for Le Mans testing. And stopped. Before they arrived Jo Schlesser had written off one car on the Mulsanne Straight and the next morning Roy Salvadori crashed the other Ford, so they had a coffee in France and flew home.

Meanwhile, Wally and Tyler were engrossed in making what was, in all but name, the first McLaren sports car. They cut out the willowy tube chassis that had started life as a 1961 Formula 1 Cooper and had since been chopped and changed about by Penske, and built a new and stronger sports car chassis between the original Cooper bulkheads. Bruce had created a small model of the chassis he wanted and Wally and Tyler did a good deal of thinking outside the square to come up with a complete car that could carry the 3.9-litre aluminium Oldsmobile V8 engine.

Bruce's Formula 1 drives weren't going to plan. A steering arm broke in practice at Monaco and he crashed heavily. He resorted to the 1963 car in the Grand Prix but retired with engine failure. In the Dutch Grand Prix at Zandvoort he finished an unhappy seventh. Fellow Kiwi Chris Amon was fifth in a Parnell Lotus-BRM. 'He's still only 20, but he drove like a veteran at Zandvoort and thoroughly deserved his fifth place and the two points that went with it.'

The Nürburgring 1000-kilometre race with Ford was scheduled for the following weekend, but Bruce first had to dash back to England to test his new car, diplomatically christened a Cooper-Oldsmobile rather than the more correct McLaren-Oldsmobile.

'My mechanics, with some bits and pieces donated by John Cooper, built a new chassis for the 1962 Formula 1 suspension to hang on, installed a 4-litre aluminium Oldsmobile V8 in the back, re-fitted the body shell and had it down at Goodwood for me to test — all within three weeks! Mind you, they didn't get too much sleep.'

There was no time to fabricate an elegant exhaust system so the decision was made to send the car to its first race at Mosport near Toronto in Canada with eight separate vertically aimed stack pipes. The chassis was completed on a Sunday morning and I was despatched to find some paint. Forty years ago, Sunday was still a day of rest in the real world, but we weren't living in any sort of real world. We worshipped the god of motor sport. The only open shop I could find sold garden seeds and tools…and paint for garden gates. I didn't have to spend much time choosing a colour — there was only a single tin of bright green. I don't recall the comment when I got back to the grader shed, but I'm sure it was to the point. From then on the new car was nicknamed The Jolly Green Giant.

Ever the diplomat, Bruce held the company line before the first race for the new Ford GT at the Nürburgring. 'For some time I've been telling people what a good car the Ford GT was, is and surely shall be. But most people have been disinclined to believe me, particularly after the Le Mans test weekend when both the new cars were shunted or had accidents. I don't think it is giving anything away to say that the car was unstable at very high speed and I must admit that as one of the test drivers I am partly responsible for not noting the tendency during some of the earlier runs with the car. To me, one of the most impressive facets of the Ford organisation was that they recognised the fact that they had a problem, they made a plan to investigate it, they overcame it, and at the Nürburgring with only a few sorting-out laps the car was second fastest in practice.'

Roy Salvadori was more forthright about the new Ford. 'When I first tested the Lola-based car at Monza in October 1963, I found there was virtually nothing about it I liked. The car was unstable on the approach to the Curva Grande and the faster parts of the circuit...my initial reaction was not to blame the car and I was wondering whether I was at fault — perhaps my driving was getting rusty and I ought to give up competition driving.'

For 1964, Ford produced a GT that combined the basis of the original Lola design and updates from Ford, including their 4.2-litre Indianapolis V8.

Phil Hill and Bruce shared the car and made it to second place but had to retire after the failure of a rear suspension mounting bracket at quarter distance.

In an odd sort of juggling process that we seemed to regard as perfectly normal at the time, Bruce flew back from racing the Ford GT with its army of mechanics and technicians, to test his own brand-new car at Goodwood with just a brace of mechanics who had just built it and would run it for the remainder of the season.

At this stage Wally, Tyler, Teddy and I were renting a small house in New Malden, not far from the grader shed. Howden Ganley remembers being hired by Bruce around this time and arriving at our New Malden house. 'I was taken around to "the workshop". "Taken around, and taken aback," probably sums it up. I remember you had to wend your way through all these machines and finally in the far back corner was a little space with a workbench, a vice, a drill press and a set of welding bottles. It was one of those "At-cost" concrete buildings — a sort of concrete kitset thing that farmers used to build barns. There was just enough space for the Zerex and one of the Tasman Coopers. I had missed the engine change in the Zerex, but the big wooden crate which had been used as a chassis stand was there, still with green paint all over it!

'After sweeping the dirt floor (actually I think there was some concrete below if you excavated deep enough) Wally and I went and bought the famous olive yuck-green Mini van and then I was asked to go and get the tube from Coopers, with which we were going to make a set of axle stands. Somebody was going to cut and fit the tubes and weld them together as stands, but I did it while the others were out. When they came in the next morning they asked who had made the axle stands and, when I confessed that I had, they said, "You didn't tell us you could weld. Right — now you're the fabricator." And they got another gofer. I started building the new back end on the Tasman Cooper, then I fitted the first Hewland gearbox, then I built this and that… I gathered that I'd arrived! I seem to remember that Bruce was going to buy the concrete shed from the contractor, but the bloke had nowhere to put all his graders and things and was stalling, so the move was made to the factory at Belvedere Works in Feltham.'

Howden had raced a Lotus Eleven in New Zealand and he was amazed and delighted when, for the first test with the modified Tasman car at Goodwood, Bruce suggested that he bring his helmet so that he could try the car.

'How many employers would do that for you? He had that way of getting you to want to give 100 per cent effort all the time, and to continually lift your game. A small group of people all pulling together, led by Bruce, one of the nicest, most charismatic people I have ever had the privilege of knowing.

'I've often said that if Bruce came into the workshop one morning and said, "OK guys, today we are going to walk across the Sahara desert," there would have been no moaning and complaining. The response would have been, "OK Bruce, when do we start? Let's get going..." No matter what hours you had to work he was almost always there and joining in all the laughing and joking that kept everyone going through the all-nighters. He always had a good word, would compliment you on a job well done, and made you feel as though you were an important part of his team. He also brought back the gossip, the inside stories from each Grand Prix, or Le Mans or whatever race he had just done.'

The Cooper-Oldsmobile had been shipped to New York where Wally and Tyler picked it up and put it on a trailer for the 500-mile drive north to Toronto. It was 2 June 1964. Exactly six years later, the Bruce McLaren story would end and the legend would begin.

At Mosport, outside of Toronto, Dan Gurney put his Ford-engined Lotus 19 on pole, half a second faster than Bruce in his new car. Jim Hall was third fastest in his Chaparral. Hall's car was as complex as Bruce's car was simple. The lanky Texan had an under-the-counter arrangement with General Motors (who were officially out of and against motor sport) to use an aluminium Chevrolet V8 and an automatic transmission, which was top secret and always covered in the pit lane. The chassis was a form of plastic foam sandwich moulded as a monocoque.

The race was divided into two 100-mile heats and Bruce won both, taking Tyler on the lap of honour after the first win, and Wally on the second, carrying the chequered flag. It was the first time Bruce had raced in

Canada and he enjoyed the experience — or would have if there had been time to do so. A helicopter was waiting to rush Bruce to Toronto airport, still in his race overalls, to catch the overnight flight to London.

The Belgian Grand Prix at Spa was a tantalising race for Bruce as he came oh-so-close to winning it, but it was a lottery that seemed to revolve around fuel. 'Given another half-gallon of petrol Dan Gurney would have won; given another quart of petrol it would have been Graham Hill's race; and given another teaspoonful, *I* would have won!'

Dan Gurney had dominated the race in the works Brabham, fastest all weekend ahead of Graham Hill's BRM, John Surtees' Ferrari and Jack in the other Brabham. In the race, Dan broke the lap record three times and by halfway had half a minute on Jim Clark's Lotus. With two laps to go, Gurney pitted for a quick splash and dash, but there was no fuel in the Brabham pit and he took off again...and ran dry. Graham Hill took the lead...and he ran out of fuel. Bruce took the lead...and he *appeared* to have run out of fuel. Jimmy Clark had pitted for water and eventually he took the lead and had unwittingly won the race (the chequer was shown to Ginther in error!) when *he* ran out of fuel on the slowing-down lap. He arrived back at the pits for the victory ceremony on the tail of teammate Arundell's car!

Hill, Clark and McLaren had been racing in each other's slipstreams all race disputing second place, far behind Dan's Brabham. Gurney's fruitless pit stop for fuel had put the battling threesome into a race for the lead, with Hill leading on the penultimate lap. Bruce was delighted at the thought of second place, but that quickly dulled when the fuel pressure started to sag and he had to slow drastically and Gurney flashed past. But then Dan was parked at the side of the track and Bruce was back to second again. When he saw Hill's BRM parked in the country, he realised he was leading on the last half lap!

'I was winning the race with an engine about to fade out completely

— what a feeling! I was within 200 yards of the hairpin and the downhill cruise to the finishing line. Then the engine started to falter and cough. I dipped the clutch and tried to make the engine rev on the last dregs of petrol, then slipped the clutch out to jerk the car along on the inertia of the flywheel. I j-u-s-t made it round the hairpin, and started to coast down the hill at about 10 mph. I could see the man with the chequered flag. This is it! I've won the Grand Prix! But with less than a hundred yards to go I was blasted out of my victory speech rehearsal by James Clark, OBE, sizzling past to win in his Lotus. I hadn't even thought of Jimmy. My last hobbling lap had taken 5:30.0 — 1:30 longer than usual — and that was exactly the length of time Jimmy had spent in the pits soothing the boiling Lotus.'

Bruce did manage second. He wasn't out of petrol, his battery had flattened itself. The fuel pump had failed on Graham's BRM.

The next race in Bruce's diary was Le Mans. It was his fifth drive in the world's most famous 24-hour race and he was forming an opinion on the event, said to be a race staged by the French for the entertainment of the English, and generally too dangerous by virtue of difference in top speed between larger and smaller cars, and differences in driver experience. 'As far as I was concerned, my four-hour stint from midnight into the early hours of Sunday morning was the best 500 racing miles I've ever covered. Driving at night, once you become accustomed to it, you find that the very high speed is much safer than during the hours of daylight. The main danger at Le Mans was the little cars with a top speed around 90 mph that were cruising nearly 100 mph slower than we were, but in the darkness they couldn't help but see our lights coming up behind, and they stayed out of our way.'

It was the first time the might of Ford had attended Le Mans and they were learning as they went. There seemed to be an army of mechanics and experts in every field of engineering — except the man who mattered when the Ford Bruce shared with Phil made repeated stops with a misfire early in the race. It was finally decided that the problem was not electrical but a blocked jet in one of the Weber carburettors and the shout went out for the man from Weber. A cry from the grandstand over the Ford pit revealed that the man from Weber was in the crowd above. 'What are you doing up there?' demanded team boss, John Wyer. 'They wouldn't give me a pit pass…' came the plaintive reply.

The pair had to drive hard to catch up and Phil eventually set the fastest race lap at 3:31.29 before the Colotti gearbox failed just before dawn. Richie Ginther and Masten Gregory shared the Ford that led the early stages and Ginther was vastly impressed at the speed of his car. On the second lap he had passed the three fastest Ferraris down the 3-mile straight, getting a progressively greater aerodynamic tow from each one until, as he took the lead he was doing 7200 rpm — 210 mph!

'When Richie hopped up on to the pit counter to well-deserved applause from the huge crowd after his first driving spell, the Ford pit drill was cool and efficient. Richie was agog at the shattering performance of the Ford and was rather taken aback by the unruffled reception of the pit staff. "Well, for God's sake — isn't anyone going to ask me how the car went?" Someone immediately did, and Richie burst forth with a wildly ecstatic description of the Ford's performance in the hectic first hour.'

Rover had loaned Bruce one of their new luxury small saloon 2000 models for the season and we drove back in this, doing 95 mph on country roads across France. I was in the passenger seat and Peter Jackson of Specialised Mouldings, which made the bodies for the Ford team, was sprawled in exhausted sleep in the back seat. In an act that was clearly hugely amusing to Bruce at the time, he suddenly shouted loudly and hit the brakes. I thought the instantly awake Jackson was going to go through the roof with fright! But I sympathised with him. I think Bruce was still velocitised…high on the speed and drama of the race.

The following weekend the action was again in France with the Grand

Prix at Rouen, where Jim Clark set the pace in practice. Bruce started the race from row three, between Hill's BRM and Bandini's Ferrari. At the end of the first lap he spun and found himself in the middle of a gyrating traffic jam, but he got back into the race and eventually finished sixth for a championship point. He was most concerned for Innes Ireland, who had gone off the road just past the pits at a 145 mph right-hand curve, just before Bruce drove through the dust cloud. I had been keeping a lap-chart underneath a tree on the other side of the road when Innes suddenly landed in the ditch at high speed, wheels and bodywork flying from the destructing BRP-BRM. He emerged shaken, and ran across the road to where I was sitting. 'Bloody hell, chap!' he said. 'What happened?' I pointed out that since he had been sitting in the car at the time of the incident, perhaps he might have had a better idea than me...

In England, the McLaren empire, such as it was, was on the move. The grader shed had served its purpose, whether Wally and Tyler liked it or not. They didn't. I was despatched to find more suitable premises for a small racing team with major prospects and I turned up a 3000 square-foot factory building in a trading estate tucked in behind the main street of Feltham, a slightly down-at-heel working-class Middlesex town not far from Heathrow airport. The estate roads were puddled but compared with the premises at New Malden, the new factory was a palace. We had the place cleaned and painted and offices installed for management and designers. Bruce's office door had a sign that read 'Don't Knock — We Don't Have That Sort of Time'. A sign on his desk was, I think, cribbed from Roger Penske. It read 'Winning Isn't Everything — But It Beats the Hell out of Coming Second'. We moved in on 27 July 1964. The McLaren team had started to seriously shape up. Teddy Mayer had taken over the management reins and within a month the staff had grown to ten. Work was well advanced on the first new McLaren.

I was also on the search for a better house to rent for us somewhere closer to Bruce and Patty's Surbiton maisonette. I soon found that it was impossible for four young bachelors to rent any sort of house that we would want to live in. I sympathised with the landlords. I wouldn't have rented us a nice house either. I changed my approach and asked the next agent if he had a house so big and expensive that he couldn't rent it. He threw me a set of keys. Every other house I had looked at, the agent wanted to accompany me to make sure that I didn't souvenir any of the ornaments. This gentleman just tossed me the keys and said it was in Corkran Road in Surbiton. I asked for the number. 'It doesn't have a number, Sir. It has a name. It is called Warden.' It was enormous and very Edwardian in a grand sort of manner, being half of an elegant old stately home. It was £20 a week. A fiver each. I accepted immediately on behalf of Teddy, Tyler, Wally and myself. We each had a large double bedroom and shared the huge reception rooms on the ground floor. The house stood well back from the road, being approached by a wide horseshoe drive. We soon nicknamed it 'The Castle' and various racing identities stayed there over the next few years. I had already found a house for Chris Amon not far from us in Ditton Road, which he shared with Peter Revson, Mike Hailwood and Tony Maggs. They were known as 'The Ditton Road Flyers'.

Bruce was 26, I was 25, Wally was 23, Chris Amon had just turned 21. BP had commissioned a documentary movie called *The Time Between*, which was to chronicle the happenings in the lives of their contracted Formula 1 drivers between the French and British Grands Prix. We explained to BP that Amon's 21st would be an ideal event to film. They thought so too, and offered to finance a special birthday dinner at the Contented Plaice fish restaurant on the river at Kingston-on-Thames, conveniently located between the McLaren maisonette and the Gloucester Arms pub in Kingston that we used on a regular basis. Most of the Formula 1 drivers were at the dinner and a good time was had by all, including the BP film crew, who never shot any footage at all because they had been taken by drink. We were more or less committed to stage the dinner again a fortnight later so that BP could salvage some return on their by then considerable investment.

The British Grand Prix was held for the first time on the 2.65-mile Brands Hatch circuit, 20 miles south of London. The race was largely between Jim Clark and Graham Hill, with Dan Gurney putting up a spirited showing before his Brabham fried its electrics. Bruce started from the third row but retired after eight laps with a broken gearbox.

Brands Hatch was also the scene of the Guards Trophy sports car race on the August Bank Holiday Monday. It drew some impressive American entries, including A.J. Foyt in a Scarab, Walt Hansgen in a Lotus-Oldsmobile and Augie Pabst in a Lola-Chevy GT. The German Grand Prix at the Nürburgring was on the same weekend, so a special Wednesday practice session was arranged at Brands Hatch for the Formula 1 drivers. Bruce had set fastest lap at 1:41.2 in the Cooper-Oldsmobile and Hulme, in a 2-litre Brabham, and Graham Hill in the Ferrari 330P that had come second at Le Mans, were tied for second fastest at 1:43.0. The Americans were off the pace, requiring more time to adapt their big cars to Brands.

Over in Germany the Cooper mechanics had changed springs on Bruce's car for the second day of practice and he managed a spot on the second row of the grid with Jack Brabham and Graham Hill. John Surtees won the race for Ferrari, getting a foothold on the championship ladder that would eventually earn him the title by the end of the summer and making him the first man to win world titles on two wheels and four. Bruce retired after five laps with an engine problem. The German Grand Prix was also notable for the debut of Honda in Formula 1.

After his five-lap disappointment, Bruce had to return to England. 'Sometime in the wee small hours of Monday morning, Betty Brabham was beating on the door of my hotel room, and we were soon airborne in Jack's twin-engined Cessna 310, bound for Brands Hatch. There were plenty of feet sticking out of car windows and bleary-eyed types wandering about the paddock there, as evidence of a tiring trip back from Germany, and I took the opportunity of catching a few minutes' "kip" in the sun before the race call-up.'

The race was a walk-over for Bruce in the newly painted Cooper-Oldsmobile, green with a broad white central stripe. Wal and Tyler added to the professional touch of the little team by wearing green shirts and white trousers. Roy Salvadori (Cooper-Maserati) and Walt Hansgen (Lotus-Oldsmobile) disputed a distant second place until the Cooper broke an upright and Hansgen hit a bank a lap later. The end result was something of a colonial affair with Denny Hulme and Jack Brabham coming in second and third respectively. In another race, Chris Amon and Jack Sears had the crowd on its feet as they raced wheel to wheel in a pair of bellowing Cobras. Much was made of Chris's bleeding palms after hefting the big Cobra round the Kentish track, but he later said that he had started the race with blistered palms following his drive at the 'Ring.

It was during this weekend that Bruce was introduced to Robin Herd, a senior research scientist with the National Gas Turbine Establishment at Farnborough, then involved with design work on the Concorde project. Bruce was interested in the new science of aerodynamics as applied to motor racing and Herd was a specialist in that very field and confessed an interest in becoming involved in motor racing design.

We'd planned a 'castle-warming' for the night after the Guards Trophy race and sent out an elegant invitation to our guests. It began: 'O be it known hereby that Bruce McLaren and his Merrie Men: Young Eoin of Surrey, the Lord Mayer, Sir Walter Willmott and Alexander the Great, Knights of the Night, prescribe the presence of the damsels and gentlemen preferred hereunder'…and went on to detail the prospects of 'Balderdash Slinging, Goblet-Tilting and Wenching…Iron gauntlets, broadswords and lances must be parked at the portcullis…Raiment: Bold Knights — Suits of Armour (No monocoques). Fair Ladies — The Lady of Coventry was the Climax of Style.'

The Americans couldn't believe the opulent residence of McLaren's mechanics. They didn't believe the mock medieval 'joust' between Jim Clark and Graham Hill, either. Both men wore fibreglass helmets and breastplates. Jimmy stood on the broad stairs swinging his sword but he got a bit over-zealous and thwacked Graham around the head — and that's when it became apparent that Jimmy's sword was real and Graham's helmet wasn't. Graham was momentarily knocked out. The Americans were amazed at this 'Grand Prix' behaviour...

In the new workshop at Feltham the McLaren M1 — similar in concept to the Cooper-Oldsmobile but different in most detail, apart from the uprights and wheels — was nearing completion. By the end of August we had issued a press release: 'The chassis is a tubular space frame reinforced with magnesium sheet. Large diameter light gauge main tubes carry oil and water with smaller tubes forming the diagonals. The undertray and cockpit bulkhead are 14-gauge magnesium sheet attached to the tubular structure with epoxy glue and aircraft rivets.

'The front and rear bulkheads, which are used to carry the majority of the suspension, gearbox and steering and pedal mounting points, are fabricated out of sheet steel. The chassis side elevation is a shallow 10 inches to enable a variety of engines to be fitted and at the same time allow for the design of a small body, which conforms to Appendix C regulations. Rear suspension is midway between wishbone and radius rod type, while the front suspension has very broad-based wishbones.

'Two saddle tanks made from 18-gauge aluminium wrapped in glassfibre cloth form the body sides and front and rear wheel wells. Tank capacity is approximately 36 gallons. The 4.5-litre Traco-Oldsmobile V8 is mated to a Hewland HD4 gearbox.'

We immediately received six firm orders for customer cars. This was both flattering and frustrating, because despite the size of the new factory and the increase in staff numbers, the team was only just able to cope with working on the Cooper-Oldsmobile, the new M1 prototype, which had its first race scheduled for the end of September at Mosport, and preparing the single-seater Coopers for the 1965 Tasman series.

In August, Austria staged its first world title Grand Prix on the Zeltweg NATO air base, 140 miles southwest of Vienna. The track was notoriously bumpy and there were many chassis breakages. John Surtees looked like winning until his Ferrari's rear suspension collapsed and his young Italian teammate, Lorenzo Bandini, took over to score his first win in the team's 'obsolete' 1963 V6 car.

The attrition rate on the rough surface prompted Bruce to observe that by half-distance there were more Grand Prix drivers watching the race than normally attended a Grand Prix Drivers' Association meeting. He had retired with engine trouble at half distance.

His Cooper teammate, Phil Hill, could have done without the Austrian weekend. Phil seemed to race on his nerves; he was always tense, but his reputation demanded respect. He had won Le Mans in 1958 and 1962 in Ferraris and had won the 1961 World Championship for Ferrari. Phil grew up in California and started his racing there, too; he was passionate about the sport and its history. For some reason he and John Cooper clashed within the team and what should have been a relaxed season turned out to be a summer spent on tenterhooks. In practice at Zeltweg, Phil plucked a wheel off his car and had to start the race in a 1963 car. Just after half distance he crashed into the hay bales and the car caught fire, burning itself out before the fire marshals arrived. Phil was unhurt, but John blamed him for both accidents. There was a definite atmosphere within the team, which until then had operated on a sort of happy-go-lucky basis. Phil was delighted to see the end of the season and his Cooper contract and yet he went straight on to race one of the McLaren Coopers in the 1965 Tasman series and it was a delightful experience for all.

There were a few races to get through before that, though, including the 300-mile Tourist Trophy race at Goodwood. This would be the final race for the Cooper-Oldsmobile and Bruce was up for it. He set fastest lap on the first day of practice and the team felt confident enough to give the second day a miss. The main competition came from Jim Clark in his Lotus 30, which was gradually being de-bugged. Jim initially led but by the first time they went past the pits Bruce was in front and he set a new lap record as he built up his lead. The team had no plans to stop for an hour and a half, but the clutch started to slip so Bruce pitted. The mechanics did their best but the clutch was beyond help and after two more fruitless stops, the car was wheeled away.

Bruce climbed onto the pit counter and watched Jim drive away out in front. Lotus were in the next pit so we had a grandstand view of Jim's fuel stop…and the drama thereafter. The Lotus fuel system gagged during the stop and took on only 10 gallons instead of 25, before burping back. In the urgency of the pit stop this was not noticed until Colin Chapman realised that the 'empty' churn had gone back on the pit counter with a clunk instead of a clang. There was a great in-team shouting match and Jim had to be called in again, losing the lead to Graham Hill's Ferrari in the process. The Lotus eventually retired.

For the Italian Grand Prix at Monza, Phil was replaced by Tony Maggs. Bruce was embarrassed. 'Phil's replacement was a rather uncomfortable move — I prefer to think that it was a clash of personalities in the team, rather than a reflection on Phil's track performance. I have a very high regard for Phil's driving ability and am glad to be taking him "down under" to drive one of my Tasman Coopers next January.'

Bruce had stolen a slipstream lap to secure a second-row grid position and was amazed to find himself actually leading away from the grid and then becoming embroiled with Gurney's Brabham, Surtees' Ferrari and Clark's Lotus. The leaders dragged themselves away from the rest of the field, though Jimmy and Dan dropped out as the race wore on. Surtees scored an ecstatic win for Ferrari on home ground, with Bruce motoring in second almost unnoticed in the *tifosi*'s passion.

'We were looking on the Monza race to sort out the championship, but once again Jimmy and Graham were spectators at the finish. I heard later that a highly-chuffed Graham Hill strolled up as Jimmy was taking off his helmet and gloves, to offer sympathy, the "sincerity" of which was underlined by a broad grin!

'The annual "war" with wine-soaked knotted napkins, bread rolls and sugar lumps was waged that night between the Cooper and BRP teams allied at one end of the hotel dining room, and Team Lotus who were ensconced behind a wall of screens. The waiters seemed to take it as a matter of course, continuing to serve the non-combatants, who were crouched *under* the tables!'

The United States Grand Prix at Watkins Glen in the first weekend of October was a tedious event for Bruce, who qualified on the third row but went out with engine trouble on the 26th lap. There were no red Ferraris present. Enzo Ferrari was at war with the Italian national body over the homologation of the 250LM, so the cars of Surtees and Bandini were painted in the US racing colours of blue and white and they were entered by Luigi Chinetti's North American Racing Team. Luigi and Enzo went back a long way. Chinetti had won Le Mans for Alfa Romeo in 1932 and 1934 and in 1949 he drove a Ferrari to win the team's first 24-hour race at Le Mans.

Graham Hill won at the Glen for BRM with Surtees coming second in the Ferrari. The result took the championship right down to the final race in Mexico. Graham, John and Jimmy all had a shot at the title and it took a dramatic race to shake it out.

Bruce waxed lyrical about the flavour of the race in Mexico, 7000 feet above sea level. 'Formula 1 to North American enthusiasts means Europe and something special in racing. I'd been missing this, perhaps not so much missing as forgetting; when you are too closely associated you are so much in the picture that you can't look at it, but this year at Mexico someone planned it that there was so much "European" Grand Prix-type atmosphere you couldn't miss it. It's got something to do with a bright blue day; something not too orchestral, not too pop, just a little too loud from the loudspeakers; grandstands full of colour; and a whole stack of people who have been about for years, going about what is for them their routine jobs, wheeling the immaculate little cars out to the start line completely impervious to any of the above...'

Jim Clark led the race to within two laps of the flag when he realised that the oil slick he'd been trying to avoid was his own. Graham Hill had been robbed of his tilt at the title when Bandini under-braked and whacked the BRM at the hairpin, forcing Hill to pit in an attempt to straighten the exhausts. Bandini was again in the spotlight in the closing laps: Dan Gurney was leading in the Brabham, Bandini was second and Surtees third. John needed second place to take the title, Bandini was advised and he waved John through to the championship. Bruce motored quietly through to seventh place in the race and seventh in the championship.

∧
The 1967 Le Mans test weekend and the Ford Mk 4 GT awaits Bruce McLaren.

∧
Daytona 1967. Bruce tests the Ford J-car.

< Moving in the right circles, Bruce McLaren chats to Prince Philip, Duke of Edinburgh at a 1968 racing car show in London.

EOIN YOUNG COLLECTION

< The Bruce and Denny Show, 1968, featuring the key to their success.

EOIN YOUNG COLLECTION

^
Bruce tests the M8A less bodywork at Goodwood in 1968.

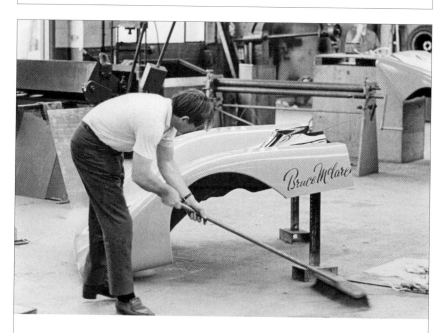

^
Mucking in: Bruce does the chores in the Colnbrook factory, 1968.

∧
The 1968 M8A CanAm monocoque takes shape in the Colnbrook factory. If inspiration was needed, one only need look at the wall.

>
Patty and Bruce
in the pits at the
Nürburgring, 1969.

^
Bruce demonstrates the lightweight nature of the 1969 Formula 1 monocoque made by Reynolds Aluminum.

<
Bruce, Amanda and Patty in 'Muriwai', their home in Burwood Park, near Walton in Surrey, 1969.

∧
Two faces of Bruce McLaren, 1969.

∧
Bruce at speed in the Formula 1 McLaren, Silverstone, 1969.

∧
Bruce in the 1969 CanAm race at Mosport, Canada, one of his favourite courses.

> Bruce takes a break
from testing the CanAm
M8B, Goodwood, 1969.

∧
Customer CanAm McLaren-Elvas being built in the Trojan factory, 1970.

13 Tyler Alexander

Tyler Alexander was and is an enigmatic, laid-back American specialist in the engineering art of motor racing. Something of a loner, Tyler tended — and I'm sure still does — to do things *his* way. He was one of the original technical trio at McLaren with Bruce and Wally Willmott and although Willmott had joined Bruce two years prior to Tyler's arrival, Tyler himself had been on the American racing scene for several seasons. It was Tyler who helped to rebuild the original 1961 Formula 1 Cooper after Walt Hansgen had crashed it in the US Grand Prix at Watkins Glen and it was Tyler who collected the same car — metamorphosed into the Zerex Special sports racer — from John Mecom's workshops in Texas in 1964. In *Bruce McLaren — The Man and his Racing Team*, I described Tyler as wearing jeans, hand-made Gucci shoes and a Rolex. I gather he still does. Tyler is famous as the only member of the modern, polished-perfect Ron Dennis-era McLaren organisation to come to work in casual clothes. Tyler is also the only link connecting the original fledgling McLaren organisation to the modern McLaren-Mercedes operation, where he heads up special projects.

Tyler just sort of drifted into motor sport. He had trained as an aircraft engineer doing a two-year course in the US and then cruised for a while. He taught himself to be an accomplished photographer and his photographs of racing in those early days have been shown at exhibitions in the US. I was delighted when he agreed to make some of his early McLaren photographs available for this book.

He was not particularly interested in obtaining a regular job as a

21-year-old and his mates in his hometown of Hingham, Mass., were into flying and racing specials they had built themselves. One of the part-time race driver/aviators was John Fields, who decided to move up to a Cooper 500 and Tyler helped to prepare it during the 1961 season, in which Fields won 15 of the 17 races in the national championship.

At the same time the Mayer brothers, Timmy and Teddy, were running a Formula Junior Cooper with Timmy driving and Teddy looking after the team management, and quite often Fields and Mayer were running in the same race, but in different classes. At a loose end with the season over, Tyler took the Mayer Cooper down to the Nassau Speed Week, where Roger Penske drove it. Timmy was otherwise engaged with his national service in the US Army. 'I wasn't really working for Teddy as a mechanic, but I just sort of ended up taking the car to several races and started working for Teddy without ever having said, "How about a job?" or anything like that. It just happened…'

Timmy Mayer had driven a Formula Junior Cooper for Ken Tyrrell during 1963 and he, wife Garrell and brother Teddy were living in a rented house on an island in the River Thames. Tyler renewed his association with the Mayers when he went to Brands Hatch with the Mecom team, who'd entered Penske in the Zerex. Tyler decided to join up with them again, so he resigned from Mecom and accompanied the Mayers to a race in Denmark instead of returning to America.

Bruce came around to one of the Mayers' riverside lunch parties, hobbling on a cane after a crash in the German Grand Prix. He wanted to continue discussions they had been having about taking a brace of 2.5-litre Cooper-Climaxes to New Zealand and Australia for the 1965 Tasman Series. Wally Willmott was building Bruce's car — a special slimline lightweight with minimum tankage for the 100-mile races — at the Cooper Car Company in Surbiton and Tyler joined him to start building a twin car for Timmy.

'To me, Coopers were a big deal in those days, because we had been running the 500, the Formula Junior and the Formula 1 car in the States, but it didn't seem to be such a big deal when I actually went into the workshop…'

When Tyler arrived, the racing factory had not changed much since they made their first 500 cc racing car. The old hands were probably critical about American racing people, who often arrived with more money than driving ability and certainly only a modicum of mechanical skills. Tyler was definitely an exception.

'I was amazed at the time, that there was a bunch of people working away in a dirty, dark corner of the world and I had been tossed in there by Timmy and Teddy to get on with the job. These people were very impressed that I could actually weld and do something. Bruce was in and out of the factory all the time while the cars were being built, but I don't ever remember being formally introduced. At that time I didn't know a great deal about him. In fact, I was fairly ignorant about the whole business, but I was keen on doing something I was interested in and these people seemed to be very serious about what they were doing, so I thought it would be a good bunch to tag along with. There were so many things I didn't know about racing cars then and this guy with the limp seemed to know a fair bit about them, so I thought maybe I'd better pay a bit of attention to him and see what was going on.'

Recalling those early days, Tyler realised he didn't get the most out of them: 'Bruce was very easy to learn from, but I find now that I didn't really learn all that much and I think I know why. After working for him for about a year and a half I found that I was doing my part of the job and he was doing his. I knew that the car had to be finished and had to be at the race and I knew how he wanted it, but we were working in parallel rather than together. Well, maybe parallel isn't quite right. Maybe it *was* together. We used to argue like hell over how something should be done, but we never seemed to get upset about it and we always ended up with a reasonable solution. He knew what he wanted and after a couple of years I believed him. It's odd, thinking back, because we used to argue like hell but we never said, "Screw you because I'm going to do it *my* way" and I guess that's why we got on so well together.

'I realise now that I should have learned more from Bruce. I got on with my own job, and never reckoning he was going to write himself off, I never bothered to get him to explain a lot of the technical aspects or engineering to me, because he knew that part. That was his department. I could cope with the detail bits and pieces and making sure that the car was built, and he did the other part, saying *we* should put that there, or why don't *we* mount that there? And I would say, "Gee. We did that last year and it was no good" and then we'd remember *why* it was no good.

'This is why I felt out of place after Bruce's death. He and I had worked so much as a team that I hadn't bothered to pay much attention to the things he did as long as the end result was right.'

When Bruce and Patty moved into their big new home, 'Muriwai' in Burwood Park, Tyler moved in and literally became a member of an extended McLaren family. The intercommunication of ideas between Tyler and Bruce became even stronger as the dinner table conversation became an extension of workshop discussions. It was probably the most lasting liaison in the team and Tyler was elevated to chief mechanic, engineer in charge of the racing operations in all fields the team entered, and finally appointed a director of the company. McLaren Racing was the only team that competed in Formula 1, CanAm sports car racing and Indianapolis-type racing, but from a mechanic's viewpoint, Formula 1 was the best background. 'We had a better team in CanAm racing because a lot of the people who worked on our CanAm cars used to work on the Formula 1 cars. The thing about Grand Prix racing that makes you a better mechanic is that it is so intensely competitive. You can't slow at all. You've got to try to be smarter. You've got to keep thinking about it. It's very hard work, but it's so competitive that you develop a very competitive spirit and with this competitive spirit you develop a very competitive attitude. If you miss by a second because someone's forgotten something, you don't make the race, but in CanAm you could miss by ten seconds and still get in the race.

'It's difficult to explain. If you're good, you're good. If you're not very good or you're not as good as the other people in the team, it shows up and there are always a lot of people who are willing to work harder and take your place. Formula 1 cars are easier to work on than CanAm cars, but in Formula 1 you have to work much harder and faster. A CanAm sports car is more work, taking it as a vehicle, and we probably did more work between races on the CanAm cars than we did in Formula 1, but with Formula 1 the competition is so keen and so competitive that you've got to do things quickly and be sharp. Really on the ball. You can't mess around trying to make up your mind about what to do when something goes wrong on the morning of a Grand Prix. You've got to say, "Do you think that's going to be better? Well, try it. Quick. Now!" Because when you operate like that it could mean half a second somewhere in the race.'

Bear in mind, Tyler is talking of 1970, discussing the racing that he and Bruce and the McLaren team had been involved with, but the broad principles remain the same today. If you're good, you're good.

'If you're a good Formula 1 mechanic, you're pretty good at almost anything, but Indianapolis is a completely different deal. It's another kind of motor racing and patience is something you need there more than at any other race. The best thing about Formula 1 is that you can get on with it, but at Indy everything is such a long, drawn-out process. Some of their rules are justified, because Indy is a very dangerous place. You go very fast in a confined area, much more so than on any Grand Prix or CanAm road circuit. The difficult thing for a mechanic is that, in any other form of racing, if you have a problem you drag out your tool box and get after it, but at Indianapolis you have to pack everything up on the pit front and drag the car away to the garage area and do a fifteen-minute job in two hours. At a Formula 1 race there's no way you could take that long because you just wouldn't make the race…'

Tyler liked to hark back to his aircraft engineering background. 'If someone was to ask me what was the best training for a racing mechanic, I'd tell them to go to an aircraft engineering school. You learn to be a lot more careful and more precise, because when one of those things quits in the air you don't just get out and fix it. So you have to make sure that it doesn't quit. After a while you develop the attitude that it's not so much knowing what's wrong when it goes wrong (although it does help!) as doing it right in the first place so that it doesn't go wrong.'

Bruce liked to employ young Kiwis who had grown up as mechanics in New Zealand, but for Tyler, being a racing mechanic was a world away from a commercial garage. 'Alistair Caldwell, our chief Formula 1 mechanic, possibly knew more about cars as cars than I did, because he was an apprentice in a big garage in New Zealand and when a Jaguar came in making a weird noise he knew that it had a busted framstat. I wouldn't have a goddamn clue what was wrong with it because I've never had anything to do with standard road cars. It's either been a racing car, or I'd just as soon not bother…'

Team Lotus, Colin Chapman and Jimmy Clark were the class act of the 1960s and Tyler used them as an example. 'Lotus have very good racing mechanics. It seems to me that when they first go there they don't have anything over anyone else, but they *know* that Colin Chapman is very good — they may not like him, but they know he's good — and quite a few of the Lotus mechanics have ended up being very, very good. They respect Colin Chapman because he's had years and years of experience. They believe in him and learn from him. Maybe part of this is that Lotus have always had very good drivers and when you're working with someone who is capable of winning a race and is giving it 100 per cent, then you give him *your*

100 per cent. If you're working for a driver who isn't going to make it, it's easy to say, "Ah, why the hell bother working all night for him — he's not going to win the race anyway…" Chapman has always managed to have that air of success about him, or at least had good people about him or had good people driving for him, and…y'know…I think good people go together.

'I always felt that when I was working with Timmy and later with Bruce. I didn't know anything and Timmy didn't know anything, but we said we'd have a stab at getting to the top together. I suppose it ended up happening with Bruce, because later we used to laugh and say, "We're on our way. Let's not stop now. We'll bust our ass till we beat them all…"'

14 McLaren Racing to the end of 1965

The week after the 1964 Formula 1 season finished Bruce was back at Feltham working out a deal whereby Frank Nichols and Elva Cars would make customer versions of the M1 McLaren sports-racer under licence at their premises in Rye on England's south coast. Bruce and Frank had settled on the mechanical side but the name was still up for grabs. I spent the best part of an afternoon discussing this with Peter Agg, managing director of the Lambretta Trojan Group, which had taken over the Elva company in 1961. The name was a corruption of *elle va* — 'she goes'. Peter wanted the car to be called an Elva-McLaren, while I was adamant that the car would be a McLaren-Elva or the whole deal would be parked at the kerb. Peter was very old-school and proper and he probably thought I was an unpolished colonial, but we agreed to disagree and the customer cars were McLaren-Elvas.

The new McLaren M1 was painted deep red with a silver stripe up the nose and was first run in the Canadian Grand Prix for sports cars at Mosport early in October. 'It was the first race with the car that we built ourselves from the rubber up and we were delighted with its performance and potential. We didn't win, but we certainly didn't leave Canada with our tails between our legs. We learnt two important things. Firstly, we have to find more horsepower and secondly, we had a convincing reminder that Jim Hall, the lanky Texan builder of the Chaparral sports car, didn't go to school just to eat his sandwiches.'

Bruce had won at Mosport the previous year, but in 1964 he had his work cut out with some stiff competition. Jim Clark was there in a works Lotus 30, Jim Hall drove his Chaparral, there were three Brabhams from Britain and three Ferraris from the North American Racing Team, as well as a number of American cars.

Hall had qualified his 5.5-litre Chaparral fastest, ahead of Bruce in the 3.9 McLaren-Olds. Come the race, Bruce led away, Jim Hall crashed on the second lap and on the third lap Bruce was shown a 'Clark Out' signal. For 55 laps Bruce cruised, trying to stay concentrated…and then the engine started to stutter on six. A link to one of the four carburettors had broken. Bruce sat in the pits for four laps while the team fabricated a new link, then got straight back into the fray, fighting to make up lost ground. He eventually clawed his way back to third, knocking a second off the lap record and generally making a name for the first true McLaren.

More horsepower was available for the Riverside race as Tyler and Wally had installed a bigger 4.5-litre Traco-Oldsmobile engine. Bruce was in the lead when a water hose blew off. He pitted for the problem to be rectified, battled back to third place, and then the hose blew off again. These were routine teething troubles on a new car, but despite them Bruce proved a point every time the car with his name on the nose was in front.

It was the same story at Laguna Seca; on the pace in practice, up front in the race, then sidelined with a minor gearbox problem. It would get better.

The Nassau Speed Week, held at the end of the European season, was the brainchild of Captain Sherman F. 'Red' Crise, who promoted motor races on the island's airfields to bring tourists to the Bahamas. His series began in 1954 at Windsor Field, but in 1957 he moved to Oakes Field, closer to the Bahamas' capital town of Nassau with its big hotels.

'The races start when everyone is about ready. And the start could be from a grid, a rolling start, or even a Le Mans start, depending on how "Red" Crise felt at the moment.'

The cars were brought to the island by a huge landing craft that carried over 100 racing cars in a 24-hour tow by tugs from Miami. Bruce was entered in a McLaren-Elva, a Ford GT and a Formula Vee. He finished third in the Vee race and was promoted to winner when the first two were disqualified for technical infringements. 'My winner's cheque was well over what a Grand Prix winner could expect to receive in Europe!' In all, the scrutineers had to tear down *eight* Vees to establish the first three legal cars!

The Ford GT broke its suspension in a qualifying heat and Bruce was a spectator for the rest of the weekend, making the most of the elegant and exuberant cocktail parties held each night.

'We rented a grand beach house for our team, attached to the Balmoral Club at Cable Beach, and from there we could phone for a speed boat to take us water-skiing or whatever took our fancy.'

The sports car race started in a tropical downpour. 'It was a sodden shambles from the start. We stood across the road from the cars, getting soaked as we waited for the starter and then we were running, scrambling into our cars, firing the engines and accelerating away with wheels spinning. At least that's what should have happened. I managed all the first bit, but the engine didn't fire and I was a little late getting under way. The track was like a skating rink and there were cars spinning in all directions. The safest thing seemed to be to stay out of everyone's way until the rain stopped and the track started to dry.'

Penske managed to crash one Chaparral and took over the other from Hap Sharp. He went through to win the race from Bruce in the McLaren-Elva, who in turn was two laps ahead of Pedro Rodriguez in the Ferrari.

'After this annoying motor-racing business had finished, we were able to spend another day at the beach before the grand prize-giving ball, where all the cheques and trophies were dispersed. The next day my crew started to split up. I had some business to attend to in chilly London, some of the mechanics were taking a well-earned holiday in Nassau and others were on their way back to Australia and New Zealand to prepare for the Tasman series, starting early in January.'

Teddy Mayer kept the McLaren ship financially watertight back in Britain while Bruce was away for increasing lengths of time. Harry Pearce, who had worked as Tommy Atkins' mechanic on loan to Bruce in the past, joined the McLaren team as workshop manager. He was ideal for the job because, while Teddy was new-Yank and abrasive in his way of doing business, Harry was motor racing old-school, well versed in the ways of getting things done on the old-pal's act.

Harry started in motor sport on two wheels, setting an all-time 250 cc lap record on the original grass track at Brands Hatch. When the track was sealed in 1950, Harry rode his Triumph to win his heat and the final at the first event on the new surface. One of the riders he beat that day was a young John Surtees. Harry worked as a toolmaker for Tommy Atkins, who had also been an amateur motorcycle racer and would later enter cars for Roy Salvadori, Graham Hill and Bruce. Harry eventually became General Manager, a position he held until his retirement in 1980, when Ron Dennis took over the McLaren team.

The 1965 Formula 1 season — the last summer of the 1500 cc formula — started on an odd note in South Africa. Practice was held on the East London circuit in 1964 and the Grand Prix ran on New Year's Day, which just happened to be a Friday! Bruce had a new teammate, the volatile Austrian Jochen Rindt, and Jackie Stewart had graduated from Formula 3 to Formula 1, driving for BRM. Bruce started on the third row and finished fifth. The following weekend he was in New Zealand and in trouble.

Phil Hill was Bruce's 1965 Tasman teammate and they had modified their two Coopers to take Firestone tyres. In the first of two race heats Bruce was chasing Clark's Lotus when the car's tail came round on a patch of oil in the Esses. Suddenly, Bruce was on the grass, trying desperately to miss an ambulance that had drawn up to attend an earlier victim of the oil.

'There's nothing like that blank flash of despair when it dawns that you might be going to hit something hard and there isn't a thing you can do to avoid it. Except to get down in the cockpit and pray. The rear wheel of the Cooper snicked the footplate of the ambulance and the car was thrown into a five-foot drainage ditch. I slithered hurriedly out on to the bank to watch the car sinking slowly in the muddy water, with the right rear wheel floating, attached only by the brake hose...'

Submerged beneath the Cooper was a Lotus 27 that had spun into the ditch before Bruce had arrived!

The Cooper could obviously not be repaired in time for the race (Bruce was amazed later to receive a bill from the ambulance company for damage to the footplate!) so it was decided that Phil would race in the second heat and Bruce would use Phil's car for the Grand Prix. In the race itself, Bruce once more left the track, but this time he had Jim Clark for company. The two had made contact while disputing the lead on the first lap going down to the hairpin. Jimmy stalled, but Bruce kept his engine running, got back into the race in fourth place and had made it to second behind Graham Hill's Brabham when his gearbox failed on the unlucky 13th lap.

At Levin, Bruce came a distant fifth and Clark won. The short, tight Levin track had never been a McLaren favourite and the team had problems tuning the Coopers to the new Firestones, running on lightweight single-seaters for the first time outside the USA. At both Wigram and Teretonga, Bruce finished second to Clark.

The most excitement in the New Zealand series came on the water. 'Jimmy and I were skiing behind one boat, Jimmy away out one side of the wake and me on the other. I was skiing along quite happily when I suddenly realised that Jimmy was launching himself into a 'crossover' — a manoeuvre that requires the concentration of both parties and one ski rope shorter than the other. If I hadn't seen the Flying Scot literally living up to his name coming across the wake, there would have been a colossal crash. I let go of my rope as Jimmy flashed across the exact point I would have been in another split second. Admittedly he was no longer attached to his ski and he was about two feet off the water at the same time. He had a solo shunt while I sank voluntarily, choking with laughter...'

The McLaren fortune did not fare much better when the series moved to Australia. Bruce retired with overheating at Warwick Farm when a newspaper blocked the radiator intake; at Sandown a piece of sponge rubber sealer behind the radiator dislodged itself, diverting the hot air directly on to Bruce's feet and he finished an uncomfortable second to Clark's Lotus. Honour was regained at Longford, where Bruce won and Phil, driving the second Cooper, thoroughly enjoyed a spirited dice with Jimmy to finish third. Jimmy won the Tasman title with 35 points, Bruce was second on 24 and Phil was fifth on 15.

The season ended on a sad note following the deaths of Lex Davison at Sandown, and his young protégé Rocky Tresise the following weekend at Longford. 'Lex was a great man, one of the truest automobile enthusiasts. The spirit and courage shown by his large and wonderful family is as strong and forthright as "Davo" was himself...'

Bruce's next race was on a drenched Sebring circuit, where he shared a Ford GT with Ken Miles. Boats may have been better than cars — the water was six inches deep in places on the circuit, and a river a foot deep flowed down the pit lane! Bruce was glad he had a closed car though it did have its disadvantages. 'The windscreen wiper packed up and we were flying blind and perhaps wishing we were wet and able to see, rather than snug and dry and plugging on into opaque swimming gloom.'

At one stage Ed Leslie in a Cobra was searching in vain for a right-hand turn when he suddenly realised he was in among the parked aircraft half a mile from the track — he stopped hurriedly and was rammed by a Sprite and three other cars that had followed him in the murk!

It was Bruce's first drive for Carroll Shelby's Ford team and he was impressed at the experience. 'As I see it, it's a team of chiefs who work like Indians. The men doing the job have all the knowledge, experience, intelligence and enthusiasm you could hope for: mention anything you like and they know what you are talking about; if you want something special to try, they get it set up — and quickly.'

Bruce and Ken finished second, four laps behind Hall and Hap Sharp in the Chaparral.

At Goodwood Bruce gambled with the weather and lost. With black clouds threatening, the team waited until the last minute to decide whether to fit wet tyres or dry. Bruce was on pole and when a few spots of rain started to fall, they hurriedly fitted wet tyres to the sports car. Big mistake. In the Formula 1 race that followed, Bruce ran a lonely sixth until retirements further up the field elevated him to fourth place, his engine misfiring by flag-fall.

At Monza for the 1000-kilometre race, two Ford GTs raced off against a small army of Ferraris. Bruce and Ken Miles were paired again and Shelby told Bruce that they were to try to take control of the race from the start. The problem was that it had rained in the final practice and they had been unable to bed brakes or scrub tyres so Bruce started the race with new tyres and brake pads.

'I out-braked a couple of Ferraris easily going into the hay-bale chicane — I couldn't stop! — scraped through the first part of the wiggle-woggle, but with about 60 mph more than I needed to get through the second bit I didn't have any option but to punch an easier route through the bales. It's amazing what happens when you do something like that. It was like being inside an exploding haystack and I was spitting straw and dust for the next few laps!'

Ferraris finished first and second with the McLaren/Miles Ford in third place.

The 1965 season was to be Bruce's last with the Cooper team and he was pressing ahead with projects for his own team, including a secret open version of the Ford GT, which was being built behind closed doors at Feltham. Robin Herd had joined the McLaren crew and was penning what he and Bruce hoped would be the ultimate Grand Prix design for the 3-litre formula starting in 1966. They were aiming much too high. In *Bruce McLaren — The Man and his Racing Team*, I wrote: 'The first McLaren sports cars were very obviously Cooper-based with McLaren ideas superimposed, and it was not until Robin Herd joined the team bringing with him advanced — and not always practical — theories from the Royal Aircraft Establishment, that the true McLaren stamp became apparent. Their first Formula 1 car was so bundled up with accumulated ideas on how to go Grand Prix racing with a brand-new car that it was little better than a failure. The main cause of the disastrous un-competitiveness of the [Formula 1] M2B was the dead weight of the 3-litre version of the four-cam Indianapolis V8 engine, but in other areas the car also ignored later McLaren principles of developing an established theme. The lesson was learned well.

'Looking back, Herd remembers that their thinking when he joined the team early in 1965 was very much influenced by Jim Hall and his Chaparrals. "Jim was going through a phase of being a really outstanding designer and constructor and our emphasis tended to be more on the elegance of the chassis structure rather than on the design of a really quick racing car. I now find this rather surprising, because Bruce's sense of values in relation to the design and engineering of a racing car was first class. He never, after our first few months together anyway, lost sight of the immediate aim, which was to design a car which crossed the finishing line first. On our initial design we erred from this and tended to go towards technical ingenuity and bullshit rather than race-winning engineering." '

Herd says that Bruce had a big influence on the way he carried out his detail design but he also feels that to a degree he changed Bruce's thinking.

'Bruce's designs would tend to be very easy to make, sound, reliable, perhaps not very light, and I think it's fair to say not particularly elegant, whereas mine were the other way round. Between us we made up for each other's deficiencies with our experience and ability, such as it was then. Bruce gave me an immensely free hand in the design and when I talk to other people — like the way Maurice Phillipe worked with Colin Chapman at Lotus — I realise just how good Bruce was in this way, although perhaps I didn't fully appreciate it at the time. He had the experience I didn't have and he really was a super bloke to work with.'

Gordon Coppuck, a Farnborough man who had worked with Herd, also joined McLaren, but late in 1965. When Herd left to join Cosworth in 1968, Coppuck became chief designer. 'Bruce was very good at vehicle dynamics,' recalled Coppuck. 'This is the theory of why vehicles do certain things — vehicles generally, not just racing cars. Whereas most racing drivers could tell you whether the car was over-steering or under-steering, Bruce understood about centres of gravity, moments of inertia and things of that nature — and he could apply these. This was something that was of great benefit to the firm. I don't know where he learned it, or whether he just evolved it himself. I don't think he would have learned it at school because it isn't taught in school. He most likely evolved it by applying a basically good education and a good mind.'

The team had been experimenting with Ferguson automatic transmission and after Amon set a test lap record at Oulton Park, Bruce decided to race the prototype automatic McLaren in the Tourist Trophy there in May. The race was held in two heats and Bruce never finished either because of transmission troubles. 'Despite having led the first heat and set a new lap record in the second, we had plenty of people saying that we were foolish to have raced with a component that wasn't sorted out. That's certainly not the way I look at it. You can't progress by standing still and watching someone else experimenting…'

The sports car race at Silverstone fell to Bruce in the M1 fitted with a regular Hewland transmission after a wheel-to-wheel battle with John Surtees in the Lola-Chev. John broke down with three laps left and Bruce stopped to give him a lift back to his pit on the slowing-down lap. The new lap record of 1:31.6 (115.03 mph) was set by Bruce midway through the race. The non-championship International Trophy Formula 1 race was a slog to sixth place in the works Cooper. Jackie Stewart won in the BRM and Denny Hulme had a drive for Brabham, standing in for Dan Gurney who was qualifying at Indianapolis that weekend.

Monaco was always a McLaren favourite with memories of his Grand Prix win there in 1962 and Bruce enjoyed the whole supercharged atmosphere of the weekend.

'Monaco's memory for me this year was a noise like a runaway express train as Dickie Attwood's Lotus-BRM went bellowing by me on full noise, heading straight for Nice with a back wheel hanging off. I had just begun to swing into the hairpin when a little voice whispered that perhaps I shouldn't lock over. The wall of hay bales around the hairpin upset Dickie's trip to Nice and the Lotus reared in the air, scattering hay and pieces of motorcar in all directions, but somehow a very lucky Mr Attwood stepped out unscathed. The wheel had broken adrift under braking from somewhere around 100 mph for the dead-slow hairpin, and the brake hose parted as Dickie had been heel-and-toeing a down-change. When the brake pedal went to the floor, the accelerator did too. Nasty…'

Graham Hill scored a hat-trick of wins at Monaco, but took his last the hard way. Bruce wrote: 'Graham Hill and Jackie Stewart in the BRMs were wandering away with the race in the opening laps when they hurtled down into the chicane as near as dammit flat out to find Bob Anderson's Brabham limping through to accidentally but very effectively close the barn door on Graham. Graham had a split second to decide whether to go around Bob, over him, or stop, and he chose the latter course. He didn't have all that much room to stop either, but the heavy black marks leading into the little escape cul-de-sac told their own story. He hopped out, pushed the BRM back to the track and was in and off again half a minute later. Half a minute happens to be 30 seconds long, and the story of Graham's pursuit while he hauled everyone else in and won the race is just fantastic. He thoroughly deserved the wild acclamation he received when he took the chequer. He had driven a race in the style of the grand old days, when men were men and racing cars were monsters.'

This race also saw Australian Paul Hawkins hurtle into the harbour at the chicane and it was Denny Hulme's first Grand Prix for Brabham, again standing in for Gurney who was racing at Indianapolis. Another Indy absentee, Jimmy Clark, won the '500' that weekend. Bruce and Denny had both started from the fourth row of the grid, and finished fifth and eighth, respectively. Two years later Denny would win at Monaco and go on to become World Champion. Three years later he would be driving for and with McLaren.

While the Formula 1 folk were at Monaco, Chris Amon was flying the McLaren colours at Ste Jovite in Canada, where he won the sports car race from Hap Sharp's Chaparral. Bruce swept into Canada to carry the standard in a sports car race at Mosport, driving the McLaren-Elva fitted with a 5-litre Traco-Oldsmobile engine. Unfortunately, boiling brake fluid and a broken gearbox dropped him out of both heats. He flew down to Detroit to test the new 7-litre Ford GT that he would race at Le Mans and then it was back to Europe for the Grand Prix at Spa.

'At Heathrow I went through the usual rigmarole. Did I have a British passport? No. Did I live in England? Sort of. How long was I staying? Three hours. That destroyed official composure, but it was quite true. Just time to leave a few notes with my busy merry men at Feltham, then off to Spa…'

There, on a circuit he professed to hate, Jim Clark took victory again, making it *four* Spa wins in a row! Bruce again started his Cooper from the fourth row of the grid, this time beside Jack in the Brabham, and crossed the line third after a wet race.

Le Mans had an air of familiarity about it for Bruce: 'I led the whole, historic affair from the first hour and a half, stopped for dinner at the Shelby farm behind the pits, heard that our racer had broken its gearbox, had a pleasant evening at the Hotel de Paris and flew back to London in time to watch the finish on television. Just like I did the year before, and the year before that, and the year before *that*.

'Between four o'clock and five on the Saturday afternoon my Kiwi teammate Chris Amon and I enjoyed some real motor racing with the 7-litre Ford GTs. Chris led away from the start but I cruised by as we pulled out on to the Mulsanne Straight and from then on we were able to resist the temptation to make those electrifying opening laps a carve-it-up sprint. We were too far out in front for that! We were both running with 400 revs in hand, as instructed, and changing gear and braking ever so gently, yet still drawing away at around 4 seconds a lap.'

Most of the McLaren team were using their 'home' driving licences — New Zealand or American — but when the company arranged a corporate motor insurance policy, it was pointed out that all employees should have UK licences. Which meant a UK driving test. Bruce thought it hugely amusing: 'Dropping from 200-plus mph on Mulsanne to a brave and anything-but-competent 25 mph in my wife's Mini-Cooper with a driving examiner at my side was a little unsettling when I got back to England. I'd taken the precaution of sneaking a lesson with an instructor friend of mine, who showed me how you are supposed to pass your test. I think the examiner was probably as embarrassed as I was, but I managed to say and do all the right things, carefully avoiding cross-arms on the steering wheel in favour of the shuffle, and drove away a fully-fledged English road-user with a licence to prove that I could competently handle a heavy locomotive, a tractor, a mowing machine, an electric milk float, or a motor tricycle weighing not more than 8 cwt unladen. And a 7-litre Ford GT...'

The French Grand Prix was held for the first time on the sinuous 5-mile Clermont Ferrand course, 2500 feet up in the Auvergne hills. Jim Clark dominated the race in his Lotus, starting from pole, winning and breaking the lap record 15 times! Bruce started from his familiar fourth-row spot and retired on the 24th lap with broken suspension.

In July, Bruce raced one of his own sports cars at Ste Jovite and scored a narrow win over Jim Hall's Chaparral. They had run nose to tail until the lanky Texan missed his braking and dented his nose against the McLaren's tail.

Jim Clark was still stringing Lotus Grand Prix wins together, taking his fourth British Grand Prix in a row at Silverstone. He and Bruce took the chequered flag nose to tail, the problem being that Bruce was two laps down, having pitted with a gearshift problem in the Cooper. Bruce took rueful credit at being the only driver to feature in a photo finish with Jimmy that summer.

The following weekend they were back at Silverstone, having entered the sports car for the Martini Trophy. During Friday practice a loose carburettor union sent petrol spraying over the engine and Bruce's back and it caught fire.

'There's nothing quite so terrifying as a fire in a racing car. I've always been a great advocate of wearing safety clothing in racing cockpits, but on this occasion I was wearing a nylon jacket (rather foolishly) and no gloves (again rather foolishly) and the burning nylon was melting through my overalls despite my efforts to beat out the flames with my bare hands while also trying to get the car stopped. Lesson learned: (1) don't wear a nylon jacket in a racing car; (2) wear driving gloves — even if they aren't worth half a second as the adverts might lead you to believe, they will certainly save you from a painful scorching should you be involved in a burn-up.'

Chris had only done a couple of test laps on race morning to make sure the car was running properly after the repairs and he started from the back of the grid, but within just four laps he was on the tail of Surtees in the leading Lola and when Sortees' engine blew on lap seven, Chris took over to win.

At Zandvoort for the Dutch Grand Prix Bruce started on the fourth row of the grid yet again and retired with a gearbox problem on the 37th lap. Jim Clark won in the Lotus from Jackie Stewart's BRM.

The Guards Trophy sports car race at Brands Hatch was not much of a birthday treat for Bruce, despite the fact that there were six McLaren-Elvas, six Lolas and six Lotuses. Bruce finished second to Surtees, who was driving a new Lola in both race heats and the little team went back to Feltham wondering how or where to find two seconds timewise.

'After my day of second-placing racing and my distant lesson on how a sports car should be made to motor by J. Surtees, Esq., I remembered it was my birthday, so we set off into a three-hour traffic jam and took over the Contented Plaice in Kingston for a rowdy sorrow-drowning, wine-downing dinner that rollicked into the beginning of the next day.'

The German Grand Prix on the Nürburgring was another forgettable race for Bruce. He started on the third row of the grid and dropped out with gear-change problems after eight laps. Clark won again in the Lotus.

Colin Beanland, who'd accompanied Bruce on his first trip to England in 1958, had sold his Auckland parts business and shifted to the UK to work once again for McLaren. He'd been put in charge of fabrication for the new single-seater being constructed amid great secrecy at Feltham. Ostensibly the car was a test vehicle for Firestone, but it must have been apparent to the outside world that it was a prototype for a 3-litre Formula 1 car. The new car was a well-kept secret. I fielded several phone calls asking whether we were building a Formula 1 car, but I could always deny it, secure in the knowledge that it was really a tyre-test car…

The news broke in *Autosport* on 17 September with a piece headed 'A

McLaren single-seater — Secret Formula 1 Firestone Project for 1966?' The report carried enough detailed technical information to convince Bruce that it must have been an 'inside job' and he worried that the team had a 'mole' within the ranks.

'The first McLaren single-seater, believed to be a prototype 1966 Formula 1 car, carried out some tyre tests for Firestone last week. A Traco-modified Oldsmobile production unit currently powers the latest McLaren. This is of monocoque construction with many indications of the aircraft design influence brought to McLaren by ex-Farnborough designer Robin Herd. The monocoque structure is built of laminated sheeting comprising outer layers of aluminium with end-grain balsa wood between. The sections are both bonded and riveted together, and to the lightweight diaphragms which are also constructed according to aircraft practice. One of the most striking features of the car is its low frontal area, said to be no more than that of a Lotus 33. Fuel capacity is currently 35 gallons but apparently more can be housed within the monocoque structure without increasing overall size. The low fuel capacity adds weight to the rumour that McLaren will use an American (presumably Traco-developed) 2-o.h.c. V8, which would give more mpg than the higher-revving 16-cyl. BRM unit; the power disadvantage might well be offset by the low weight — in present trim the car is down to the minimum weight limit of the 1966 formula.'

We never did find out how the story of the 'secret' single-seater reached *Autosport*, but the assumption in later years was that Robin Herd might have discussed the car with someone who passed on the information.

By late August the car had been christened the M2A, the new M1A sports cars were built for the series in North America, the secret Ford GTX car was nearly ready to test and the single-seater Mallite car was also completed. A second Mallite car was fitted with a 4.5-litre Traco-Oldsmobile engine and testing was carried out at Goodwood, Oulton Park and Zandvoort. Initial problems were found with the Hewland transmission, so ZF transmissions were ordered from Germany. The team also tried a wing on a frame over the gearbox during the tests at Zandvoort and lap times improved by three seconds, but the desperate problems with the Ford motor in 1966 meant they never had the opportunity to use the wing.

The team also moved to a larger 7000 square foot factory building at 5 David Road, near the little old village of Colnbrook that had grown up from a coaching stop on the road from London to Bath. It was ideally situated close to Heathrow and convenient for freight and team travel. It was actually off the end of the main Heathrow runways and we soon grew used to pausing in conversation as a Boeing roared over on take-off, and picked up the conversation as though it was perfectly normal, when the plane had passed over.

Looking back now, I'm amazed that Bruce chose to go the Ford route, reducing a 4.2-litre four-cam Ford V8 originally built for Indianapolis, to 3 litres for Formula 1. The obvious advantage was that Ford gifted four engines for the project in March 1965, but that was where the advantage ended. The McLaren men were ideally placed to use a 3-litre version of the aluminium Oldsmobile V8 that Traco had built for them, but Bruce was anxious to involve Ford. He wouldn't — couldn't — have known that while he was aiming at Ford in Detroit, Colin Chapman was putting a Formula 1 proposal to Walter Hayes at Ford in Britain. The Chapman-Hayes project yielded the Cosworth DFV V8 that came to totally dominate Grand Prix racing. He couldn't know, either, that his old friend and rival, Jack Brabham, was planning to use the Oldsmobile V8 as the basis for a Formula 1 engine built by Repco…and they would win the World Championship in 1966 and 1967.

Hindsight is a wonderful asset. Late in 1965 Bruce was deep into the challenge of Formula 1 but, like other teams at the time, he was aiming too high. Lotus had proved that the monocoque had to be the way to win. Brabham and his designer Ron Tauranac went with a simple space-frame and the simple Oldsmobile for the new 3-litre formula. Tauranac always maintained that the fastest thing about the monocoque Lotus was Jim Clark. He was right for the time. Jim Clark was the only driver who ever won a World Championship Grand Prix with a Lotus 25.

The German engineer Klaus von Rucker took on McLaren's project of reducing the 4.2-litre Ford engine to 3 litres and the work was carried out by Gary Knutson and Tyler at Traco Engineering in California. The whole Formula 1 project had started to fall behind Bruce's schedule and it was February 1966 before Willmott arrived at Traco with the Mallite chassis and the 3-litre Ford engine fired in the chassis for the first time.

It was a disaster, much like Bruce's 1965 Formula 1 season, which was slowly slipping away from him. The Cooper spark had gone. At Monza Bruce sat on the fifth row of the grid beside Hulme in a Brabham and finished fifth while Jackie Stewart won his first Grand Prix. At Watkins Glen Bruce again started from the fifth row, but retired with no oil pressure. For the final race of the season, in Mexico, Bruce and teammate Rindt both started from the lowly eighth row, and Bruce again retired, this time with gear selection problems. Despite starting on the second row, Richie Ginther led from start to finish, winning his first and only Grand Prix and scoring the first Grand Prix victory for Honda and for Goodyear.

Bruce was philosophical about his last race with Cooper. Part of him must have been delighted to be leaving a team that had faded in the latter seasons, but he had grown up in Grand Prix racing with the Cooper organisation.

'Sadly, a professional association that has lasted eight years will come to an end, but I am sure that the social association will not cease. Anyone who has known John Cooper has liked him, and anyone who has known him as long as I have, cannot help but have considerable regard for him. The heat of Grand Prix racing is something like the heat of battle — it either welds people together or breaks them apart. In the eight years that I have been with Coopers I have to think very hard to remember a cross word between John and me. In motor racing that's something of a record — perhaps eight years with a Formula 1 team is something of a record too...

'When I started to race with John I was very young and I blush to think of some of the stories that he can, and is liable to, tell you of those early days when I was very much a green Kiwi. With Coopers I learnt a lot about racing cars and racing people, and I spent those formative years from age 20 to 26 with people like John and the men around him — Brabham, Salvadori, Ken Tyrrell — and Charles Cooper, who started the whole story with the car he built for John. It's due in part to the influence, the example and the success of these people that makes it possible for me to attempt Grand Prix racing with my own team.'

15 Le Mans winner 1966

The new, official, McLaren team started its Formula 1 programme poorly, with a less-than-inspiring performance at Monaco, where the smaller-engined cars dominated. In contrast, the Le Mans 24-hour race was a sensational 'up' for Bruce and Chris. Their victory marked the first time Ford had beaten Ferrari on the most public and important international motor sporting arena, and it has gathered drama as the years have passed. Ford went on to win Le Mans in 1967, 1968 and 1969, but that first win was the stuff of legend.

Bruce thoroughly enjoyed indulging himself in his *Autosport* column, but it seemed that he deliberately avoided the political situation that bubbled during that long race. The Ford team was contracted to Goodyear for its tyres, for example, and a special dispensation had been made whereby McLaren and Amon, who had major personal contracts with Firestone, could use Firestones on their car. Viewed from today's water-tight commercial contracts, this was an incredible arrangement. I think it was agreed between the two American tyre companies that if the McLaren/ Amon Ford won, Firestone could not advertise the victory. It turned into a problem that came close to costing them the win. Compare Bruce's rose-tinted review of their race with Chris's recollections nearly 40 years later, and you would think they were talking about different events. Bruce's race was a breeze. Chris's version was a race riddled with politics and intrigue, and not a little rage and sorrow in some quarters after the event. It was certainly no stroll in the park, even though Bruce endeavoured to present it that way. Or was it just that Bruce was doing his diplomatic bit and protecting his Ford association, while Chris, who switched to Ferrari at the end of that season and led Ford's opposition in endurance racing, enjoyed the luxury of looking back from a considerable distance.

It was not a matter of Ford simply tolerating the situation. They positively welcomed the Kiwi duo, painting the Ford Mk 2 black, with central silver stripes and a silver fern on each side.

'It makes a change to be right sometimes — after Daytona, I said that Fords could and should win Le Mans. No one in England would believe me. They said Le Mans was different. Le Mans was a car killer. You couldn't beat Ferrari — and now it's history! It's by far the biggest race I've ever won and the same goes for Chris, but the whole thing seemed to be so simple,' said Bruce.

Ford had effectively entered three separate teams. Shelby American entered three cars — McLaren/Amon, Miles/Hulme and Gurney/Grant. Holman and Moody entered three Mk 2s and two more were entered by Alan Mann. Add in five privately entered GT40s and there were actually 13 Fords in the race. Ferrari had entered only three cars, but they were in disarray before the race started, when John Surtees stormed out of the team after a disagreement with team manager Dragoni.

'The pattern for the whole race was set on the Tuesday night. The car was absolutely ready to race so team manager Carroll Smith suggested we take it out on the road and set the lights as we pleased. To have the time to let a couple of finicky drivers mess about — to the left a bit, no, back a bit, now up a bit — is unusual. To have that job done three days before the race is exceptional, but that's the way the whole week went. I took the Ford out for its first practice run and it felt taut and precise.

'The engine would have pulled up to 6500 rpm if I'd left my foot in it, but I felt this was two or three hundred rpm faster than we should run it. The best we had used before was 6200 rpm (about 200 mph), but now we had about another ten miles an hour in hand. Ford's engine people said the last batch had been the best yet. "We haven't made any changes — we're just getting to know them a bit better," was the way one of them put it.

'The history of these 7-litre Ford GT Mk 2s is interesting. The first ones ran at Le Mans last year and Chris and I had a glorious hour-and-a-bit out in front at the start. A Mk 2 GT won at Daytona earlier this year and at Sebring, the 7-litre GT-X, the car that my team built in England, led the field home. The basic chassis and suspension parts of the GT are built in England. This is handled by Ford Advanced Vehicles, a division run by John Wyer. The engines come from Ford's Engine and Foundry Division in America, coming over completely ready to race. They weren't exotic racing engines as a lot of people seem to think.

'You could lift the bonnet of a Ranchwagon and find the same lump, with its pushrods and one big carburettor. The transmissions come from another Ford offshoot, Kar Kraft, where Roy Lunn does all the advanced concept work, and the complete cars are assembled at Shelby's plant in Los Angeles under the direction of chief engineer Phil Remington. The cars and 21 tons of spares were then air-freighted to Le Mans!

'The Shelby crew changed the gear ratio after practice, which dropped the revs back to 6200 at 210 mph. There were a few final adjustments made at the track during practice — shock absorber settings, tyre pressures, roll stiffness bars to balance the car up for easy handling in the low-speed corners, rear spoiler setting to keep the car stable in high-speed corners, and the brake ratio set front and rear.

'There was hardly any need to practise again on Thursday night. Without extending man or machine it appears that the Fords could run three or four seconds a lap faster than the Ferraris. This might not sound a lot, but for the first time we had more Fords than Ferraris on the entry list, and rumours about weaknesses in the Ferrari transmissions were combining to keep Ford enthusiasm high.

'On Saturday afternoon at 2 o'clock, we had a Ford drivers' meeting and project manager John Cowley said he would like us to start lapping at around 3:38.0, which was about eight seconds slower than we knew the cars would run. But the impressive thing was his whole attitude to the business in hand. He said he had appreciated that we had all been racing longer than he had, but he wanted the cars to finish and he respected our abilities to help him in this aim. During this last year the attitude shown by the "top brass" to team mechanics, engineers and drivers has been such that it gets the best out of each individual. You wouldn't hear someone saying, "Do this", or "Do that" — rather, "Let's get it done." This "togetherness" was apparently a lot different from the rows and personality clashes in the Ferrari camp.

'I did the start. Last year Chris and I had been hurtling round in front, but this year it looked as though we had a chance of being up front at 4 o'clock on the right day. It looked like rain, so we had fitted rain tyres.'

Note that Bruce made no mention that their wet-weather tyres were Firestones, while the rest of the team were on Goodyear.

'In the last two big races — Indy and Spa — half the field had been knocked out in first-lap shunts, so when the flag dropped I was very careful not to break a leg or otherwise injure myself running across the track and clambering into the car. I shrugged the shoulder harness on, buckled the lap strap, fired the engine and turned sharp right to scuttle along the pit wall rather than push my way into the mêlée in the middle of the road.

'Not very much happened for the next twelve hours or so…'

I suppose it rather depends on what Bruce meant by 'not much'. Chris remembers the panic pit stops as the Firestone rain tyres chunked catastrophically, throwing their early race plans to the winds.

'It didn't rain so we changed off the rain tyres at our first fuel stop, and at the second fuel stop an hour and a half later, Chris took over. Three hours later he handed over to me again, and three hours after that I gave it back to him. Our conversations were brief. "Is it OK?" "Yeah, fine," and so it went on. Which I suppose is the way it ought to be. Most of the time we seemed to be lying fifth or sixth but we were on the same lap as the leaders which meant that a couple of hours of concentrated effort would have pulled us up among them at any time.

'I didn't try going to sleep until 7 o'clock on the Sunday morning. I don't trust the cars I drive at Le Mans, because as sure as hell if I go to sleep in the caravan behind the pits, they'll break down! Seeing that we were still mobile at dawn, I figured forty winks wouldn't do me any harm, and I slept until 9 o'clock. I wandered out bleary-eyed to ask someone how we were placed, and they held up one finger. We were leading!

'We swapped the lead with the sister GT driven by Ken Miles and Denny Hulme for the rest of the day until it became obvious that one or other of us was going to have to win the race. This was quite a political situation, for obviously we all wanted to win, and equally obviously we all couldn't!

'The French organisers thought the idea of a dead heat was a good one, and it certainly seemed to be the easiest and fairest way around the ticklish problem, so that's what we tried to do. As it turned out, it was just as well we did trickle over the line at 70 mph instead of battling across at our usual 140 mph. There were police and mechanics crowding out into the road and I'm sure there would have been a terrible accident if we had been racing for the line! We don't win races like this every weekend, and at least someone could have told us that we would only have half the road to use.

'From there on it was chequered flags, champagne and chauffeur-driven cars. Chris and I were flown to the States to attend Ford receptions and generally received the full royal treatment. The enormous Lincoln that collected us at New York airport was flying a New Zealand flag on one wing and the Stars and Stripes on the other. In the plush drawing-room about thirty feet behind the engine, we swept through New York, feeling very much like the reigning monarch with all the peasantry peering in.

'Now I *know* how tough it must be at the very top...'

Bruce told the *real* story of the race in a letter to his father in Auckland: 'I pulled the car into the pits at one o'clock Saturday afternoon. In the previous five laps Miles had caught up about 30 seconds, when we were all supposed to be lapping at 4 minutes and no faster or slower. He [Miles] also had a very rapid pit stop and handed over to Denny.' Bruce went on to explain the Firestone chunking problem and the switch to Goodyear tyres, pointing out that he and Chris were Firestone people in a Goodyear team. 'My car was in the pits when a Goodyear man said "Change that wheel." At the time I thought there was something fishy about it. I didn't realise till I thought about it, that he hadn't looked at the wheel! Chris went out in the car. We were now about 40 seconds behind Hulme and supposed to lap calmly at the same speed till 4 p.m. I asked Shelby how the race was going to be finished. It had been decided, he said, to let the car that was ahead after the last pit stop win, so that it would give the crews on each car a nice feeling! Chris didn't know this. He wasn't allowed to lap faster than 4 minutes without the EZE board coming out. Miles must have ignored the board for five laps and this, combined with our tyre change, put us 40 seconds behind. Fifteen minutes before, we had been 30 seconds ahead. I didn't even bother to think about working out who, how or what had and was going to happen.'

Bruce approached the Ford team management and presented his views strongly. 'I said, "You are going to put the drivers that run to the pit signals in second place — I could have run at 3:25.0 for the last hour if you wanted, and both cars have been running 20 seconds a lap slower than they could. Why don't you bring the cars over the line together? It would be much better public relations. In fact, with all three cars up, you are paying dearly for the pictures in the papers, so get a good picture..."

'Well, you know the story from there — I didn't think ten minutes of politics could win a 24-hour race — but there you are. Nice guys don't win ball games, they say...'

Chris Amon's recollections are somewhat different: 'At Le Mans in 1966 Bruce and I decided we weren't going to worry about pacing ourselves. We were just going to get on with it and *race*. We were running Firestones while the rest of the team were on Goodyears, and we had major tyre problems in the first hour and a half and lost a lot of time. We started on intermediate tyres because it was sort of showery and the bloody things started chunking. Bruce had done the start and after 10 laps or so he came in with great chunks of tread off the tyres. This happened on the first and second sets and after the second set chunked, I took over while Bruce attempted to sort things out and, as I recall, I was called in early in my stint to change to Goodyears, this being the result of Bruce's negotiations in the pits. By then we had probably stopped three times compared with one stop for the others in the team.

'Because we had got ourselves well behind, we said to hell with it, we're gonna go for it for the rest of the race. And we drove as though it was a Grand Prix distance and we had a lot of fun. We made up significant time during the night and we were leading by a reasonable margin, certainly in excess of half a minute, when the EZE sign came out some time after lunch on Sunday afternoon. We slowed, but the Miles/Hulme car, which at that time was being driven by Ken Miles, didn't.

'It didn't really detract from anything as far as I was concerned, because we had been way behind, we had caught up, and Bruce was driving the last stint. I had a feeling that Bruce had made up his mind that we were going to win anyway, despite any arrangements the team was trying to make about crossing the line in a photo finish.

'The unfortunate aspect of this whole saga is that over the years, people who were not even vaguely connected with events at the time and not even present, have suggested that the wrong pair won. Examination of the facts doesn't support that, but I think some of it stems from Ken Miles' death a few weeks later. I never really discussed things with Denny at any length. I think he moved on from it very quickly...'

Inside the team there was yet another slant on the situation. Carroll Shelby, who had won at Le Mans in a works Aston Martin with Roy Salvadori in 1959, and was managing the 'works' Ford team at Le Mans in 1966, said: 'Ford didn't cost Ken the race at Le Mans, I did — and I regret it to this day. They [Ford] came to me and said, "Who do you think should win the race?" I thought, "Well, hell, Ken's been leading for all these hours — he should win the race."

'I looked at [Ford competition director and GT40 project chief] Leo Beebe and said, "What do you think ought to happen, Leo?" He said, "I don't know. I'd kind of like to see all three of them cross the line together." Leo didn't tell me what to say or do, so I said, "Oh, hell, let's do it that way then," not knowing that the French [race organisers] would interpret the rules the way they did. Ken [and Denny] should have won the race and in most everyone's minds he did win the race. I take full responsibility for it and I'm very sorry for it because Ken was killed at Riverside [testing for Ford] two months later...'

In his book, *Bruce McLaren — Life and Legacy of Excellence*, Karl Ludvigsen, who was working in the upper echelons of Ford in the 1960s, wrote: 'Carroll Shelby told Bruce that team orders were for the car leading after the last pit stop to be the winner. Bruce took the matter to the Ford men, who called the top shots and suggested that a photo finish would earn Ford more publicity. They agreed. Bruce reckoned that Henry Ford wasn't really too concerned who won as long as one of his cars did, and Bruce didn't see why Chris and he, as Firestone-contracted drivers in Shelby's Goodyear-sponsored team, should be penalised...'

In his biography, *Forza Amon*, Chris said, 'Bruce made bloody sure he was in front [at the finish]. He made absolutely certain that it was no dead heat, because he crossed the line two or three lengths ahead of Miles.

'It rained on and off for the whole race and I find it difficult to sit back now and think that we actually averaged 125 mph for 24 hours when 15 hours of the 24 would have been in the wet. They were *so* fast, those 7-litre Mk 2s. We were doing 220-something miles an hour down the Mulsanne Straight…'

16 Going Grand Prix racing 1965–66

The Ford-engined M2 Formula 1 prototype was first tested in California early in 1966. Robin Herd remembers towing the car through the streets of Los Angeles in order to try to start it. 'That was what one did in those days, but either the oil was so cold or the oil pressure was so high, that it actually burst the oil cooler as we towed it. Once it finally got started, Bruce drove it back in the dark to the garage where we were working.

'We tested for a couple of days at Riverside. It made a *beautiful* noise. You could hear the car coming out of the last corner and you'd wait for it to come into view. The noise was *tremendous* and you were expecting a missile to flash in front of you…but then the car arrived doing about the speed of a Morris Minor. The engine and gearbox weighed more than the rest of the car and it soon became apparent that all wasn't going to be as we'd hoped…but at least we could claim to have led the Formula 1 world with wings, even if we didn't have the chance to prove it!'

With his aircraft design background, Herd had been keen to experiment with wings on the Formula 1 car and had originally designed a flat sheet of Mallite on a mounting that would adjust up to 90 degrees. This meant it could also be used as an air-brake, such as Mercedes had used on their 300SLR sports-racing cars at Le Mans in 1955. 'We didn't get around to contouring the wing then. If you didn't put too much angle on the flat sheet, the air flow still stayed attached. Most of the down-force was generated by a Gurney Flap. We'd tested it with the Oldsmobile engine at Zandvoort late in 1965. The Olds engine didn't have much power, but at least it was light. Bruce got close to the lap record at Zandvoort using the wing and at that stage we felt we were ready to win the World Championship in 1966…but the engine didn't let us…'

Bruce spent a lot of time in the States early in 1966, worrying over engine development at Traco and driving the 7-litre Mk 2 Fords with Chris Amon at Daytona. In the 24-hour race at Daytona the Fords finished one-two-three-five, with the New Zealanders in fifth behind the Rodriguez/ Andretti P2 Ferrari. They were to have driven the new J-car at Sebring too, but Ford decided to save that for the Le Mans tests, and Bruce and Chris were put on the reserves bench so Bruce went back to base.

'Chris was vastly impressed when Miles and Ruby won in the GTX — the open Ford that we had built and developed while we were at Feltham and the car that Chris had raced at Mosport, Riverside and Nassau. We developed the car as a long-distance machine rather than a competitive sports-racer for sprint events and, although Chris suffered a weight handicap in the fall races (and the car received the nickname "Big Ed" with reference to an earlier not-so-successful Ford — the Edsel), it certainly came through with flying colours at Sebring.'

Ford had re-christened the GTX the X-1 roadster and seemed strangely coy about acknowledging McLaren's contribution to building the car in the first place. After the win that seemed to confirm the potential of the car, it was officially destroyed!

Bruce was aware of the building pressure on his team. 'At the moment down in Colnbrook everyone is working hard on a variety of deadline projects. There are three monocoque Formula 1 chassis taking shape in our "Keep Out" shop, two McLaren-Elva sports cars are being built up for Snetterton and we have a small production unit building space-frame Formula Libre single-seaters. I heard one of our dawn-till-after-dark toilers saying he had to go outside to yawn in case someone thought he was tiring on the job. The Formula 1 boys are working with Monaco very much in mind, the 5-litre sports cars have to be ready for Snetterton on Good Friday and customers always seem to want their cars delivered yesterday...'

The famous 'Whoosh-Bonk' cars were the result of a conversation between Bruce, Ron Smith and Patsy Burt about a single-seater version of a CanAm car being ideal for hill climbs. Bruce commented on them at Goodwood, where he'd carried out pre-delivery tests on one for Swiss hill climber Harry Zweifel. 'Basically the car is a single-seater version of our sports car — it has a conventional space-frame chassis, sports car running gear, a ZF gearbox and an engine bay that will accept any of the big American V8 engines. I wouldn't call it a lightweight, but it is certainly strong. We reckon it should be able to bounce off a mountain without requiring a major rebuild, which must be a point worth considering by people who go rushing up hills for only congratulations and trophies.'

The Archie Scott-Brown Memorial Trophy, held at Snetterton on 10 April 1966 went to Denny Hulme in the 6-litre Lola. Both 5-litre works McLarens suffered engine problems. The second heat featured an all-Kiwi front row, with Denny on pole in the Lola and Bruce and Chris beside him in the McLarens. Bruce was adamant that, when it came to engines, light was right, but he had some non-believers within the team who were determined to prove him wrong. Or at least prove to Bruce that there was another way to do it. One such person was Kiwi Bruce Harre, who worked with Amon on the Firestone test sessions. He could not understand Bruce's determination to stick with the aluminium Oldsmobile V8 engine, which, though it had grown from 3.5 to 5 litres, was being out-gunned by the 5-litre Chevrolet V8s.

'I asked him why he persevered with this bloody Olds engine,' Harre recalled. 'He'd tried to get it up to 5 litres with fuel injection and spent a lot of time and money at Traco Engineering in Culver City, California, but the thing kept breaking and wouldn't run properly. Chris and I were scheduled for a three-day test at Silverstone with the M1B sports car, so we went to a plumber's supply shop in Surbiton and bought some sheets of lead. We worked out how much heavier a Chev engine was than an Oldsmobile and how much heavier a ZF gearbox would be than the Hewland HD4. When we had finished the Firestone testing, we strapped the lead around the chassis frames on each side of the engine to represent the increased engine weight and tied it all around the gearbox with lock-wire. Chris went out and drove more than one second a lap quicker with the Oldsmobile engine and all the extra lead weight. Bruce wouldn't believe it. He just *wouldn't* believe it. His pet theory was always that lightweight was the way to go. He had some pet ideas and they were fixed. He would go to the ends of the earth and he reckoned that Amon had been driving at eleven-tenths to go quicker, because it *must* be slower if it was heavier. He thought Amon and I were bullshitting him, but the Firestone timekeeper was an independent observer and Bruce eventually had to succumb to the Chev engine and the bigger gearbox…'

The opening Grand Prix of the 1966 season was also the first race for the new 3-litre formula, doubling the capacity from the previous 1.5-litre formula that had ruled from 1961 to 1965. For Bruce, his first Formula 1 car was the ultimate challenge, but it would also turn into his ultimate disappointment.

'I rather think we expected bells to ring and trumpets to blow, but 22 May came and went just like any other day. It was Monaco, our first Grand Prix with our first Formula 1 car, and it was a day we had been aiming at for nearly a year. We had been building up our hopes and a car for this race in the expectation that the opening round of the new 3-litre formula would be different from all the others — but it wasn't. It was just like any other race, in fact more so! No one had to worry about a tense last-minute scramble to qualify as there weren't enough cars anyway, and before the race was half over, most of the drivers were spectators or waiting while their cars were rebuilt.

'It seems that every time we build a new car we find something new that can happen in the first few laps. The first few laps of the *race*, that is! This particular fault will never occur during testing or practice when you are pounding on mile after mile after mile looking for something, just like whatever will lay you low in the race, to raise its ugly head. When it doesn't really matter, you can have the most reliable car in the business…but I suppose it's racing that makes racing cars.'

Bruce noted that BRM had spent the last year honing their sleek 1.5-litre V8s and had then taken them — in enlarged 2-litre form — to the Tasman Championship, where they had cleaned up. The minimum weight limit for the new formula was 1100 lb whereas in 1965 the 1.5-litre BRMs and Lotuses only had to weigh 1000 lb. 'Add something like 20 lb for the mods to bring the BRM and Climax engines up to 2 litres, just enough to tip the scrutineer's scales, and you've got a machine with 250 horsepower that is more than competitive with most of the new 1300 lb, 300-plus horsepower cars. If someone had tried to build an 1100 lb car with a 300 horsepower engine, they would have been in very good shape — and it would seem that Brabham has tried to do this.'

Bruce could have done exactly what Brabham had done with his engine for a fraction of the anguish and cost involved in trying to make a Grand Prix engine out of the big four-cam Indy Ford engine…

'I'll tell you something — being a Formula 1 constructor isn't easy (not that I'd kidded myself it was going to be). Racing tends to be a *question* of how much engineering you can do on how little money. Now I'd like to add a third rider: and in how little time!

'Not unexpectedly the 2-litre cars were fastest in practice, with the Surtees 3-litre Ferrari getting in amongst them at the last minute. The first few laps of the Thursday practice were in the rain, so no one could tell for a while how the new cars would fare. When the track dried, my car felt pretty much like the Cooper last year, but through the climbing right at

Ste Devote and through the chicane you could feel you had a heavier car. It wasn't so long ago with the smaller cars that you could sort of "straight line" the chicane without much bother, but now with the wider track, longer wheelbase and bigger tyres you had to make two corners of it, first left and then right.'

Bruce had what he described as a failure in the footwear department for the final practice session on Saturday, leaving his racing boots in the hotel room. His Hush Puppies were comfortable touristy sort of shoes but they had not been created with the cramped pedal box of a Formula 1 car in mind. Bruce hacked the toes off. Patty was *not* impressed.

'What a shambles the race was! It looked for a while as though nobody would finish. An oil pipe union came loose up front in my car and squirted half the oil on the road and the other half over me in the cockpit. Oil is uncomfortable on the road, but I can assure you it's even worse in the cockpit — and after it had been through the engine it was a little on the warm side, too!'

Bruce had qualified tenth beside Richie Ginther in the second works Cooper, which had been fitted with a hefty Maserati V12 engine. He was out after 10 laps. That brief debut meant few spectators got a really good look at the livery of the McLaren, which was probably a relief to top motor racing artist Michael Turner. Turner designed the McLaren team badge featuring the kiwi and he also designed the colour scheme for that first McLaren Grand Prix car. He was taken aback at the Monaco race to discover that his carefully styled colours had been abandoned to suit a movie...

'When I designed the bodywork for Bruce's Formula 1 car, anything on the grid which was "British" was painted green, so he asked me to come up with a colour scheme that reflected the New Zealand racing colours — green and silver — and looked different and less boring than the competition of the time. Bruce was obviously able to think of presentation as being important, as well as good engineering.

'The scheme we agreed on had the car with a green top decking and silver lower sides, divided by a horizontal band of warm yellow, which spread out around the hole in the nose. This was evolved over the winter of 1965–66, and when I went to Monaco in May 1966 I was rather looking forward to seeing the new car, resplendent in its new colours. I was really disappointed to find the car painted white with a green stripe down the middle, and asked for an explanation. I think it was Tyler who explained that John Frankenheimer had paid them a lot of money to paint the car this way so that it tied in with the Japanese team in the *Grand Prix* movie. The movie was being shot during the 1966 season using genuine race footage as well as a fleet of Formula Junior cars dressed up to look like Formula 1 cars. Of course I accepted that, to the new team, an injection of cash over-ruled any patriotic or aesthetic principles, but I was a bit disappointed. In any case, the body-styling and front intake had been simplified and with that big Ford engine the car did look a bit of a lump and not as neat as when it had first tested at Zandvoort.

'As a post-script, I had already produced the artwork for the 1966 German Grand Prix poster, well in advance of May and Monaco, and I had indulged my insider knowledge by tucking the new McLaren wearing its new colour scheme, in behind Surtees' Ferrari and alongside Hill's BRM. Unfortunately, as nobody actually saw the car in its intended colours, it caused a bit of a puzzle, as nobody knew what it was. The same artwork was used for the 1967 Nürburgring poster and for several subsequent years, but to my dismay someone whitened out the mystery car...so collectors should note that the 1966 German Grand Prix posters are a bit special!'

Turner wasn't the only person to get a bit of a schock at Monaco. Howden Ganley remembers the 'down day' after their Monaco debut. 'That Monday morning after the Monaco Grand Prix, when it was realised that the Indy engine was, to put it mildly "over-weight and under-powered", we all assembled on the terrace at Bruce's hotel. That would have been Teddy,

Wally, Tyler, Robin, Johnny Muller and me. Bruce asked everybody, one by one, to give their opinion on the best way forward. We were all given our opportunity to speak and each suggestion was given due consideration. Even if one's own ideas were not adopted, you knew that your voice was heard and you were not "just" another employee. As a way of building a team it was superb and a lesson I took on in my own race car business in later years. When you were making anything, if you had an alternative idea, Bruce would always listen, discuss it with you, and then between you a consensus would be reached. I recall that every morning he would come into the workshop, cheery as ever (whereas I was usually a bit grumpy in the morning) and go from person to person, looking at what they were doing, suggesting, encouraging…'

'We knew Formula 1 wasn't going to be a piece of cake, but we didn't expect the cake to be quite as hard as it is,' Bruce wrote. 'We ran into bearing troubles with our Indy Ford engines, and development and testing to try to cope with this has gobbled up time in a ridiculous fashion. The days explode into weeks and suddenly you find the months are flashing by.'

The big Ford needed more development. That bullet had to be bit. An alternative power unit became available when a 3-litre Italian Serenissima V8 was offered for the Belgian Grand Prix at Spa and there was a rush to modify the back end of the Mallite chassis to accept the new motor, which had low exhausts — the Ford V8 had a high exhaust system that cleared the monocoque sides. 'We knew it wasn't going to give us any more power than the Ford, but the plus features were lighter weight and a better power range.'

They jumped from the frying pan into a hot place. Bruce never managed a decent practice lap at Spa before the oil pressure zeroed and the team took the decision to withdraw. It was a good Grand Prix for Bruce to miss, as a deluge on the opening lap caused chaos, cars spinning and crashing all over the back of the track.

'When you're out on the track racing this sort of thing doesn't bother you — usually because you don't know anything about it until the race is over, and you don't have time to worry until then anyway. Sitting at the pits amid all the fingernail-biters was a bit scary, I can tell you. Jimmy's Lotus had expired not far from the start and we consoled each other with the fact that the race we were missing wasn't a very pleasant one anyway…'

Bruce also missed the Belgian and French Grands Prix, but was cheered to a degree by winning the mid-season sports car race at Ste Jovite with the McLaren fitted with a 5.4-litre Chevrolet V8 in place of the gallant Oldsmobile. The Amon/Harre experiment with the plumber's lead had paid off!

'It didn't take us long to get the handling acceptable with the increased weight in the rear and the increase of 100 horsepower over the Oldsmobile certainly made it a very different car on the straight. Of course, the whole question is why didn't we use it before? Well, I guess we were wrong to stick with the Oldsmobile for so long. In the early stages of sports car racing, development of tyres and transmissions wasn't up to the stage where 500 horsepower could be used reliably. Now I think it is.'

Jack Brabham won the 1966 British Grand Prix at Brands Hatch and Denny Hulme was second. Bruce pointed out that Jack's last British Grand Prix win had been in 1960 when Bruce had been fourth, disappointed at his placing then because he had been leading the World Championship points. In 1966 things had changed and Bruce was delighted to finish sixth for just a single title point. The main achievement was to have finished a Grand Prix in a car with his name on the nose. He was running a car designed for 400 horsepower with an engine that delivered only 260. Dark skies hinted at a wet race, so Bruce fitted rain tyres and prayed that the clouds would burst. In fact, it only rained in the opening laps and Bruce had to change his prayer to help the Italian Serenissima V8 keep running to the finish.

The team passed up the Dutch, German and Italian Grands Prix, but came back with the Ford engine re-fitted for the US Grand Prix at Watkins Glen in early October. The engine had new connecting rods and a new crankshaft and there was talk of 321 bhp at 9000 rpm on the Ford dynamometer. The biggest prize money ever offered in Formula 1 saw a total purse over $100,000 and $20,000 for the winner. This was of little interest to the McLaren team and Bruce spent the race chasing Jo Siffert's Cooper-Maserati, eventually finishing fourth, three seconds behind the Swiss. Jim Clark won to give the H16 BRM its first and only Grand Prix victory.

For the last Grand Prix of the season, in Mexico, Bruce started fourteenth and was out after 40 laps, the power from the noisy Ford finally ebbing for the last time and closing a disastrous chapter in the McLaren book. Jack Brabham went on to win the world title in his own car with its Oldsmobile-based Repco V8 engine.

Robin Herd was philosophical about that season and his first Formula 1 design. 'The Mallite car was a fairly sorry tale. A lot of work went into it and there was precious little reward, but I guess we learned a lot in terms of experience. The reaction to that first car was interesting. One would have thought that after a dispiriting year like that everyone would have been depressed and wanting to jack it in, but the result was completely the opposite. Everyone was ten times more determined to do better next year. It's strange that when you are successful it's difficult to be determined, but when you're not successful it's dead easy to be determined...'

Taking a different line
In mid-season 1966 I made the decision to leave the McLaren team and set up my own business and I thought long and hard before I wrote this letter to Bruce:

Dear Bruce

I'm not intending this to be so much a letter as a collection of thoughts on something that I've been giving a considerable amount of thought to. Basically, what it boils down to is that I would like first of all your views on the matter, and, if you agree with me, your permission to leave the company. I would naturally appreciate it if you kept this confidential until we have talked about it.

You are as well aware as I am that the company has mushroomed far beyond even the remotest expectations we may have had back in February 1962, and I'd like to think I've played a small part in getting it along in those four years. However, where my talents as a journalist and a very basic book-keeper were probably useful in the beginning, they are obviously falling behind with the growth of the firm. I've never pretended to know anything about things mechanical, or aspired to any great heights in financial wheeling and dealing. On my own grounds of press and publicity work I like to think I'm reasonably efficient, but it is very obvious that I can't expect the company to keep me on at a wage of £30 a week. It has been made very apparent by Teddy that I don't work hard enough, and that what work I do is usually aimed in the wrong direction.

When you and I worked together, I think we made a fair sort of combination, but things were very small potatoes then as compared with company activities now. Teddy is the right man for the position he is in, and I think you'll agree there, but I'm afraid I just can't continue working under him. In short, I think I'm wasting my time and the company's money being Teddy's office boy, sorting out the loose ends of any problems he doesn't want to handle, and doing his typing for him. Please don't think I'm talking out of turn or being high-handed but I think the company would be better off employing someone with a better knowledge of parts, engineering, or mechanics, and also book-keeping and general office management. Someone like this would come considerably cheaper than £30, and would be better value in the long run.

I've saved up a small amount of capital while I've been with you, and what I'd like to do is invest this in a small consultancy business doing press work and ghost-writing and publicity for drivers. By that, I mean operating as a freelance journalist for my various papers and magazines, and to extend operations to cover ghost-writing and publicity/public relations work for other people on a proper basis.

If you have been agreeing with me on most things up till now in this letter, I would be very grateful if you would allow me to carry on doing your *Autosport* and New Zealand newspaper stuff in addition to general public relations for the company.

Like I said before, I don't want you to take this as an ultimatum and think that I'm stepping out as from the time you read the last line. I'd like to talk with you, and arrange some sensible sort of set-up whereby I could slide out of the company after someone else had taken over the reins in my office. The very last thing I would want is for you to think I was intending to walk out and leave you high and dry.

I'd also like you to know that I don't think I'm running off to make a million pounds on some fly-by-night idea. I've been thinking about it for quite a while, and I feel sure that, while I won't be making as much on my own to begin with as I was working full time for the company, I will have the chance of making a better future for myself if I have a personal ambition to achieve. I think you will know what I'm talking about here as this is what you are doing at the moment. My future (and I'm talking a few years hence) is about as bright under Teddy as yours was with Coopers. You made a break and by working hard to achieve a personal ambition, you are succeeding. I'd like to think that in my field I could do the same thing.

It really is a matter of what you are cut out for, I suppose. I wasn't meant to be a bank clerk in New Zealand any more than I'm supposed to be a sort of company secretary in a company expanding as fast as yours is.

If Teddy had not come into the company we wouldn't be where we are, or are heading at the moment. This I fully appreciate. But I also feel that, personal differences with Teddy aside, the company and I would be better off if I wasn't in it.

Bruce, I do hope you can see what I'm trying to get at. I'm trying to say that the last thing I want to do is to leave your company (as opposed to Company) and I can't thank you enough for the things you've done for me and things we've done together over the past few years. I'm well aware that I wouldn't be here now if it wasn't for you. It probably seems a bit stupid for me to write you all this, but you will, after all, have a couple of clear days to digest it before we all descend upon you in Monaco. I *do* want to set up a small business of my own, and I *would* like your support by letting me do your press and publicity stuff to start me on the road. I just hope you don't think I'm letting you down. I couldn't have begun to explain all this to you in the office, and I wouldn't even have attempted to explain it to Teddy.

Anyway. Please do me a favour and keep this under your hat until we've had a talk about it.

Sincerely

Eoin

17 The CanAm trail 1967

History shows that the CanAm series of sports car races started with six races on its North American circuits in 1966, but for McLaren fans the *winning* story started in 1967.

In 1966 John Surtees emerged as the first CanAm champion, taking three wins in his Lola. Other winners were Dan Gurney (Lola), Mark Donohue (Lola) and Phil Hill (Chaparral). Bruce and Chris made the front row everywhere except Las Vegas, but they could not turn that qualifying pace into race wins. It was a continuation of the team's appalling fortune in that summer of '66 when the Formula 1 programme floundered. The works McLarens scored three second placings and three thirds and Bruce was third overall in the inaugural CanAm championship.

Pete Lyons, son of Ozzie, the celebrated American motor sports photographer of the 1950s, chronicled the CanAm series, as he had done for European Formula 1 for several summers. Pete was one of the ultimate racing wordsmiths.

'They were the fastest, grandest cars in the world,' Pete wrote in *CAN-AM*, his 1995 history of the series. 'That's what everyone remembers about the original, almost limitless CanAm. Critics found things to say against the series itself, but its fans — yes, I was one — loved the cars. It's been a human generation since these wild racers last roared in rage, but you can still interject their wondrous memory into any bench-racing session and watch eyes and mouths open.'

Pete regarded his motor sport as a religion. He didn't just follow it. He lived it. The CanAm series was his world. 'It was an automotive adventure, a noble experiment in virtually unrestricted technology which gave us the most powerful, fastest road course vehicle that had ever been seen. Track for track, year for year, these "Big Bangers", at their best, proved themselves quicker than Formula 1 cars.'

There was no maximum engine size, no minimum weight. There were no limitations on tyre size, structural material of the chassis or restrictions on turbocharger boost pressure.

'Imagination was free to roam in nearly every direction, so the boundaries of performance were being stretched in every dimension, and I had the giddy good fortune to be able to watch. The CanAm gave us the biggest Ferrari V12 ever created and the turbocharged Porsche flat-12, the mightiest power plant road racing had ever seen.

'But always, the very air trembled to the thunder of the *real* CanAm Motor — the big-block American V8. They were so raw! Even at idle, the sound could send shivers from the soles of your shoes all the way up your spine. Sometimes I'd kneel behind a big Chev being warmed up, right in close where the acrid blast from those cannon exhausts could beat on me, my body rocking to the throbbing of each of those mighty pistons, the sharp fumes crinkling my nose and watering my eyes. I could take about ten, maybe twelve seconds of it.

'The CanAm car combined rarefied aerospace with the red-meat muscle of the dragster, the sophisticated European method with gaudy Indy showmanship. It all added up to the greatest auto racing show in the world, or so many of us thought, and for those of us who loved the CanAm in its prime, nothing ever quite filled the void after it was gone.

'Maybe I was a wide-eyed youth, but I used to think that cowering behind a guardrail as a CanAm car slammed by with its dander up was one of life's great experiences. It almost did move the earth…'

Bruce McLaren had found his forte and in 1967 he would demonstrate that he and the team had learned valuable lessons in 1966. 'We had tried hard but we hadn't won a race. It had been a season of "ifs", but "ifs" don't put money in the bank or encourage sponsors, as we rapidly found out. We had learnt quite a lot, particularly about how to make our own Chevrolet engines. It had been a bit like our Formula 1 year — no results worth mentioning, but a lot of lessons learned. No matter who tells you, or where you read it, there is no substitute for going and trying it, seeing it and measuring it for yourself.'

They feared a strong opposition in 1967, encouraged by the $500,000 prize purse offered, but the opposition probably scared themselves away with those same fears. The McLaren team stepped up strongly and simply took over. Goodyear came on board and proved to be an important technical and financial partner to the team in Europe as well as in North America.

The fact that the V12 BRM Formula 1 engine was impossibly late (promised in February, delivered in August) was, ironically, a huge boost to McLaren's CanAm sports car programme.

'For a completely new car, the M6A wasn't really very new. With the exception of the driveshafts everything else was a development of something we had done before. The basic layout of the rear bulkhead was identical to that of the new M5 Formula 1 car. The idea of tying the side-stress boxes into the front engine mounts came from the 2-litre BRM-engined Formula 1 M4A. The front suspension was a mixture of the production sports car and last year's Formula 1. The scheme for the fuel injection came mainly from the Formula 2. By the end of March, Robin Herd had a design together that we were happy with, and a full-scale wooden mock-up to assist with details was made. This was later used as the basis for making the clay body mould. Our design philosophy? Simplicity, light weight, and a rider that I stressed fairly hard — strength.'

They tested the car without the body for a month to get the handling perfected and then worked on the aerodynamics with the body fitted. They played with various wings but finally opted for a fairly conventional duck-tail rear spoiler. Designer Robin Herd had ridden backwards in the passenger's seat to check the measurements of the rear suspension movement and had an interesting perspective on life when Bruce inadvertently spun the car!

Chris Amon had signed to drive for Ferrari in 1967 but Bruce was delighted to have Denny Hulme on board to drive the other M6A. The bright orange hue of this car startled the purists, but team manager Teddy Mayer never worried overly much about what purists thought. He was strictly business and he reasoned that a bright colour would show up better in the mirrors of a driver about to be lapped, than the dull, darker colours they had been using.

It was the start of an exciting era for the McLaren team. Denny would win the World Championship in Formula 1 for Brabham, but he also cemented a successful relationship with his fellow Kiwi that would see him switch to the McLaren Formula 1 team in 1968.

Pete Lyons struck the theme for the McLaren CanAm domination when he wrote 'Denny Hulme drove one of Bruce's cars to victory in the first race of 1967 and that began a domination by the distinctive yellow-orange factory McLarens that lasted right through 1971. Their thirty-seven wins in the forty-three races of those five seasons came to 86 per cent. They had a run of nineteen straight at one point, including all eleven races held in 1969, the CanAm's peak year. During the same period they strung together twenty-four consecutive pole positions. "The Kiwis," McLaren himself and Hulme, alternated the championship for three years. The Bruce and Denny Show, we called it…'

The first CanAm race in 1967 was at Elkhart Lake where records immediately started to topple. Bruce put his car on pole 10 seconds faster than the lap record and a tenth faster than Denny. Gurney's Lola was nearly 2 seconds slower on the second row. Denny won, Bruce having dropped out with an oil leak. Denny set a new lap record and his average speed for the 200-mile race was faster than any previous lap record! He crossed the line 93 seconds ahead of Mark Donohue, the new USRRC Champion, in a Lola. John Surtees, the incumbent CanAm champion, was a distant third, also Lola-mounted.

'You've got to demoralise 'em straight away,' said Denny.

Bruce lasted only three laps at Elkhart Lake. 'I'd lost oil from an oil cooler leak. I didn't know whether to cry, shoot myself, hurl rocks at the Lolas, or what... Eventually I settled for walking back to the pits, sitting there getting more and more nervous, inventing trivial problems that might cost Denny his lead and biting my nails down to the wrist. But this time Lady Luck was with us and I'm pleased to say she has followed us around since. Believe me, she's the best pit popsy a team could have. You still have your problems, but you have them in practice or before the race if she is smiling at you!'

The second round was at Bridgehampton. Denny was quickest in qualifying, 3 seconds faster than Jim Hall's Chaparral had been for pole in 1966. The front row was Hulme-McLaren-Gurney. Bruce had suffered snapped cylinder head studs on the first practice day, which were traced to poor heat treatment, but all was ready for the race.

Denny stormed away into a lead that allowed him the luxury of a mid-race spin without losing first place and he won with ease with Bruce in second place. George Follmer's Lola was a lap down in third place and John Surtees' Lola took fourth. It was the McLaren team's first CanAm one-two. It would certainly not be the last.

Don Grey wrote in *Motoring News*: 'Once again it was a McLaren ball game and no one else was even dressed for the game.'

The Mosport course in Ontario, Canada was an old favourite for Bruce but it was Denny on pole again, his time of 1:20.8 some 2.1 seconds better than Hall's pole with the Chaparral in 1966. The race afforded a direct comparison between the McLaren-Chev CanAm car and a Formula 1

Lotus, as a month earlier Jim Clark had taken pole position in the Canadian Grand Prix with a time of 1:22.4.

Though the figures show that the McLarens were vastly superior, they were still prone to freak problems. 'An hour before the race the mechanics went to lower my car off its jack stands and a leak appeared. The car had been sitting with full tanks since early morning. If we'd found the leak ten minutes earlier it wouldn't have been dramatic — ten minutes later and it would have been, like, forget it…

'Fifty gallons is an awful lot of petrol. Getting it out of the tanks involved filling every vehicle we had around and some we didn't. When we got to the stage where we were pumping it out faster than we could empty the cans into cars and trucks, we simply tipped it over the fence. By the time we had fitted a new rubber fuel bag, filled the tanks and got the engine running, the race had started. Just 40 seconds earlier to be precise! This was just the exact gap that could be made up without going completely crazy. I made it to second place with just ten laps left.'

Denny was well out in front but as it turned out he needed that cushion. He'd had a spin that he hardly noticed, but towards the end of the race his steering rack started to work itself loose and he ploughed off the track, folding the left front corner of the bodywork in on the wheel. He had a lap and a half left — and a punctured front tyre — but he set off with typical determination and drove to the finish and the chequered flag to win with smoke pouring from the jammed front tyre. Bruce was second, and observed that had the race been a lap longer he would have won.

The team had three wins in a row and Denny seemed to have the title wrapped for delivery halfway through the series.

'It doesn't really seem all that hard, either,' Bruce wrote in his *Autosport* column, 'although I did make the mistake of saying that aloud in front of one of the team. "Hard…?" he queried with an incredulous look on his face. "I didn't see you in the garage at four o'clock this morning!"

'Before Bridgehampton the mechanics had three nights in a row to 3 a.m. and then an all-nighter before Mosport. Now it seems just too easy to forget the little meeting we called at the Colnbrook factory in early July. All holidays were cancelled, Saturday was to be a full working day, and 5 p.m. was considered the middle of the afternoon. It speaks volumes for these people who work their way into motor racing that there wasn't a murmur...'

Laguna Seca in California, 100 miles south of San Francisco, is a picturesque but tight circuit for the powerful CanAm cars. 'Denny's luck left him in practice on Friday [13 October] when his fuel injection metering unit failed, then his brake pedal bent, we were having a problem with cracking wheels putting 500-plus horsepower through those big Goodyears and the chassis was starting to split around the engine mounts as a legacy of his late-race shunt in Mosport.'

Bruce, by comparison, was sitting confidently on pole position, half a second faster than Gurney's Lola. Denny was third fastest on the second row with Parnelli Jones' Lola. Race day was so hot and the track so dusty that Bruce knew there would be problems and they arranged for the crew to keep a bucket of water ready in case either driver signalled for a dousing. The two Lolas jumped the two McLarens at the rolling start but after 10 laps Bruce and Denny were running one-two again. By twenty laps into the race Bruce was literally baking in the cockpit. He pulled his face mask down and gulped in air, but it was superheated and simply made him hotter and more uncomfortable. He shut his mouth and breathed through his nose, but that was just as bad.

Bruce signalled to the pit and next time round he startled the spectators by slowing beside the pit wall, where a bucket of water was sluiced over him. He was still leading and was now gloriously refreshed...for about 10 laps and then the cockpit heat came baking in again. Denny had retired with engine failure, leaving Bruce to take his first win of the season. But by the finish, Bruce was finished too. His sunburned lips had blistered and suddenly winning seemed like an extremely painful business.

Denny spent the following weekend in Mexico for the Grand Prix, clinching the World Championship for Brabham. A week after, the Bruce and Denny Show was back on the CanAm trail, this time at Riverside in the outer suburbs of Los Angeles.

Dan Gurney had won at Riverside in every kind of car. It was his local track and he knew every inch of it, which helped him to pole position, the first time that season that something other than a McLaren had been fastest in practice. Bruce was beside him, three-tenths slower, while Denny had been parked up with a gearbox problem. Bruce's Saturday practice session was not without problems either, his motor having to be changed after it had started smoking.

When the race started Gurney stormed into the lead and Parnelli took Denny, as he had the previous weekend, but the Lola clipped a tyre marker into Denny's path and he had to pit for repairs. He stormed back down the pit lane to rejoin the race but was stopped by officials because there was too much bare front wheel. The air was apparently blue as Denny disputed the call. Gurney and Jones were soon out and the race was left to Jim Hall in the high-winged Chaparral and Bruce. Both men enjoyed laps in the lead, but at the finish it was McLaren who won the race and a stash of dollars in prize money. The winning margin was only three seconds… but it was a win nevertheless, and Bruce was leading Denny on title points 30 to 27.

The battle against the tall Texan in the winged Chaparral picked up again in practice for the final race at Las Vegas. The race history shows that Bruce started from pole, his time a slender three-tenths faster than Hall's; Denny was back on the third row beside Peter Revson's Lola. Hulme had been fastest until a broken valve follower sidelined him in the important closing stages.

In fact, this final race was an anti-climax for the previously dominant McLarens, despite flattering performances from both cars during a few laps on the morning of the race.

'What I didn't know was that a grey-brown foam had been exuding from my engine breather, which could only be oil and water mixed. There wasn't time to pull the cylinder heads off and certainly no time to change engines. The only thing we could do was add as much cylinder and gasket sealing goo as was feasible to the water and keep our fingers crossed,' said Bruce.

Parnelli jumped the start in his Lola and led early. Bruce let Denny through to pursue him, but an early race accident had thrown debris on the track and Denny picked up a rear puncture. 'In the final stages of the race Mark Donohue was leading Surtees, both in Lolas, and Mike Spence was third in a McLaren M1B, but for an hour or more, Denny was gathering them in at a second and a half a lap after his early pitstop…until his engine exploded in front of the pits and he joined me as a spectator.' Surtees won in his Lola leaving Bruce to take the championship despite both of his cars being non-finishers.

'It's not the way I would have chosen to win the title, but I can't really complain. In the six CanAm races our team collected six fastest laps, qualified six times on the front row, took five pole positions and won five races.

'Trying to learn how to go motor racing properly over the last couple of years has worn us down nearly to our knees, but the 1967 CanAm series stood us back on our feet again, and now we're going to try even harder to walk tall…'

18 The summer of '67

Bruce was glad to bury the M2 Formula 1 project, along with its complicated Mallite construction and various power-plants. The difficulties of working with sheet Mallite to form a monocoque and the battle to squeeze any sort of usable horsepower from the recalcitrant Ford engine were overwhelming. The team's answer was to switch to Formula 2 and Robin Herd designed a tidy, simple and light bathtub monocoque — the M4A — which could also serve as a Formula 1 car when fitted with a 2.1-litre BRM V8 engine. The wheelbase was stretched three inches to accommodate the bigger engine and side sponsons were added for extra tankage.

'Having similar cars for both Formula 1 and Formula 2 is a good thing in that we are able to apply lessons learned from the Formula 2 car almost directly to the 2.1-litre V8 car and this has cut down our testing requirements considerably. Of course, we don't imagine we're going to stay in the Formula 1 power race with the 2-litre engine and we have been working on a new chassis for the V12 3-litre BRM. Contrary to a lot of the tales I've been hearing, we are not dropping the V12 engine into our Formula 2 chassis. We have nearly finished the first of the new M5 chassis for the V12 and as fuel capacity is a problem we have gone to double curvature on the sides, rather similar to Gurney's Eagle,' noted Bruce.

Chris Amon had signed for Ferrari and led the team into the opening endurance race at Daytona in February. The previous year the Ford team had steamrollered the race, taking the top three spots, but 1967 was dominated by red cars: Ferrari finished one-two-three, with Amon and

Bandini winning in their P4. The Fords were crippled with transmission problems and the 7-litre Mk 2 Bruce shared with Belgian Lucien Bianchi was the best-placed of the blue-oval cars, taking seventh place. Amon scorched Ford management by echoing Ettore Bugatti's views, observing that last year's Ford handled like a truck compared with his Ferrari. (Bugatti had earlier been even more scathing, calling the Bentleys the fastest lorries in Europe.)

Bruce spent a lot of time flying back and forth between the Colnbrook factory and Daytona, where he was testing Fords. 'I've got to the stage where I know Daytona forwards, sideways and backwards — in fact, backwards at 180 mph in one particular incident, which is probably best left undescribed...'

In the Sebring 12-hour race Bruce and Mario Andretti took victory in a new Mk 4 Ford, an updated version of their Le Mans-winning Mk 2, with a better body shape. Ferrari didn't compete, so the Ford victory was not that significant, but it was a win nevertheless, with some good racing against Phil Hill and Mike Spence in the Chaparral in the opening hours.

Driving the works Brabham, Denny Hulme won his first Grand Prix at Monaco in a season that would see him become World Champion. Graham Hill was second in a Lotus-BRM V8, Amon was third for Ferrari and Bruce was fourth with a stop-gap M4B, the V12 engine not being due for delivery until July. The Kiwi dominance did not go unnoticed by Bruce: 'Three or four years ago, Denny had used up all his own money racing a Formula Junior car. He couldn't get anyone to give him a works drive so he stopped racing for a year and worked in Jack Brabham's garage, servicing customer cars. Now he's just won the Monaco Grand Prix. And look at Chris Amon — he had a year when nobody had a car for him to drive and last year we spoilt his Formula 1 season along with our own — he finished third at Monaco in his first works drive for Ferrari.'

A broken shock absorber mounting had cancelled out Bruce's first practice session at Monaco. Nonetheless, he'd qualified on the fifth row, which gave him a grandstand view of the mayhem on the opening lap — Bruce *thought* he drove up the kerb to miss the clogged-up cars on the track. He was definitely hastened on his way as a result of being shunted up the back by Siffert's Cooper-Maserati!

Stewart and Hulme disputed the lead in their BRMs and Brabhams, Bandini and Surtees argued over third place for Ferrari and Honda, and Bruce sat at a strong fifth — if you can call fifth strong. After his season in 1966 it must have felt like *winning*. Bruce moved into fourth place when Surtees' Honda had engine problems. Behind him, Jim Clark pressed on hard in his Lotus until a broken shock absorber ended his race, leaving Bruce in a comfortable fourth spot. Until the BRM V8 started to misfire…

'I couldn't believe it — the first time the engine started missing I hoped I'd imagined it, but the second time was really definite and in a couple of laps it was losing all its power and sounding terrible. The fuel pressure was well down. The pit crew were ready for me because they'd heard it too. I pulled into the pits and said, "It's fuel pressure." We'd been throwing quite a lot of fuel out of the overflow early in the race, so in case we were short of fuel, five gallons went in immediately. In the meantime I was jabbing at the starter button to see if the battery was flat. Jack Brabham had come into our pits shouting, "It's your battery, it's your battery!" Good old Jack. It *was* the battery and we quickly whipped another one in, but we had lost a lap or so. I charged back into the race and had gone about four laps when Bandini crashed the Ferrari at the chicane. I don't know exactly what happened, but it was certainly a bad crash and it looked at first as though there was more than one car involved, but the smoke and flames were all coming from the straw bales and the blazing Ferrari. During my pit stop Graham got by into third place in the Lotus-BRM, then Chris had to change a tyre on the Ferrari, which dropped him from second to third, and I finished fourth. It was so nearly a one-two-three Kiwi benefit at the world's most prestigious Grand Prix, but I guess we can't complain about a one-three-four finish!'

Lorenzo Bandini died of his injuries a few days later.

Bruce raced the M4A in Formula 2 events to keep himself in trim for Formula 1 and for the endurance races with Ford, although he didn't need to be particularly fit at Zandvoort for the Dutch Grand Prix because his race lasted only two laps! The race marked the debut of the Lotus 49 fitted with the new 3-litre DFV V8 Cosworth, sponsored by Ford and exclusive to Team Lotus for the 1967 season. Bruce qualified on the sixth row, Zandvoort favouring the raw power of the big 3-litre cars over the nifty and nimble attributes that best suited Monaco.

'The Dutch Grand Prix for me was a short, hectic race. You see, there was this oil on the road on the second lap that hadn't been there on the first lap, and then I was climbing out of a rather bent racer feeling a real idiot and trying to figure out how I'd managed to get tangled up in the wire fence! I had taken out a long stretch of heavy wire fencing on the inside of the corner, but the monocoque section of the car was completely unharmed. All we had to do was unbolt the damaged suspension parts and bolt another lot on. It turned out that the oil had been an overflow from the catch-tank of Denny's Brabham, who'd been hammering along to make up for the time he'd lost trying to dodge a slow marshal on the grid.'

Jim Clark gave the new Lotus-Ford a win in its debut race. Bruce described the new car as being built right down on weight and right up on power.

For the 1967 Le Mans Bruce shared a new Mk 4 Ford with Mark Donohue, but the car was plagued with cracking windscreen problems, necessitating a huge rescue arrangement on the part of the American screen-makers. A set of replacement screens with softer glass on the outside was constructed, and flown to France by TWA. Before they arrived Bruce managed one clear practice lap with a sheet of Perspex slipped in behind the cracked screen.

It was pitch dark, but he ran at 220 mph down the Mulsanne Straight and turned a 3:24.0 lap to take pole position! The new Ford could out-accelerate, out-brake and out-corner everything, including the Ferraris, and on the straights it was 20 mph faster than anything else.

Eight hours into the race the McLaren/Donohue Ford was running a comfortable second behind the Gurney/Foyt car when Bruce picked up a puncture. He hobbled round to the pits to hand over to Mark, grabbed some sleep and when he took over again in the early hours of Sunday morning they were still second. During this spell a clutch problem brought Bruce back to the pits and while the mechanics worked on the car, the race caution lights came on and news filtered back that three Fords had crashed in the esses. It turned out that Andretti had gone out with new pads and crashed heavily; McCluskey had spun into the bank trying to avoid Andretti's wreckage and Schlesser had crashed his Ford trying to miss the two others.

In a later race, Bruce would be amused to find a note taped to his steering wheel which read NEW PADS MARIO!

When he got back on the track, Bruce's Le Mans mayhem continued, as he first realised the clutch problem had not been cured and then picked up a puncture from the Ford wreckage in the esses. The pit stop to correct these problems took half an hour, so the team decided to lap 10 seconds faster than they had been to catch up their second place behind the leading Ford.

By Sunday morning they'd slotted in to third place. Bruce took over again, confident that the car was running well. Suddenly there was an almighty *BOOM!* 'I pushed the clutch in at once and waited for the tail to go light as the oil hit the tyres. But not too much happened. The car waved round a bit, but the oil pressure seemed normal as the car slowed and there weren't any rude noises from the engine as I blipped the throttle. I waited for the runkadunkadunk-*crunch* of a broken gearbox, but that didn't happen either. Then I looked in the mirror and there was lots more daylight than usual. The whole tail of the car had blown off! I drove back to the pits where everyone shouted at me to go back and bring the tail in so that they could fix it on again. So I drove back out on to the straight again to where a crowd of Frenchmen were shouting "Ici, Ici" and so on, and then in the spirit of the regulations they all stood back and let me put the tail back on, not willing to assist in case I was disqualified.

'It was a bit of a performance, as it's normally a two-man job and I had to stand inside the tail on top of the gearbox, lower it down on its rearward mounts and climb out over the engine to lower what was left of the front down. I lashed it across with elastic cords and drove gingerly back to the pits. After about 45 minutes of doctoring back to racing order, the car looked like a wounded soldier, but instead of bandages it had grey tape. Now I know what GT stands for — Grey Tape!'

When it looked as though nothing else could possibly go wrong, the big Ford engine died out on the back of the circuit and Bruce coasted to a halt. His first problem was that the tools were in the luggage trunk in the tail, which had been taped securely shut. There was an engine access panel in the back of the cockpit and Bruce discovered that the coil mounting bracket had broken, probably when the tail broke loose, the coil had dropped down and the high-tension lead had pulled out.

'I ripped off some of the ever-useful grey tape and bound the coil on to one of the water pipes, pushed the lead back in, pushed the panel back, threw the seats in and fired the engine. You should have heard the French spectators cheer…and I was pretty pleased about the whole thing myself.' Bruce and Mark eventually finished fourth, but the team was happy because Gurney and Foyt had scored a repeat win for Ford.

The elegant little M4B McLaren-BRM V8 Bruce had started the Formula 1 season with had been written off during the Goodyear tests when it was gutted by fire, so Bruce marked time before Dan Gurney was able to loan him one of his Formula 1 Eagles. He missed the Belgian Grand Prix, but was ready for the French Grand Prix, held on the short, 2.75-mile Le Mans circuit.

'I put one of my fibreglass sports car seats in the huge Eagle cockpit that was normally filled by Gurney's 6 foot 2 inch frame, and sort of sat in the middle of it. In the space that was left, you could have held a Grand Prix Drivers' Association meeting!'

On the first day of practice Bruce suffered a broken oil pump that damaged the engine and transmission, but on the second day he got to grips with his borrowed Eagle and qualified on row two alongside Jim Clark in the Lotus-Ford. It was as high as he had been on a Grand Prix grid since he could remember. Dan was on the outside of the front row, Graham Hill was on pole in his Lotus-Ford and Jack was sandwiched in the middle in his Brabham. The race went to the Brabhams, Jack and Denny finishing one-two. Bruce's Eagle ground to a halt with an ignition problem, while Dan retired with a cracked fuel union.

A satisfying second place in a Formula 2 race at Rouen followed, Bruce driving his own M4A McLaren and enjoying the relaxed atmosphere. 'Most of us were staying at the same hotel so that Jimmy Clark, Graham Hill, Jackie Stewart, Denny Hulme, Jochen Rindt, Alan Rees, myself and a few others ate together and swapped jokes together. It was one of those meetings that makes motor racing seem very worthwhile…'

The British Grand Prix was drama piled on drama for the McLaren Eagle. In the final practice session the Weslake V12 engine broke a connecting rod, forcing the mechanics to work through the night to fit a new engine. It sounded a tad noisy when it was fired up on race morning and on the warm-up lap it cut out twice, the fuel pump sucking air through a loose union.

'We fixed that and I did another lap round to the dummy grid, but when I stopped there seemed to be oil coming from everywhere. A marshal demanded that I get the oily thing off his clean track, so I pushed it to one side and slid underneath to find that the oil pressure line had worked itself loose...' Just try to visualise any of today's Grand Prix drivers working under their car while the grid waits for the off!

Bruce eventually started on the third row of the grid, but on the fourth lap the Eagle's clutch started slipping and it wasn't long before he retired in a cloud of smoke. Bruce watched the rest of the race from Becketts Corner, impressed at the battle for the lead. 'Denny Hulme, Jack Brabham and Chris Amon turned on a spectacular show behind the Lotuses, Denny using full-lock slides that had everyone gasping and made me leap back from the wall a couple of times!'

Bruce had missed the German Grand Prix the previous summer but in 1967 he took the Eagle to the Nürburgring. Again the Weslake V12 engine caused problems, refusing to start for the first practice session. They towed the car half a mile down the road outside the circuit before the engine finally fired. From then on, Bruce was in flying form. He equalled Gurney's best lap, but because he set his time later, he had to start from fifth place from the second row of the grid. Where times were tied, the first to set it got the higher grid position. Bruce made an excellent start and went into the first turn on the tail of Clark and Hulme. After half a lap Dan, driving the other Eagle, had closed in on him and Bruce let him through ('You never know — I might want to drive Eagles again some time!'). Brabham caught him too, took a tow in the slipstream, and pulled past at the end of the long straight. Bruce stayed with him and pulled the same move on Jack on the next lap.

'The 'Ring is a great place to race if your car is going well, and this Eagle felt really healthy. At least it did until I was coming up the hill to the banked Karussel corner and something smelt hot. Either the Germans were having a fry-up in the woods or I had a problem. I had a problem!'

Bruce stopped in a cloud of smoke with a major oil leak and hitched a ride back to the pits to tell them the bad news. Meanwhile, Dan was out in front, leading the race in the other Eagle…until *his* engine broke just two laps from the finish. Denny won, Jack was second and Chris was third in the works Ferrari. It was another Antipodean one-two-three.

Back at Colnbrook, the new 3-litre V12 BRM engine had arrived, enabling the M5A to be completed in time for the Canadian Grand Prix in August. The chassis had been sitting empty since April. The usual new-car teething troubles saw BRM take the engine back for final fettling before the M5A (painted red with a silver and green stripe) was loaded on an Air France Boeing on the Wednesday before the race. It was the first Formula 1 race in Canada and the first Canadian Grand Prix to count towards the World Championship.

Qualifying saw Clark and Hill fastest in the Lotus-Fords, with Denny on the outside of the front row. Amon (Ferrari) and Gurney (Eagle) sat on the second row, with Bruce just a tenth slower than the Eagle on row three.

It started to rain as the cars took the grid and several cars spun on the warm-up lap.

'Back on the grid you could see each driver asking the other if they'd noticed how slippery it was, and using lots of highly coloured exclamations to describe conditions.'

The modest power of the V12 (around 360 bhp) was ideal for the conditions and Bruce was soon among the leaders, but the track caught him as well and he spun, losing a lot of ground due to a long wait to get back into the traffic. He made his way up to tail Clark's second-placed Lotus, Jim being unhappy with the all-or-nothing power delivery of the Cosworth in the rain. Bruce got by him, which just left Denny's Brabham in front…and then the rain stopped. As the track dried Jim re-passed Bruce and then the BRM started to misfire and the oil pressure began to plummet as the car went around the corners.

'My only salvation would be if it started to rain again. It's not very often during a race that you want it to rain, but this was one of those rare occasions. It started to rain again, but by now the battery was so flat that the engine would barely run and I began to drop back.'

A pit stop for a battery change dropped him to seventh. Bruce felt that they might have out-smarted themselves by leaving the alternator off to save weight. Another possible reason for the flat battery was that the oil catch tank had been positioned directly over the battery and the blow-by gases from the engine were heating the tank enough to boil the battery dry.

The Italian Grand Prix at Monza followed and after early concerns that the BRM V12 was a little short on horsepower the team had found an extra 19 bhp and Bruce qualified on the outside of the front row beside Clark and Brabham. The Italian organisers had tried to persuade the team to repaint the car green (it was red — the 'Italian' racing colour), but once they saw that the McLaren was the only red car on the front row, the complaints melted away.

The start was a shambles and Gurney came off the second row in the Eagle to lead the first lap, chased by Jack in the Brabham and Bruce. When the race settled down the two Lotuses and two Brabhams were out in front, with a following group of Bruce, Surtees (Honda), Chris (Ferrari) and Jochen Rindt (Cooper-Maserati) slipstreaming each other.

It was a race for the history books. Clark stopped with a puncture and came storming back into the race a lap down. The BRM V12 blew on lap 47 of the 68-lap race and Bruce arrived back at the pits on foot to watch Jim unlap himself, catch up to Brabham and Surtees and take the lead again in an incredible charge. But it all went for nought when a fuel-feed problem slowed him on the last lap, leaving Surtees and Brabham to charge for the lead.

'They went into the last corner of that last lap side by side, both knowing that the inside was oily, but with Surtees getting the jump and

Jack, committed to the slippery area, going sideways. They came out nose to tail, with Jack just inches from the Honda exhausts as they screamed up to the line. He dived out of the Honda slipstream just before the flag, but he was too late; Surtees had won a classic Grand Prix in classic style, first time out in the new car!'

Although Denny Hulme was racing against Bruce in Formula 1, he was part of his team for the CanAm series. He won the first three CanAm races for McLaren while he chased the World Championship into the final races at Watkins Glen and Mexico.

At the Glen, Bruce had engine problems in practice and started down on the fifth row beside — and faster than — Jackie Stewart in the works H16 BRM. The problems continued in the race, Bruce retiring after 16 laps with overheating. Jim Clark went on to win with his left rear wheel at a drunken angle; Hill's Lotus was second and Denny's Brabham third. With one race left the championship was still undecided. It was between Jack and Denny in the Brabhams. If Jack won at Mexico, he would be champion for the second season running — provided Denny didn't finish higher than fourth. It was a tense weekend in the Brabham pit.

In Mexico, Clark and Amon took the front row, with the two Brabham title contenders side by side on the third row. Bruce was a row behind with Surtees and the Honda. Denny had announced that he had worked out his tactics: 'If Jack finishes seventy-ninth, I'll be eightieth...'

He was pretty close. Jim built up a big lead after a tangle with Gurney's Eagle at the start, and won as he pleased. Bruce became embroiled in a hectic struggle with Pedro Rodriguez in the Cooper-Maserati and Mike Spence in the H16 BRM, but the McLaren faded with falling oil pressure.

Jack finished second and Denny third, a result that saw him clinch the world title. Jim Clark invited him inside the huge laurel winner's wreath on the rostrum. Bruce proudly flew back to Las Vegas with his CanAm teammate, the new World Champion.

19 GP champion and Ford engines in 1968

Before the 1968 season started, Bruce discussed his Grand Prix plans with *Autocourse* journalist David Phipps: 'The first thing is obviously the Cosworth engine — *five* Cosworth engines. The next in importance is Denis Hulme, and after that we have to put a chassis between Denis and the engine — that's about third in importance as I rate it at the moment. I think we can knock up a chassis that will work fairly well. It may not be as brilliant as we would like, but we're going for a fairly well-proven type thing — in other words a Brabham approach, which we feel with a Cosworth engine and Denis driving is the most sensible way to go at the moment...'

Bruce said he was looking forward to having the new McLaren-Ford ready for the Spanish Grand Prix in Madrid or perhaps the Race of Champions non-title race at Brands Hatch. 'We were toying with the idea of trying to do South Africa at the beginning of March but the CanAm series taught us that testing and development work and getting ready for the season really helps in the long run.'

Did Bruce think drivers were overpaid? 'No, I don't think so. The drivers are the stars of the sport and they are definitely the people who bring the crowds through the gates. I think perhaps that some of the drivers don't put enough back in terms of what they do from a public relations standpoint, although a lot of them do try. Graham Hill and Jackie Stewart, for instance, both try very hard to give motor racing a good image. But drivers are not highly paid in relation to other professional athletes — particularly baseball players and golfers, people whose names are used worldwide. And quite apart from their publicity value, drivers do take some fairly extreme risks; every time one of the top six or seven drivers makes a fastest lap or does something of that nature he is extending himself pretty much and he is taking a lot of risks.'

Phipps asked Bruce whether he thought motor racing was dangerous; in retrospect his answer was poignant, considering what would happen to Jim Clark within three months…and to himself within two years.

'No, the risks are entirely as great as you make them, but the risks for the top drivers are lessened only by their extreme ability, by their dedication to keeping fit and knowing what they're doing and being right on the ball…'

No mention of the chances of a sheer, fluky accident.

The season had started for Bruce in New Zealand, where he had agreed to race a 2.5-litre version of the V12 BRM in the first half of the Tasman Series, teaming up with works driver Pedro Rodriguez. The water-skiing was more entertaining than the motor racing. The BRM was a dog, plagued with fuel pressure and clutch problems in the Grand Prix at Pukekohe. Bruce started fifth and was out after 15 laps. Pedro managed 30 laps. Chris Amon won in his neat little 2.4-litre Ferrari, Jim Clark having set the pace in practice in his Tasman Lotus. At Levin, Bruce retired after 56 laps with boiling fuel! At Wigram he qualified seventh, despite being plagued with fuel pick-up problems. He eventually managed to finish fifth by using two fuel pumps wired in series instead of parallel, with a third keeping the catch tank full.

The Wigram event changed the face of racing. Jim Clark's Lotus appeared in the bright new colours of Player's Gold Leaf tobacco, instead of its traditional green with a yellow stripe. Commercial sponsorship of motor sport became a reality that weekend.

'The Lotus looks great painted in the red, white and gold colours of the new Player's Gold Leaf-Team Lotus sponsorship. This is what Grand Prix racing is going to look like, and I'm all for it. I can imagine that some of the purists will have a fit when they see it — the Lotus looks like a small Indianapolis car with its stylish paint job and decals — but let's not forget that advertising contracts are going to bring new life to motor racing, along with extra finance, and instead of being on the verge of a slump, I reckon we're just entering an even bigger and brighter boom period for the sport.'

Rather to Bruce's surprise he won the race at Teretonga but not before the sort of dramas that he had almost come to expect. The 10-lap heat was held on a rainy race morning and Bruce was running fourth behind Clark, Amon and Rodriguez with two laps left when he followed Pedro into the hairpin. 'I lifted off the throttle and nothing happened. Or should I say nothing happened for a split second and then everything happened at once! Spray and grit had fouled up the throttle linkage of the BRM and jammed it solid. By the time I'd switched the engine off and had all the wheels locked trying to stop, the track turned left and I was heading straight into one of Teretonga's ditches. I went into it with quite a thud, nearly pulling a front wheel off, destroying the nose and wrecked the radiator.'

The mechanics fitted a new radiator and repaired the nose and the suspension. Bruce made a reasonable start and was running fourth when his luck started to change for the better. Amon's Ferrari and Frank Gardner's Brabham-Alfa took each other off the road, and shortly after Clark's Lotus spun wildly off the circuit — on the straight! Bruce motored on doggedly, took the chequered flag and won his fifth feature race at Teretonga.

The Race of Champions at Brands Hatch in March brought Bruce a win on the debut of his new Cosworth-engined M7A. He had been testing the new Formula 1 car since his return from New Zealand and had become accustomed to the on-off power of the engine, which induced seemingly random wheelspin. 'With just the slightest bit of oil down it was possible with the Ford engine to get wheelspin all round the Brands Hatch circuit. I had been testing our car for a month and I'd got used to this business of feeling that the car might fly off the road when the wheelspin started, and also, when it was bounding up and down on the bumps, having built it I was pretty sure it wasn't going to break.'

On the other hand, Denny Hulme hadn't driven the new McLaren before and he found the power behaviour of the Ford-Cosworth to be on the extreme side, especially following his Tasman Series in a Formula 2 car, and the smooth delivery from the modestly powered Repco engine he'd used the previous summer.

Bruce took victory in the Race of Champions from Rodriguez, his Tasman teammate, in the BRM. Denny was third in the other new McLaren and Chris Amon was fourth in the Ferrari. As usual Bruce was proud to acknowledge the Kiwi one-three-four success.

The next event for Bruce was the BOAC 500 endurance race at Brands Hatch, where he drove the sleek new Ford F3L sports prototype GT, along with Mike Spence. They led the Porsches for 30 laps until the car broke a driveshaft and they were forced to retire. Bruce said his goodbyes to the Alan Mann team and the Ford crew and set off on the drive home. It was on that journey that he heard on the news that Jim Clark had been badly injured in a Formula 2 race at Hockenheim.

'Suddenly my elation from leading the race was gone. When I got home I learned the crash had been fatal. I was stunned. Jimmy ranked with, perhaps even outranked, Nuvolari, Fangio and Moss, and I think we all felt that in a way he was invincible. To be killed in an accident with a Formula 2 car on a straight is almost unacceptable. But tragically it's true.

'Too often in this demanding sport, unique in terms of ability, dedication, concentration and courage, someone pays a penalty for trying to do just that little bit better or go that little bit faster. And too often someone pays a penalty just for being in the wrong place at the wrong time when a situation or a set of circumstances is such that no human being can control them. However, that's the way it is. We accept it, we enjoy what we do, we get a lot of satisfaction out of it, and maybe we prove something, I don't know…

'I'd raced against Jimmy since 1958, when he drove a Lister-Jaguar in the TT that year and, strangely enough, I was driving a Lotus 15 sports car. I'd driven with him, too, at the 'Ring in one of John Ogier's Astons. He hated difficult conditions or dangerous motorcars as much, or perhaps even more, than the rest of us, but he was at his best in the worst conditions. A couple of times at Spa in the rain he made the rest of us look silly. His ability to control a car in the wet was almost supernatural.

'He couldn't swim worth a damn, but he'd put a life-jacket on and go water-skiing — he loved that and on this last Tasman Series we had some fabulous water-skiing sessions. Off the track Jimmy could be a good friend, and we'll all miss that. On the track he was obviously a competitor you would fear more than anyone else. Fear isn't the word I want and "respect" isn't either, but you know what I mean. In the world of motor sport it's not going to be necessary to comment on Jimmy's ability or his courage — he won 25 World Championship Grand Prix and that's description enough.

'When Stirling Moss had his accident, an era ended, and from then on it was Jimmy's lap times you used as a yardstick. The Lotus/Clark combination was fantastic. It was a case of the best driver in the best car, and I think it will be a long time before we see another partnership as powerful as the Colin Chapman/Jimmy Clark duo.

'Why do we do it? Is it still worthwhile? Yes. Of course it is…'

At a time of high emotion like this Bruce had a captivating way of expressing his inner thoughts with a blinding honesty that few journalists would have been able to convey. His thoughts on Jimmy ended with him convincing himself that the return was worth the risk. Clark's would not be the last death Bruce would have to face. A month to the day and Mike Spence, who had shared the Ford with Bruce at Brands Hatch that afternoon, would also be dead, killed while testing a Lotus at Indianapolis.

But racing was his focus and the new Ford-Cosworth engines had at last put the McLarens into a competitive situation in Formula 1. In the International Trophy at Silverstone Denny and Bruce finished first and second, with Chris third in the Ferrari. Unusually, goggles played an important part in this race. Bruce had led away from the start, but Mike Spence, driving a BRM V12, pressed him hard. The first half of the race was a battle. 'It was so hectic that my account of it doesn't seem to coincide with some of the people who were watching. In fact, it was so exciting that not many of them seem to agree either.'

Oil dropped on the track enabled Spence to take the lead, but when it dried, Bruce retook the lead and looked around for his teammate. Denny eventually came through, but his irregular pace worried Bruce. In fact, Denny had collected a stone thrown up by Spence's BRM, which had smashed a lens in his goggles. He had slowed while he was getting used to driving with one eye half-closed! When the BRM expired Bruce came under pressure from Amon's Ferrari, but that faded when the strap on Chris's goggles snapped and he had to struggle to put on his spare pair.

The first Grand Prix for the new McLaren cars was on the Jarama circuit outside Madrid, a track that's much too tight for Formula 1 cars. Bruce said it seemed to be one corner that was a bit too slow for Grand Prix cars followed by another corner that was a bit too slow for Grand Prix cars. 'It was like Monaco without the houses. We had to use low gear twice a lap and transmissions were taking a pounding.'

Bruce plunged into the catch fencing in practice when he struck oil dropped by Jack's Brabham. He recovered to line up on the second row of the grid. His time was equal to that set by Denny — who sat on the outside of the front row — but Bruce had set his time later in the session so sat further down the grid. Chris was on pole in the Ferrari, with Rodriguez second fastest in the BRM V12.

Pedro led the early laps but then put the BRM in the safety fence. Bruce lasted until later in the race and was in fifth place when he saw his own smoke in the mirrors. 'I tried to ignore it but I knew that I would be in trouble before long. By half distance the oil pressure started to fluctuate. A little while later Chris dropped out, as did John with the Honda and I found myself third. With 20 laps to go I thought there was a chance of finishing in the money. I was coasting every time the oil pressure dropped to zero in the corners, but eventually it reached the stage where the gauge registered zero just too often and the engine was starting to feel tight. These engines cost £7500 each, and third prize just didn't measure up to that sort of money so I stopped.'

Graham won the race for Lotus with Denny second, having driven the last ten laps without second gear. It was the team's best Grand Prix finish to date. Better was to come, and sooner than even Bruce had imagined.

Not at Monaco, though. This was a race that Bruce preferred to forget, mainly because after a tangle with Jacky Oliver's Lotus on the first lap his race was over! Graham won his fourth Monaco Grand Prix. Denny was fifth and last. There were 16 starters and only five finishers.

The Belgian Grand Prix at Spa was completely different. Bruce emerged, much to his surprise, with a win! Chris had a wing fitted on his Ferrari — the first time one of these appendages had appeared in a Grand Prix — and had taken pole with a blistering lap of just over 150 mph average. It was instantly assumed that his speed was due to the wing, but he would say later that he had been just as fast without the wing and wished he hadn't used it in the race.

Bruce was never happy at Spa. Something about the 8.76-mile circuit spooked him. 'The very nature of Spa, with its long, fast straight and high-speed curves, with nothing but pine trees for company if you happen to go off the road, is such that it's hard to get excited about racing there. The circuit is certainly a challenge and a fast lap is pretty thrilling, but it's also pretty damn dangerous, particularly with these light 3-litre cars with so much power. In someone else's slipstream down the straight it was possible to touch 200 mph. The straights were very bumpy and the big wheels and tyres we now have just don't stay on the road very well at that sort of speed.'

Chris led until he took a stone through the oil radiator of the Ferrari. Five different drivers led through the race, with Jackie Stewart heading the final lap until his Tyrrell Matra cruelly ran low on fuel on the final lap. Bruce won without realising it!

'I crossed the finishing line, gave a bit of a wave at the chequered flag, braked hard, pulled in behind the pits and tried to drive the car back up to our transporter. Second place wasn't too bad. I'd got boxed in quite badly at the start and had to get through most of the field but, after my previous two Grands Prix, I was feeling really pleased. Our crew seemed pleased too and they had been jumping up and down as I crossed the line. There were so many people milling about at the back of the pits that I had to stop the car and climb out.'

Convinced that he had finished second and happy with that, Bruce couldn't understand what one of the BRM mechanics was telling him. 'Then he shouted, "You've WON! Didn't you know?" I didn't, and it's about the nicest thing I've ever been told.' He had won a World Championship Grand Prix in a car with his own name on the nose, a car built by his own company.

The team's elation was short-lived. Though the first day of practice for the Dutch Grand Prix at Zandvoort flattered the McLarens, with Denny comfortably fastest and Bruce second fastest, equal with Graham Hill's Lotus, it was downhill from there. When the grid formed up on Sunday, Bruce and Denny were side by side back on row three with Ickx's Ferrari. Chris's Ferrari was on pole. And it was raining.

'I arrived at the end of the pit straight after 20 laps, put the brakes on, and the front wheels locked. If the car didn't actually accelerate when that happened, it certainly didn't seem to slow down appreciably! I let the brakes off a couple of times and then squeezed them back on to try and get turned, but there wasn't a chance. All I could do in the brief fraction of a second was pick the softest bit of sand dune and safety fence and aim for them! I ducked well down in the cockpit and waited until everything had stopped flying through the air. It didn't really do much damage to the car, but it put me out of the race and I felt pretty bad about it for a while. It seemed a stupid thing for me to do, but then I started watching the antics of the others. About ten of them either slid straight off, spun or careered virtually sideways into the fence. A couple of them did it more than once, but probably if I'd been able to back out the first time, I would have done it again...'

Denny retired with engine problems on lap 10.

The rain followed them to France for the Grand Prix at Rouen les Essarts. Bruce started off on the third row of the grid, three-tenths slower than Denny on the second row. Both McLarens started on dry tyres and both pitted to change early in the race. Bruce had to stop again because the car was handling oddly and the crew found that one of the fresh tyres had a leaky valve. Meanwhile, Ickx, who had started on rain tyres, confidently motored through nonstop to win his first Grand Prix. Denny finished fifth and Bruce was a distant eighth.

It wasn't raining at Brands Hatch, but there were big black clouds about and after their experience in France, Bruce decided to start on wets. Luck refused to sit on his side. The black clouds came and went a few times during the race but it never rained and, handicapped on the wrong rubber, Bruce came home seventh. Denny finished fourth, a gearbox problem having cost him third place. The race had been held on a Saturday and was followed by a champagne party at Graham Hill's country home. Sunday saw sore heads among the racing fraternity as they gathered for the cricket match between a Grand Prix drivers' team and a local team — which included Prince

Charles! — captained by Lord Brabourne. As World Champion, Denny was captain of the drivers' team.

'Captain Hulme lost the toss and the others went in to bat while we fielded. I'm not sure whether they'll come and close down the factory, take away my passport or just lock me in the Tower…anyway, I caught Prince Charles out. He didn't seem to mind very much, though, and he had batted very well. To be fair, he was one of the best batsmen that day, and during my epic innings (in which I made a stylish duck) he got his own back, by asking if I played much…'

The German Grand Prix was another one for the McLaren men to forget. The weather was the worst they'd seen for thirty years, with heavy rain and thick fog when the race finally started, having been delayed an hour. The McLaren drivers could barely see the starter's flag. Denny was eleventh on row five, Bruce sixteenth on row seven. They finished seventh and thirteenth. Small wonder there was no McLaren column in the magazines the following week.

Motor racing has an ageless record of being fickle. Up one weekend, down the next. The McLaren lads were in the depths in Germany, but within a week they were walking tall, having made a clean sweep of the opening CanAm race at Elkhart Lake and winning the Italian Grand Prix at Monza!

As always the Monza grid was decided in the last ten minutes of final practice after two days of trying to avoid giving anyone else a slipstreaming tow.

'Up until the last ten minutes everyone is rather shy of towing you round. This is understandable. If you tow someone who has a good car, he is going to be faster than you are. With ten minutes to go on Saturday, there's no time to be shy and you're all trying to get a tow off each other. Generally it's just a question of luck at picking just the right moment. On the very last lap I managed to get a good tow from about three people. I passed two cars on the lap and hammered around the corner as fast as I'd gone before, but Pedro managed to get in the way on the entrance to one of the corners and held me up just fractionally. But even so I finished up with second fastest time…which surprised everyone except me.'

Surtees had pole position in his Honda; Chris was on the outside of the front row in the Ferrari and Bruce was sandwiched in between. Denny sat in the middle of row three, half a second slower than Bruce. But it was Bruce who made a perfect start, storming away into the lead from Amon and Surtees. The lead group stayed that way for nine laps until the hydraulic pump operating the Ferrari's wing suddenly sprung a leak, squirting fluid onto the rear tyre and spinning Chris backwards into the barriers. Surtees crashed as he tried to avoid the Ferrari. The high-speed impact launched the Ferrari into the air and it somersaulted through the high branches of the trees in the public car park, before crashing down on its wheels. Chris emerged, shaken but unhurt, to see Surtees peering over the guardrail up at track level!

Up ahead, Bruce looked in his mirrors and saw nothing but a long gap back to Stewart's Matra. On the next lap he backed off for the yellow flags, but Stewart had seen the accident, knew the form and closed on Bruce, cancelling his lead. Denny also caught up to the lead group and he and Bruce tried to slipstream each other away from Stewart and Siffert in the Walker Lotus, but Bruce had a problem:

'My car was snapping into vicious slides for what appeared to be no reason at all. Then I could smell engine smoke and I thought it must have been Stewart or Siffert for sure. It was a couple of laps before it dawned on me that it was *my* engine smoke. When I looked in the mirrors accelerating away from the slow corner I was just billowing oil smoke. Oil must have been spewing out of somewhere every time I braked and it was getting on the left rear tyre so I stopped at the pits, but a quick check didn't show anything obvious so I tried another lap. It was pretty hopeless and I must have been losing oil at a fair old rate, so I retired...

'It was bad enough biting my nails on the pit wall watching Denny do battle with Stewart and Siffert, but when the other two both dropped out, the suspense was even worse as Denny barrelled on through the closing laps, well in the lead.'

Denny's winning average speed was 145.41 mph — faster than Jimmy's lap record in his catch-up race the year before!

The next Grand Prix was at Ste Jovite in Canada, but the team also had CanAm races to prepare for. In the Formula 1 race, Jochen Rindt set the practice pace for Brabham; both McLarens started from row three, a tenth apart, with Surtees' Honda between them. On race day the leaders wilted and the McLarens came storming through to finish first and second, with Denny a lap ahead of Bruce, who in turn was a lap ahead of Rodriguez in the BRM.

At Watkins Glen there were three works McLarens on the grid, with Bruce repaying Dan Gurney's Eagle favours and giving him a drive in the orange M7A. They qualified on row three (Denny), row four (Dan) and row five (Bruce). Mario Andretti had made Formula 1 history by taking pole in his very first Grand Prix in a works Lotus-Ford. Despite the numbers it was an unhappy race for the McLaren men. Bruce never got settled and Denny found himself in the wars.

'Denny ran hard and fast right behind Graham's Lotus during the opening stages until he spun and crushed a brake line on some rough ground in the process, and a repair to this put him well back. Then with just a few laps to go he spun off when an output shaft from the gearbox broke, turning him left when he really wanted to turn right, pretty much writing off his car. I ran out of fuel because a breather had managed to block itself off on the reserve tank and Dan had a puncture in the last couple of laps. It wasn't our weekend.' Dan was fourth and Bruce finished sixth, for a solitary championship point.

Down Mexico way there was still a chance for Denny to defend his world title against Graham's Lotus and Jackie's Matra. Once again the Ford engines suffered from the altitude, but it was a problem for everyone. Siffert and Amon put their cars on the front row, Denny made the second row, Dan the third and Bruce was back on the fifth.

Denny made it to lap 12 before a fiery accident ended his race. Battling through the field behind him, Bruce had a close view of Hulme's crash: 'Denny's race ended with a bang when something broke and he made violent contact with the wall around the big Indy-style turn before the pit straight. When I came past, Denny's car was skating along in front of the pits with the back half of it on fire. I could see Denny was okay, providing he didn't break a leg or something in the rush to abandon ship!'

Bruce survived the mechanical carnage among the front runners in the final laps and he finished second to Graham in the Lotus, who took both the Grand Prix and his second World Championship. 'Graham really deserved to win the championship, and so did Lotus. They have had a hard year and the championship must be slight recompense for their tragic loss.' There was a feeling that Graham had won the title for himself, the team…and for Jimmy.

Graham had scored 48 points, Jackie 36. Denny was third with 33 points, Jacky Ickx fourth on 27 points and Bruce was fifth with 22 points.

20 Grand Prix season 1969–70

The McLaren M7As were fitted with tall, upright-based wings for the first time in the opening Grand Prix of the 1969 season in South Africa. Denny put his car on the outside of the front row, while on the third row, Bruce kept company with Mario Andretti and Graham Hill in their Lotus 49Bs. The race went to Jackie Stewart in a Matra, with Denny third and Bruce fifth. It was Bruce's hundredth Grand Prix and Denny's fiftieth.

The tall wings were the tech talk of that opening round of the championship and Bruce was excited at the challenge: 'Talk about wings! As the cars started to arrive at the circuit for Wednesday's practice at Kyalami in the South African sunshine — Oh, that *wonderful* sunshine — it was very apparent that big wings, the bigger the better, were in vogue. It was also apparent to us that unless a lot of people knew things that we didn't, some wings stood a fair chance of falling off.

'We had done quite a bit of basic research in January and motorists in the Colnbrook and Staines area must have wondered what was going on… In technical terms I guess you'd call it an environmental aerofoil evaluation facility, but we just called it our Minivan with a wing on the back! We took a fairly large wing, mounted it above a Minivan and took a lot of measurements. We also had a day at Goodwood when the snow cleared, running a couple of different wing set-ups on racing cars. It's got to the stage now where you can put a fairly accurate figure on the advantage of the wing. While the actual wing detail and mounting set-up has become fairly standard, the method of operation has certainly shown some variety.

'The design that would get the prize for the most complicated wing in the South African race would certainly go to the one on John Love's Lotus. It was operated pneumatically, with a high-pressure air bottle and four slave cylinders, one on each corner of the front and rear wing. The operation was automatic on selecting fifth gear; there would be a hiss and a puff like the brakes on a heavy lorry and the wings front and rear would suddenly flatten out. Marvellous. I think we'd still get the prize for the simplest set-up, with just a little hand-lever and a couple of other details that I won't go into.

'On the first day's practice, things looked good, Denny being fastest in what was basically last year's car with a big wing and the tyres that had been developed in the test sessions a month earlier. We had also swapped over to sports car hubs and axles. Tyre and wheel sizes are continuing to grow and with the extra loads imposed by the extra grip available from the big wings, we felt it expedient to make this move.'

After the sunshine of South Africa it was back to the rain and fog of England for the Race of Champions at Brands Hatch. Stewart again took victory in the Tyrrell-Matra MS80 and Denny again came third, but Bruce could not repeat his fifth place, being forced to retire with an engine failure.

The Spanish Grand Prix was held on the Montjuich circuit in Barcelona. The 2.3-mile long track was laid out on a hill almost in the middle of the city, incorporating part of a public park, impressive buildings, stone walls and plenty of trees. The circuit wound downhill, featuring hairpins and S-bends much like Monaco, then went back uphill with a couple of long, very fast left-handers.

For this race Lotus made their front and rear wings bigger and bigger and on the grid went faster and faster during practice until Rindt took pole and Graham Hill took third spot with Amon's Ferrari in between them. Bruce had trouble finding his way around what was to him a new circuit, and started well back on the grid.

The start was chaotic and after nine laps Graham crashed heavily. The rear wing of his Lotus had collapsed and he hit the Armco barrier, scattering bits of his car a hundred yards down the track. Fortunately Hill was unhurt. A few laps later his teammate and race-leader Rindt suffered a similar wing failure on the same part of the track.

'His car hit the inside guardrail, a little earlier than Graham's perhaps, and ricocheted across to the double railing on the outside. Behind the railing were trees, lampposts and spectators crammed along the fence only a few feet back, so thank goodness the railing was there. The car, according to witnesses, smote Graham's already wrecked car, rolled over and came to rest as though it had been through a crusher, with Jochen still inside it.' He escaped with a broken nose, a cut face, a spell in hospital and a concern for the construction of his car.

Amon had built up a huge lead in his Ferrari when the engine seized, enabling Bruce to move yet further up the field. 'The handling had gone a bit funny and on a couple of parts of the circuit it felt as though someone was pounding the back of the chassis with a pile-driver. It was almost shaking my teeth loose. I guessed that probably an engine mount had broken (it had) and I should stop and have a look, but with people dropping out all over the place, it seemed worthwhile hanging on. In the event, Jackie scored a convincing win.' Bruce finished two laps down in second place and Denny was fourth after a long pit stop.

Monaco was a race worth forgetting for the McLaren duo. Wings were banned halfway through the weekend and Denny was suffering from a viral illness. Bruce and Denny started on the sixth row of the grid and finished fifth and sixth, a lap apart.

Things improved slightly for the Dutch Grand Prix at Zandvoort where both men started on the third row of the grid and Denny finished fourth. Bruce, however, was sidelined after 24 laps after a bolt in his front suspension broke.

By the French Grand Prix at Clermont Ferrand, Bruce understood how the rest of the field felt about his domination of the CanAm races, since Jackie Stewart had won a string of Grands Prix in Ken Tyrrell's Matra-Ford.

'Running off and winning them all like this is getting a bit tedious. On the other hand, to get serious about it, the whole point of being in a race is to win. The Olympic spirit is great for the also-rans, but the winners invariably went there with the intention of winning all the time, and when they do they should be commended for doing it.'

This time, though, Denny put his McLaren on the front row of the grid alongside Jackie; Bruce sat on row four next to Hill's Lotus. As the race progressed Bruce started to reel in Amon's Ferrari until — of all things — he started to feel carsick!

'I was collecting the odd couple of seconds here and there until about halfway through the race when suddenly the run down the corkscrew hill from the highest point on the circuit to the lowest — the best part of a thousand feet in not much more than a mile with about ten turns in it — started to have some considerable effect on me. First of all my stomach started to hurt and then I started to feel sick and giddy.

'I kept trying to tell myself that this wasn't really happening, but I got to the stage where I just didn't want to go down that hill any more. The rest of the circuit, difficult as it was, was something of a relief compared with the drive down the hill. I didn't know it at the time but Jochen was feeling so bad that he was seeing double and Stewart said after the race that he was glad he hadn't had any lunch! I felt just awful and eased right back towards the finish.

'It took more than that to stop Denny. A bolt sheared off in the front rollbar assembly while he was in second place chasing Stewart and, by the time this had been repaired, he had lost three laps and finished eighth, although he deserved to place higher. I finished fourth.'

On his return to Goodwood, Bruce took the team's four-wheel-drive

Formula 1 car out for its first test drive. In what must have seemed like a good idea at the time, the team had been lured into the complexities of building an all-wheel-drive, as had Cosworth, Lotus and Matra.

'One of the things that will determine the performance of any of the new four-wheel-drive cars will be the ability of the driver to adapt to it. It just doesn't go round corners the same way as the conventional two-wheel-drive cars. An excess of power doesn't make the rear end break away — I don't know whether that's good or bad!

'It rained late in the afternoon: that was an eye-opener. I thought this would be my chance to try to lose control where there was plenty of road, and just see what happened. I went into the corner a little bit slower than usual, leaving myself plenty of room on the outside, locked hard over and floored the throttle at the same time. A manoeuvre like that with the Formula 1 or CanAm sports car would leave you spinning like a top, but all the four-wheel-drive car did was rocket on round the corner. Very disconcerting. In fact, it was almost eerie the way it would go through puddles and over the wet track. I'm not saying that right away it's going to be faster in the rain than the two-wheel-drive car, mainly because so much of a driver's ability to go fast is a combination of experience and confidence. The confidence will be there, but the experience with a four-wheel-drive car just won't. Probably the fastest man to drive a four-wheel-drive car would be someone who had never driven one before in his life — maybe a Mini exponent...'

The four-wheel-drive Formula 1 cars all turned out to be abject failures and embarrassments and were quietly put away in museums.

Bruce had a frantic fortnight between the French and British Grands Prix. 'After the French Grand Prix on the Sunday I got back to England in time to test the four-wheel-drive car on the Monday. On Wednesday while Denny was at Silverstone testing with the Formula 1 car, I was at Watkins Glen, New York, testing the CanAm car. Practice was Thursday, Friday and

Saturday, we cleaned up the race on the Sunday and the following Tuesday we were running the four-wheel-drive car again at Silverstone. As team manager Teddy Mayer said, "This is ridiculous — what happened to last Monday? That was one whole day when we weren't running a car!" '

At Silverstone, Rindt put his Lotus on pole and Stewart put his Matra into the bank, right in front of the pits! Bruce saw the whole thing.

'We'll never know quite how it started because, if something goes wrong with the car, the designers or mechanics will generally deny it. If something goes wrong with the tyres, the rubber company won't even talk to you. And if a bit fell out of the track right in front of the car, the circuit owner will barely accept that there's a track there! Anyway, one of these things happened and sent Jackie into a monumental spin in front of the grandstands. One thing about the big tyres these days, providing you keep the brakes on and you're spinning, you lose speed very quickly. He must have dropped from 160 mph down to about a 20 mph impact with the bank in not much over 100 yards. You couldn't really hear the squealing of the tyres for the squealing of the spectators. The commentator said in all seriousness, as the car plugged itself into the bank, "Oh, well held, Jackie!" Too much...' Or as we would say in today's terms, 'Yeah, right...'

'When I hear something like that I think of one of Reg Parnell's best-ever comments when a driver once tried to suggest that his car had been in a controlled spin. I can't remember which driver it was, but he said he had been steering it backwards in the middle of a spin and Reg replied with a big shake of his finger, "You were steering it bloody nowhere...!" '

Despite his spin Jackie went on to win the Grand Prix in the Matra with Ickx second in the Brabham and Bruce close behind in third place, a result that left him lying second in the World Championship. At the Nürburgring for the German Grand Prix the leaders switched, Ickx winning in the Brabham, Jackie second in the Matra...and Bruce third again in the McLaren.

The Italian Grand Prix at Monza was a slipstreamer that Bruce very much wanted to write about. 'It will certainly go down as one of the greatest motor races of all time. In my book, anyway. We had a 200-mile race and for the best part of 180 miles there were seven cars nose to tail and side by side, swapping positions every lap. Even on the very last lap there were four cars in the dash to the line and out of it came the new World Champion, Jackie Stewart, to take first place by just a hair's breadth from Jochen Rindt's Lotus, Beltoise's Matra and my McLaren.

'The Autodromo at Monza has been the scene of a lot of good races. I gather the last scorcher like this was way back when Ascari, Fangio, Farina et al. were hammering at it, but I'm sure this race must have been even better. Fangio was watching and he would probably agree.

'It *could* have been terribly dangerous, and in fact it took the best part of half the race before I was convinced that there wasn't going to be an almighty shunt. To be quite fair, I don't think there has been an era of racing before when there has been such a group of capable, professional Grand Prix drivers and good, evenly matched Grand Prix cars. We had Stewart, Rindt, Courage, Hill, Siffert, Hulme and Beltoise, each with three years or more of racing every weekend under their belt, and this makes a difference when you're chopping and changing positions going down the straight, gaining maximum advantage from the slipstreaming tow. I did my best to get up among the first three places a couple of times, but I just seemed to run out of revs, so I was sitting back in fourth, fifth or sixth depending on the ever-changing order, and I had a close-up grandstand seat of the action.

'Practice at Monza is always a big out-guessing competition, trying to tag onto another car and borrow a tow down the straight, but you can't spend all your time trying to do this because you've also got to find out just how fast you can run by yourself and arrive at some decision about gear ratios and whether or not you should have wings. It didn't seem as clear cut as last year. Our wing technology has advanced a little since then and for a given amount of down-thrust now we haven't got anything like the drag penalty we had this time last year.

'About half the field decided to run with wings this year. In our case we were losing about 200 rpm down the straight with the wings — the low flap on the tail and the little nose fins — but the advantage we gained on the corners, and consequently on lap times, more than negated the slight disadvantage on top speed. What's more, it pulled our revs back into just the right range, so we decided to run with the wings on. It's easy to be wise after the race, but what we should have done was use the wings with a slightly higher top gear, and in that tremendous slipstream battle we would have been well placed.

'Stewart and Rindt ran their cars bare to give them the best possible top speed on the straight. Stewart had a high ratio in as well, but Rindt had one slightly lower and he was in the same dilemma as we were — just plain running out of revs at the top end when the group of cars started to suck each other along faster than they could have gone individually.

'A couple of times during the race I almost found myself in the role of excited spectator. There I was, at 180 mph on the straight, with four or five cars in front of me all having such an enormous race that it was hard to remember you were supposed to be in it instead of just sitting back and watching...'

Denny had qualified on the front row with Rindt, and Bruce had equalled Piers Courage's time in the Brabham, but Piers had set his time first, so he started alongside Jackie on row two, with Bruce on row three.

'Neither Jochen nor Denny made a very good start, and Stewart had no choice but to shoot between the two of them and I did my best to follow through if there was room. There wasn't a great deal. In Jackie's squeeze through he scraped the Matra rear wheel against Denny's left nose fin and bent it upwards, but it didn't seem to affect the performance of Denny's car much, and within a few laps he was right up with us and led for a while. Unfortunately his brakes started playing up and that's what dropped him back to seventh towards the end of the race.'

Sadly, from there the season went downhill. At Mosport Bruce finished a lonely fifth and at Watkins Glen and Mexico he never even had the chance to be lonely. His engine blew on the warm-up lap at the Glen and in Mexico another engine quit when the fuel pressure disappeared, also on the warm-up lap, meaning he failed to start in either race.

However, Denny gave the team a boost when he won the final race of the Grand Prix season in Mexico. 'I was delighted to see our car working so well, and even more delighted to see Denny driving harder and faster than anyone else. I walked from the hairpin round the track, through the sweeps and esses that lead up into the short straight and the Indy-type curve before the pits. Denny was smoother and using less road than anyone through the esses, and in the big curve he was noticeably quicker, apparently using his Indy experience to advantage on the banking.

'When you are planning ahead for a new season you need a boost for your enthusiasm, and a win in the last race is just the answer.'

Bruce had won the first Grand Prix of the 1960s in Argentina and his McLaren car had won the last Grand Prix of the decade in Mexico.

At the black-tie Dorchester dinner for the British Racing Drivers' Club in December, Bruce shattered the formal atmosphere by going up to collect his BRDC Gold Star wearing a blond wig, aping Jackie Stewart's long hair. He was in good form, telling a joke about Jackie shopping for snow skis in Geneva: 'The man in the shop couldn't understand why Jackie only wanted one ski, but the Scot explained that if he liked skiing he'd come back later and buy the other one!'

Bruce also offered a new song for Dunlop competition boss, Dick Jeffrey, to sing to the Tyrrell team: 'These boots were made for March-ing.' And he commiserated with Graham who was there, large as life in his wheelchair, still recovering from breaking his legs when he was thrown from his Lotus in the US Grand Prix. 'I hope Graham finds time to visit the hospital now and then…'

Over the brief winter the team had built new M14A Formula 1 cars, which were developments of the M7 series, but with inboard rear brakes, slightly revised front suspension and increased fuel capacity.

The new off-the-shelf March cars appeared for the first race of the 1970 season, the South African Grand Prix at Kyalami, with Chris Amon in the works car, determined to prove his point and beat Jackie Stewart in a Tyrrell-March 701. It had always been Chris's contention that he was as fast as Jackie if he could get an equal car. Now he had one and the pair of them set identical fastest time in practice! Jackie started on pole by virtue of having set the time first. Denny was on the third row, with Bruce on the fourth.

'When they dropped the flag the dash down to the first corner was frantic. Exactly what happened down there depends on who you talked to. I did remember seeing quite a bit of the underneath of Jochen Rindt's Lotus at one stage, but until I really thought about it, all that I recall instantly was him spinning off to the left somewhere halfway through the sharp right-hander. In these situations, everything happens so quickly that it's almost impossible to recall accurately, and anyway you're busy enough trying to do two things: (A) you're trying to avoid it, and (B) you're trying to take advantage of it. By the time you've thought "Oops, that's going to hold everyone up" and "If I duck through that gap there…" In fact, you don't have time to think like that, because you've done it already!

'Now if you talk to Brabham he says it was Rindt's fault and if you talk to Rindt he says it was Amon's and if you talk to Amon he says it was Rindt's. We all figured out that it *had* to be Andretti somehow, but he was completely innocent.

'By the time the pack got to the middle of the first corner, Rindt had spun at least twice, Amon had hit him at least twice, Rindt's Lotus had bounced over Brabham's front wheel and a few cars had turned left into the rough to avoid the mêlée. Stewart was ahead of it all, having arrived there first and got clear, and it left a good group of us all together contesting second and third for a while.'

Bruce's engine blew on the thirty-ninth lap, but Denny went on to finish a strong second in the new McLaren behind his old boss, Jack Brabham.

After the crash carnage at the Barcelona Montjuich circuit the previous year, the Spanish Grand Prix returned to Jarama. There was more carnage to come. In those pre-Bernie Ecclestone days the race organisers tended to knit their own regulations over the weekend and there was plenty of drama as the rules for qualifying seemed to change from hour to hour and day to day. At Jarama Denny qualified fastest in the first session on Friday so decided to pass up the second session to concentrate on preparing for the Saturday sessions…only to find that the first Friday session times had been declared unofficial. He was not pleased. There were supposed to be ten guaranteed starters and each team had nominated their top driver, which for McLaren's was Denny. Bruce had to qualify. It was a shambles.

'Never before have there been so many capable constructors, so many capable racing drivers and such a tremendously competitive field of Grand Prix cars. The organisers are now in the position where they have got a real spectacle to put before the motor racing public but they don't seem to be able to cope with it. Shame, shame, shame.

'The administrators of some other major sports must get a big laugh out of the ineptitude with which we allow our sport to be handled. It was perhaps with a slight awareness of this feeling that some efforts were made to get the entire entry of 20 cars into the field, but all this did was create more chaos. Up to five minutes before the start on race day it appeared that the organisers would let all 20 cars run. In fact, the cars had been prepared and were actually on the grid with the drivers strapped in, and then in the most high-handed manner imaginable they were literally dragged off.

'They even attempted to remove Graham Hill, car and all, and he was one of the guaranteed entries! Perhaps realising their mistake there was some story that the six policemen were trying to drag Graham, bodily from his car — still recovering from breaking his legs at Watkins Glen — because he was being rude. Graham probably has an infinite capacity for being rude, but at the time he had a Nomex mask on and a full-face helmet. Unless they could mind-read in English there was no way the police could tell what Graham was saying inside that blue helmet...'

The race was dominated by a ferocious crash that tested the fire-fighters. Bruce had a grandstand view of it: 'I was in midfield and Jackie Oliver was a couple of cars in front of me in the BRM. As we went into one of the hairpins something let go on the BRM and he bounded across the corner, passing a couple of cars in the process, shot back on the track, T-boning Ickx's Ferrari and rammed it against the fence on the outside of the corner. The whole lot blew up in flames.

'I continued the lap fully expecting the whole corner to be blocked next time round. They were spraying everything imaginable in the direction of the fire, but there was still a gap for a car to get through and, like show business, the race had to go on. There was so much foam and water over the track that you almost had to come to a standstill.

'If anyone ever wanted action for a motor racing movie, here it was. Amazingly, both drivers had escaped virtually unscathed. One lap was particularly terrifying. The corner was a banked hairpin with the two cars burning on the outside and just as I arrived the Ferrari, still well aflame, started to slide down towards the apex of the corner. There was only just room to scrape under it and Graham followed me. He described it being like a fire ship in the days of Drake, drifting eerily across the road. Poetic sort of chap, Graham...'

Jackie Stewart won the racing, taking the only victory March would ever achieve. Bruce was second, a lap down and Andretti was third in another March 701.

'Afterwards I got the feeling that I'd been letting the McLaren side down slightly by flogging around Jarama all afternoon and only getting second. At Riverside the same Sunday, John Cannon had won in his Formula A McLaren, Peter Gethin had won at Zandvoort in a Formula 5000 McLaren and Sir Nicky Williamson had won a hill climb in *his* McLaren!'

The Monaco Grand Prix was next on the calendar. Once again the March-Ford 701s of Jackie Stewart and Chris Amon were on the front row of the grid. Denny was on the second row beside Brabham and Bruce was down on row five with Piers Courage in the De Tomaso. Looking back, it is chilling to think that just six weeks later both drivers would be dead…

On lap 19 Bruce smacked the barrier at the chicane, stopped at the pits to check for damage, drove for one more lap and retired. Denny finished fourth. Monaco was the jewel in the crown of Grand Prix racing and both Kiwis had won there, Bruce in 1962 for Cooper and Denny in 1967, the season he won the World Championship for Brabham. It was Bruce's last Grand Prix.

21 The CanAm trail 1968–69

'Motor racing does not lack for stories of periods of domination — Bentleys at Le Mans, Mercedes in pre-war Grands Prix, Alfas in post-war Grands Prix, the Offies at Indianapolis, and so on — some of them perhaps a little embellished in the retelling. One to be added to the repertoire must be the story of the M8 McLarens in the Canadian-American Challenge Trophy Series between 1968 and 1971. This is based on very firm fact: in those four seasons the McLaren team gained 32 victories in 37 CanAm races run.

'This is an outstanding record by any racing standard or precedent. It was achieved by a small company which was also heavily committed to other racing classes, particularly of course to racing a Grand Prix team, which was backed by commercial giants yet had to win prize money in order to make viable its CanAm operation, several thousand miles from its main factory. The results were achieved by a tight-knit little team that was professional to the core, with cars which were in no way extravagant or exotic, but in their heyday were the most powerful road-racing cars ever built.' Thus wrote the English motor racing historian, David Hodges, in the lead-in to his study of the M8 McLaren CanAm cars.

The M8A evolved logically from the M6A, with the broad concept for the car coming from Bruce himself. When Robin Herd left McLaren to join Cosworth — in order to design their ill-fated four-wheel-drive Formula 1 car — Gordon Coppuck took over the McLaren design office, working with Jo Marquart, who had come to McLaren from Lotus. In effect, Coppuck was responsible for the rear of the car, Marquart for the front.

Marquart had an interesting background. He was born in Switzerland and came to the UK to work for the Scottish Omnibus Company in Edinburgh as assistant to the chief engineer. His father was an engineer in the local bus company, so young Josef had an early interest in things mechanical. In his spare time, he helped a friend to build a racing special and soon found that he knew much more about engines than he knew about chassis construction. 'I didn't even know how to fix wheels on to the chassis, or how to make suspension work!' he told me back in 1968. Jo came a long way in a short time. He went to Lotus Developments at the end of the Elan Plus 2 road car project and later moved to Team Lotus to work in the drawing office under Maurice Phillipe. When Herd moved to Cosworth, Jo applied for a position at McLaren and began work on the M8. Bruce told an amusing story about one of the early meetings they had with the designers, engineers and management. They were going into some detail about a new hub and upright when team manager, Teddy Mayer, cut across the conversation to remind everyone that they couldn't race hubs and uprights. Jo had a quick Swiss answer: 'Better we race hubs and uprights than drawings only...' Bruce never told me what Teddy offered by way of reply.

Outwardly sleeker than the M6, the new car differed from it principally in using a light-alloy Chevrolet V8 instead of the iron 1967 unit, and using it as a main stressed member. The monocoque hull was made up of 20 swg sheet aluminium for the inside members and magnesium for the undertray and the outer skins around the 28-gallon side fuel tanks. The sheets were riveted and bonded with a cold-setting epoxy adhesive, which relieved the rivets of some loadings and thus helped to maintain structural rigidity through the stresses and strains of racing life. The bare monocoque weighed only 80 lb — some 30 lb less than the M6 — and had a torsional stiffness in excess of 3000 lb/ft per degree. There were only two fabricated steel bulkheads on the M8, where there had been four on the M6. An M6 was used as a development vehicle, with an M8A rear grafted on to the rear bulkhead.

A 7-litre 620 bhp version of the Chevrolet ZL-1 alloy block V8 was used in 1968. With staggered valve heads introduced for NASCAR racing five years earlier, this was in most respects a conventional pushrod engine. Its weight was almost the same as the iron block V8 used by the team in 1967, but its dry sump made for a useful reduction in overall height. Eight long intake horns straggled above the roll-over bar, their mouths being the highest point of the car.

Engine preparation was carried out by a small group headed by Gary Knutson working in the Bartz engine development shop at Van Nuys, near Los Angeles.

The M8A was a more sophisticated machine than preceding McLarens, closely following Formula 1 practice. 'It was also something of a landmark car in racing history, for it was the first road-racing car to have a power-to-weight ratio of 1000 bhp per ton,' wrote Hodges. 'It is thus interesting to compare it with the legendary Mercedes-Benz W125, often considered a yardstick in terms of sheer power. The W125 weighed 1640 lb and had an engine which at best produced 646 bhp; the M8A weighed in at approximately 1450 lb and by the end of the season was powered by an engine giving 630 bhp. In 1968 the two McLaren M8As started in six races, gaining four wins and three seconds; in 1937 the W125s started in 12 races, won six and took nine second places…'

The opening race of the 1968 season was at Elkhart Lake in September. The team arrived a day early to prepare and the result was another all-orange front row, with Bruce on pole at an average of 110.94 mph and Denny beside him, a tenth slower. But it wasn't as simple as it might have appeared — there had been teething problems with the new cars, as Lyons noted in his *Autosport* report: 'On Bruce's car the last-minute tail-spoiler fouled the latest tyres, the handling seemed wrong, a damper was leaking, a throttle bracket was cracking and then the great aluminium engine began drooling oil from every pore (that night a holed piston was discovered; it was not the first), Hulme's car couldn't even move for hours; first a supplier error prohibited the fitting of the new wheels and then there had to be some work with chisels where the front brake discs were fouling the callipers. Once Denny started lapping, he found the differential wasn't locking properly. All these are fiddling little details common to all new machines; it was unfortunate that they had to be worked out under the public eye.'

The race was run in rain and Denny roared away into a commanding lead, but when the rain eased and the track started to dry, his big Chevy broke a valve rocker and the power-roar changed to a clatter. Nonetheless, Denny pressed on, knowing that he had a lead of almost a minute. His problems got worse when his oil pressure zeroed as he headed out on the last lap, but though he eased back he still took the win, with Bruce second for the team's first one-two of the season.

Bruce was on a high and he swept all the CanAm worries under the carpet in his column, revelling in his pole position and second place at Elkhart Lake and his opening-laps lead: 'Our win at Elkhart Lake did wonders for team morale after months of hard work and preparation for the series. It made the bank manager quite pleased too!'

At Bridgehampton the orange cars were again on the front row, this time with Denny on pole and Bruce muttering that other watches had his car faster, but heck, why argue when they had qualified one-two. But the big engines were still having big problems and the team was trying to stop oil getting into the combustion chambers.

'As an indication of things to come when the track got oily Jim Hall in the Chaparral started running faster than we could and he got into the lead for a few laps until his fuel injection started giving trouble.

'Both Denny and I had run our cars just as hard as they would go staying with Hall, and Denny's engine blew up at about three-quarter distance. With ten laps to go I thought I had it made out in front. But with eight laps to go there was suddenly a lot less power than there had been the lap before, and within a few seconds less power was accompanied by more noise and a lot less oil pressure. I only just made it back to the pits. Another lap and my engine would have had a hole in the side like Denny's!'

The team had started the season with five new engines and suddenly they were running out of horsepower, with the next race just a fortnight away at Edmonton in Canada. It was the first race on this circuit. Sam Posey took a drive out past the track and reported back: 'There's one farm about two miles away but after that the road just ends. It's kinda like the end of the world.' It was also *cold*. Bruce described it as being as far north as Teretonga in New Zealand was south.

At least the engine problem seemed to have been solved, or at least alleviated. 'Chief engine man, Gary Knutson's panic programme over the last couple of weeks had paid off. The engines were running beautifully clean. No smoke and no gasket trouble. We had managed to solve our problem.'

They had also just finished one-two in the Canadian Grand Prix so the team was on a confident high. Denny put his car on pole at 117.47 mph and Bruce was eight-tenths slower. They ran away with the race, Denny out in front and Bruce a strong second, having shaken off Hall's Chaparral. Lyons reported the race: 'Ah, but what of McLaren's engine fears? Around half distance, Hulme's began smoking and he saw his oil pressure flickering. Dumping in his reserve supply brought the pressure back up, but not far from the end the needle dropped again. Just as at Elkhart, he went into nursemaid mode, and again it worked. He took the checker at the end of eighty laps, still ten seconds up on his teammate.'

Nursemaid mode...I *like* it!

It was then off to California for the Laguna Seca race — and yet more engine problems but of different kinds. Bruce was tyre testing ahead of qualifying when he felt his engine tighten. 'It dawned on me that things weren't quite right and a quick glance at the zeroed oil pressure confirmed my seat-of-the-pants feeling and I switched the engine off. A screw holding down a splash panel inside the sump had worked itself loose and found its way into the oil pump, resulting in a severe case of mechanical indigestion.'

By Saturday Bruce was back in action again and he wrested pole position away from Hall in the Chaparral; Denny was third fastest before the oil and water started mixing in his motor. More water caused problems on race day but this time it was rain — the first they'd had in the area for eight months. 'The heat and humidity played havoc with goggles and visors. Denny stopped to change his goggles for a bubble. Donohue stopped a couple of times on the circuit to try and clear his. I tried driving for quite a few laps without goggles and lost a lot of time, so I stopped to change mine. Denny finished second and I was fifth, but it gave him enough points to get him a good jump clear of Donohue, who finished eighth and didn't score.' Hall's Chaparral had backfired and jammed the starter and had to be pushed away from his front row slot. John Cannon won the wet race in an old M1B McLaren. Bruce observed ruefully that McLarens filled the first six placings — but not the right ones!

So, the seemingly invincible orange McLarens led the CanAm championship points standing, but both drivers were well aware that there was more to looking good than just driving. There had been a variety of problems before and during the races, but they were still on top. The race at Riverside was really the first on the series where Bruce felt confident. 'We'd made first and second on the grid again and as the flag fell, I beat Denny to the first corner and decided then to run just as hard as I could. The car felt just great. After about 10 laps I had around 5 seconds on Denny and he was a similar distance ahead of Hall's Chaparral. After 20 laps my lead had opened to 10 seconds.

'The fantastic middle-range power of our 7-litre engines made passing the slower traffic comparatively easy. We now had a performance edge on everyone in the race — even Jim Hall. I enjoyed it. I was surprised when they hung out a signal "30 laps to go". There's nothing like trying hard to make a race go quickly. It was so uneventful it was ridiculous. The only thing that really worried me was whether I would run out of iced tea! We had a quart Thermos flask of tea packed with ice in the cockpit. It was fully set up with a breather system and a pipe taped on to the shoulder strap of my seat harness, so all I needed to do for a refreshing drink was to hook the end of the hose round and suck. Beautiful...'

It wasn't so beautiful for Denny, who spun lapping slower cars, whacked a half-tyre track marker and wiped out the right front corner of the body. This cost him a couple of pit stops to try to repair the damage and he dropped back to fifth at the finish. He had been a comfortable second behind Bruce, which would have clinched the championship, but it didn't work out like that.

'Over the last ten laps I crossed my fingers and eased off,' wrote Bruce. 'All the gauges said everything was OK, but when you are sitting out in front with the chequered flag and $20,000 waiting, you start to hear all sorts of strange noises that could spell trouble. But that big aluminium Chevy thundered on and I won Riverside for the second year running, to be the only two-time winner of the race.'

Riverside was the first CanAm race I had been to and I was slightly staggered by the plain uncompetitiveness of the majority of cars and drivers. I wrote in my *Autocar* column: 'To say that the works McLarens win as they please seemed to be an understatement. They seem to have the race half won from the minute they drive into the paddock. The M8As are sorted-out and ready to run while other people seem to use practice for rebuilding and development work. There are probably only half a dozen competitive car-driver combinations and the rest are painfully sub-standard. It's like making up a Formula 1 Grand Prix grid with Formula Vee drivers and cars just to bolster the field.'

With one race to go, Denny led the CanAm points table on 26 points and Bruce was tied with Mark Donohue on 23 points. At Riverside, Donohue finished 37 seconds behind Bruce in second place, prompting Bruce to note: 'We had proved that when it matters we could run either Denny's car or mine fast enough to win. Roger Penske's crew were under the impression that Mark Donohue could race with me but not with Denny, so I guess we proved a point at Riverside.'

The final race was on a circuit in the desert outside Las Vegas. To get to the pits in the centre of the circuit you had to drive across the track, halfway down the straight, observing the sign that read CAUTION — RACE CARS MAY BE ON THE TRACK.

Chris Amon finally appeared in the factory CanAm Ferrari, delighting Pete Lyons, who at last had something other than American engines to write about. He did the Ferrari justice. 'At last! Chris Amon and the long-rumoured Ferrari Type 612 had come to the CanAm, blood-red and supplying a welcome transfusion of technical interest. Not to mention emotional interest. At a raceway throbbing with big-bore V8s, the Ferrari's sound was soul-satisfying: not particularly loud, nor that eerie liquid scream of the old Testa Rossa engines, but rather a heavy mechanical rasp overlaying a frantic animal moan.'

For the fourth time in the 1968 season, Bruce qualified on pole and Denny sat alongside him on the front row. Lyons noted that the McLaren crew were really prepared for this final race. 'A spare motor hung from a crane ready to drop into either car in any last-minute panic, and a complete new set of body panels stood ready for any possible repetition of Hulme's problem at Riverside. McLaren's car — but not Hulme's — also wore a big mesh bin over its intake stack to filter out stones…the Kiwis seemed positively in touch with the occult…'

Bruce described Lyons' 'mesh bin' as 'a bird cage made from wire mesh that covered the entire induction and throttle system to keep out the Las Vegas stones. The boys had only made one and Denny didn't want it, so we put it on my car. As it turned out, it was probably a good thing.'

The CanAm title for 1968 was won and lost on the Las Vegas pit straight. Mark Donohue's McLaren refused to fire before the pace lap and it was wheeled off from its second-row spot on the grid.

'I can imagine how Roger and Mark must have felt. Someone said there was white smoke coming out of the exhaust pipes as the engine churned over — and someone else said there was also white smoke coming out of Roger's ears!'

It was left to Bruce and Denny to fight out the CanAm title. There was some confusion at the start of the race: Bruce, on pole, brought the field round on the rolling start but the starter held the flag until the last minute and the grid bunched up.

Bruce was in the middle of the mayhem, so let him describe it: 'As we roared into the first right-hander, Denny was on my left and just slightly ahead as we braked for it. I eased back to let him have the corner; then as I followed him through — as I remember it, anyway — Mario Andretti was moving across intending to use the piece of road I had to use. There just wasn't room. He had got a bit of a run as the field bunched just before the start and we made fairly violent contact.

'My car spun like a top, and in the process I visited the desert at least a couple of times. I went off into the dirt and back on to the road and then did it all again, and each time I got back on to the road I was anxious to get back to the desert again because there were a lot of other race cars trying to use my bit of track. There was so much dust that it was impossible to work out what was happening. I gather that at least half the field just drove straight off into the rough!

'I had stalled the engine and before I came to a stop, I snicked the lever back into low gear, let the clutch out and the engine started. That was a surprise. When I drove back on to the track and pointed it at the first corner it went through with no drama and I was even more surprised. The brakes worked and everything felt fine, but it had been a very bumpy ride for a few seconds and I felt sure something had to be bent. I continued round and stopped at the pits, yelling to the boys to have a pull at the wheels, then I charged out again.

'Right away I knew I had made a mistake. As soon as I got up to any sort of speed the nose shell started to lift, so that at the end of that lap I came back into the pits, they lifted the shattered nose shell off, dropped the new one on, tied it tight with tape and rubber cords, and I charged off.'

Bruce pressed on, trying to get into the first six in order to gather enough points to secure second place in the championship. Then he was black-flagged. He imagined it might have been because he had no race number on the nose, but when the car stopped, Tyler was instantly at his side, drilling holes to fit a mirror as demanded by the officials. Tyler was most definitely not amused, but Bruce reckoned he was so far back that the 17 seconds he lost in the world's fastest after-market mirror-fitting wouldn't have made much difference.

'I went out again to make my fourth start…I pulled out just behind Denny and he waved me by. He'd seen what was going on and he was worried that he had caused the first-lap shunt, but he had nothing to do with it. At one stage I got back up to about fourth, but then a brake seal blew out and for the last five laps there were just no brakes at all. It was then that Jim Hall and Lothar Motschenbacher had a very nasty-looking accident. A front upright broke on Lothar's car and it slowed abruptly right in front of Jim, who couldn't avoid it, and the Chaparral was launched into the air. It landed upside down and Jim was lucky to be rescued before the wreck caught fire. Motschenbacher was OK, but Jim had two broken legs, one of them rather bad…'

Chris Amon's Ferrari was one of the two cars taken out of the race in the first-corner chaos, with the V12 inlet choked with dirt. As Lyons noted: 'After missing five CanAms, the ill-fated Ferrari 612 had ventured 6000 miles to contest one turn of one lap.'

Denny won the Las Vegas race comfortably and clinched the CanAm title, while the brakeless Bruce finished sixth. 'As Denny at one end of the pits was already being wreathed and kissed and interviewed, Bruce's boys at the other end had to pile bodily onto his battered car to drag it to a stop,' reported Lyons. Bruce's single point rescued from that final race gave him second place on points so the season's results went as follows: Denny 35, Bruce 24, Mark Donohue 23 and Jim Hall 12.

'Naturally Denny and I and the rest of the team were delighted with the way the series turned out for us. First and second was what we had hoped for, but we weren't really very confident about it. In a way we did a little better than last year. We had pole position at every race this year, and by the end of the series we had completely licked our early engine problems.'

Bruce was delighted to receive the Ferodo Trophy at the end of the season 'for his tenacity of purpose in making and developing cars which have won Formula 1 Grands Prix and Group 7 cars which have dominated the CanAm championship'. In his reply on behalf of the team after receiving the celebrated golden spike from the chairman of Ferodo, Bruce said, 'I would like to think the company couldn't have done the job without me, but I know that I certainly couldn't have done it with them.'

Bruce mentioned that World Champion Graham Hill had once driven a McLaren CanAm car at Riverside — 'And if you ask him, he'll tell you that a wheel came off it. But that's what he says about all his cars these days!' I noted in my column that Colin Chapman was standing just in front of me while the award was being made and I noticed that he didn't exactly double up laughing at McLaren's wisecrack.

Bruce's eloquence as a public speaker came as a surprise to some, but he had been getting plenty of practice as a 'star' in the States and he was certainly a better-known personality there than he was in Europe. Jim Kaser, the man mainly responsible for setting up the CanAm series as Director of Professional Racing for the Sports Car Club of America, gave McLaren the man as much credit for the success of the CanAm series as he gave McLaren the driver and McLaren the car-builder. Bruce worked hard to ensure the success of the CanAm series, but at times he overworked himself and this showed.

'I remember how bloody tired he used to get,' Kaser recalled. 'He would really run himself down with a very ambitious programme and I remember him dragging himself off aeroplanes and getting out to the CanAm race that weekend, trying to grab some sleep, and then on Monday morning he's back on that jet again going back to England. But he was the nicest guy. He could really relax alongside the motel pool to get away from the pressures of the moment. He was a nice guy when he needed to be in front of the television cameras or the press, but he was just the same anywhere else, and that's the sort of thing you remember about an individual — what he was like when he wasn't up front, when he didn't have to turn it on…'

The M8B McLarens for the 1969 CanAm series did not appear to differ greatly from the M8A — apart from the dramatic suspension-mounted rear aerofoil 'wing'. In fact, there were over 80 design changes, covering details ranging from a new magneto drive to larger radiators. The M8Bs were slightly lighter. Larger wheels were standard and the suspension geometry was consequently revised in detail. The fibreglass body was slightly smoother and reinforced with carbon fibre. Gary Knutson had gone back to Chaparral so George Bolthoff had taken charge of the engine preparation. The McLaren ZL-1 Chevrolets were stroked to give a capacity of 7101 cc, developing around 680 bhp at 6800 rpm.

The CanAm series in 1969 was taken pretty much for granted, with

Bruce winning six of the eleven races to Denny's five and Bruce was champion for the second time.

In my *Autocar* column in April 1969 I wrote: 'Bruce McLaren must have surprised even himself after tests at Goodwood with their 1968 CanAm 7-litre McLaren-Chevy, now fitted with a broad wing mounted to the rear uprights. Last year during tests (without a wing) their best laps around the Sussex circuit were around 1:12.7. Last week McLaren turned in a couple of laps at 1:09.3! I don't think Brucie was particularly anxious for his opposition to learn about the startling drop in lap times and he fobbed it off by saying that the improvement was mainly due to continued refinements during their development programme. "Now it's going about as fast as a 620 bhp car ought to!" As a comparison in lap times, Denny Hulme has been round Goodwood in the Formula 1 McLaren-Ford in 1:12, Bruce has done 1:14 in the Formula A/5000 McLaren-Chevy and Peter Gethin has done 1:15 in the same car.'

I had forgotten that in those days all the team had diminutive nicknames, thus Bruce was 'Brucie', Denny was 'The Bear', Chris Amon was 'Chrissey', Robin Herd was 'Herdy' and I was 'Eoiny'. Bruce Harre was improbably known as 'Little Bruce', despite the fact that he was a good deal larger than the boss, to avoid mix-ups in names with 'Big Bruce'. It seems a trifle infantile looking back, but then it was a mark of being involved, of being part of the team.

The first race of the new season was at Mosport on 1 June 1969. Denny had raced in the Indianapolis 500 on the Friday, where he'd dropped out of second place in a Gurney Eagle, while Bruce had tyre tested on the bumpy circuit. The testing paid dividends in the form of pole on Saturday, set at 113.2 mph; Denny was six-tenths slower. The orange cars filled the front row yet again. During the race, Gurney, in the modified McLaren they had christened a 'McLeagle', and Surtees, in Hall's McLaren, both offered opposition but they wilted and the true McLaren men crossed the line one-two, with Bruce ahead and collecting 20 title points in the J-Wax series.

At Ste Jovite, McLaren M12 customer Lothar Motschenbacher was third fastest in qualifying, which put him on the second row beside John Surtees in the 'Chaparral' McLaren M12. Bruce took pole again at 104.035 mph, with Denny second, half a second slower...but 2.4 seconds faster than Motschenbacher and three seconds faster than Surtees.

In the race the McLaren duo felt confident enough to play with the opposition, dropping back, catching up, making a joust for the lead...until a car crashed and yellow flags came out. Surtees saw the flags and slowed, but Bruce came literally slicing through unsighted in a passing move, hitting John just ahead of his rear wheel. Both cars pitted for repairs and Bruce got back up to second place behind Denny by the chequer, but the Surtees McLaren later lost its right rear bodywork and was black-flagged into retirement. After the race, Bruce apologised profusely to John, saying he hadn't seen the yellows.

Nobody could know that Bruce had just a year of life left.

A month later the circus appeared at Watkins Glen as part of a double-header weekend that also featured the World Championship six-hour endurance race. Several of the cars took part in both races. Chris Amon had returned to the CanAm scene in the big 6.2-litre Ferrari, claiming more power and less weight than at his one-turn appearance at Las Vegas the previous season. Bruce took pole, Denny was beside him and Amon was on the second row. The Kiwi one-two-three line-up pleased Bruce, but he was even more pleased by the fact that his pole time was one-and-a-half seconds faster than the Ferrari. Surtees's McLaren sported a high fixed-angle wing, mimicking the Chaparral and the works McLarens...which had also copied the Chaparral...

At the end of the 200-mile race Bruce and Denny crossed the line less than a second apart averaging 125.99 mph. It was the fastest CanAm race in the series' history, and proof that this time they had not been playing with the field. Amon's Ferrari was third.

Bruce wrote: 'The CanAm race at the Glen was pretty much routine. One day someone is going to upset that routine and we'll wonder what's struck us. I'm still surprised at how few people make an effort in CanAm. It's not all that difficult. Like anything else, it takes time and work, but there's no super-technology involved. The Chevy engines are available over the counter. You'd think that if the Americans can put a man on the moon they could knock spots off us in motor racing. On the other hand, of course, we do use American engines, joints, hoses, aluminium, tyres and money, so maybe I'd better stop knocking…'

The troupe moved to Edmonton and for the second year running the two McLarens tied for fastest time, but Denny took pole by virtue of having set the time first. Amon was third fastest in the Ferrari, but 2 seconds slower. The new Chaparral had at last arrived, but it needed more time for development than the series allowed and an unhappy Surtees was back in fifth place on the grid.

The three Kiwis toyed with the lead until Bruce's car swallowed a piston and retired in a cloud of smoke. Denny got serious, stormed out into the lead over Chris and then settled back to win by five seconds from the Ferrari.

For the race at Mid-Ohio, Denny took pole position while Bruce sorted out new Formula 1-style front suspension on his car, qualifying beside Denny but three-tenths slower. The orange marauders stormed away with the race, with Denny leading and eventually lapping the Ferrari and letting Bruce go into the lead with eight laps left. But the action began as the race neared its end.

'The orange lights had started flashing. We've got these big orange warning lights on the dash because it's a bit expensive when we ruin an engine. The idea is that you stop right away, pull over to the side of the track and don't turn the engine another rev to minimise the internal damage. My mind went blank when the lights came on. First of all I thought it was just the light playing up because we'd had trouble with them before, but then I glanced across at the oil pressure gauge and it said zero.

'I slowed, waved Denny by and headed for the pits. I stopped more to share the news than anything else. If the engine did keep going and I'd said afterwards that it didn't have any oil pressure, they probably wouldn't have believed me! I barely came to a halt, pointed at the orange light and the oil pressure gauge and roared out again. Well, I say "roared" — I took it to about five thousand where it got smooth and used about quarter throttle, but I was turning fairly reasonable lap times. I even passed a couple of people.

'There were six laps to go, then five, then four. I thought this was ridiculous. It felt OK. A couple of times I was tempted to say "To hell with it. There's nothing wrong. It's a mistake," but then I thought that was a stupid way of looking at it and I'd better be careful. So I ran right to the end of the race in second place, with Chris Amon picking up a few seconds in the Ferrari, but I had plenty in hand. In the meantime Denny had lapped Chris, so he had to finish a lap early anyway. I stopped immediately when I'd taken the flag in second place. I thought it was a bit melodramatic because obviously the thing still had oil pressure if it was running.

'When we brought it back to the pits we started looking round it, thinking there was a blockage or something comical that had affected the gauge and the lights, like a wire shorted out across the lights and something putting the gauge on the blink as well. We couldn't imagine that it would run seven laps without any oil pressure at all. The experts in the pits were reckoning aloud that the engine was well and truly "ruint".

'Finally, when we couldn't track down anything small, we had a look at where the oil pump runs and found that the main pump belt was off and the pump itself was seized solid, so obviously it hadn't just happened then. It had happened seven laps before!

'I can just imagine trying to drive 15 miles in to London from my home with zero oil pressure at 30 mph with a normal engine. And I had been running at 130 mph! The whole thing was just unbelievable. It certainly says something for the little bit of Gulf oil that was left in the crankcase…'

The race at Elkhart Lake marked the halfway point in the series and qualifying was held on Bruce's 32nd birthday, but Denny wasn't about to give him pole as a present. He saved that for the race, giving Bruce the win.

Lyons wrote: 'After four laps of leading, Hulme dropped back into third (behind Amon's Ferrari). Lazily, it seemed Denny sat watching the Ferrari ahead for ten laps. Then, on lap 20, still with 30 to go, perhaps more to keep himself awake than anything, the Bear stretched and went Zoom! In two laps he was back on Bruce's tail, and, as if to say, "Come on, let's go, I'm bored," he passed back into the lead. McLaren took the hint and with obvious ease the pair forged away by themselves.'

Bruce might have been talking about the total Ferrari domination of Formula 1 in 2004, when he wrote after his win at Elkhart Lake: 'It seems to be reaching the Moss/Clark stage, where we are getting so much publicity that people are coming along just to see us win. It's like elephants at a circus — there might only be one or two there, but you don't feel like going home without seeing the elephants, no matter how many monkeys there might happen to be…' For the rest of their CanAm involvement the McLarens were known as the Orange Elephants.

At Bridgehampton the Bruce and Denny show played a trump card that was remembered for the rest of the series. They ran the Saturday morning first official qualifying session, set the front row times with Bruce on pole and Denny beside him…and then went water-skiing in the afternoon. It could have been regarded as the McLaren team giving two fingers to the CanAm series, but there was nothing further to be gained by staying around for the afternoon. They were saving the cars for the race, they said. Denny crossed the line a few inches ahead of Bruce and they walked away with more of the J-Wax title prize money.

The next round was a one-off CanAm race on the Michigan International Speedway west of Detroit, a track that combined bankings and infield roads to make a 3-mile course. This race was different in that Jack Brabham drove the spare works McLaren in practice and Dan Gurney drove it in the race, starting from the back as he had not practised in the car. Bruce and Denny were way out in front as Dan scythed his way through the field and then the three of them ran line astern. Lyons wrote: 'There it was: three mighty McLaren M8s running one-two-three like the parading pachyderms Bruce had written of in his column. Take that, world.' Bruce took the win.

Laguna Seca — Bruce started from pole and won; Denny started second and was second. That about summed up the weekend. It was the team's ninth win of the CanAm season and its eighth with a one-two finish. In fact, the 'spare car' had raced again that weekend. Amon had blown the final Ferrari engine so Bruce loaned him the third elephant and he, too, started from the back of the grid and came fighting up through the field until he reached Jo Siffert's Porsche 908. They both wanted the same piece of road and Chris was forced into the tyre-markers, smashing in the left front of the nose. He lost a lap and though he made up some of the time, he hadn't quite reached his Swiss aggressor when the McLaren's differential broke.

CanAm descended on Riverside. Denny had won the Mexican Grand Prix the previous weekend so he was in a good frame of mind and it had generally been agreed that, as he had never won at Riverside, he would be allowed this race. The team was *that* dominant. On paper. In fact, Bruce had a couple of engine failures in practice but the elephants still filled the front row, with Denny on pole at 126.342 mph. The big aluminium Chevy had been so reliable that Bruce started the race mindful that there could be trouble in store and he kept an eye on the gauges and conserved his revs.

'It happened with a quarter of the race left on a flat-out left-hander just after the pits, that we take at about 140 mph. I heard a loud bang. The car almost leapt round backwards and I sensed it was charging up the hill towards the safety wall. It hit the wall tail first — I think — and then scraped along it crashing and banging, and I had time to wonder whether the next bit was going to hurt. It was a funny sensation, not fright, just a kind of wondering. Then it went round again a couple of times and the noise stopped. I realised immediately that I'd been way up the earth bank, along the wall, and back down on to the track again. If it hadn't been for the dust I could have seen it all happening. The accident started coming out of Turn 1 and the car had finished up with all four corners smashed in, immobile across the middle of the road at Turn 2!

'I flicked the seat harness undone and stood poised to jump out, but having got that far unhurt, I waited for the dust to settle before abandoning ship. I had no intention of leaping in front of another car! There was one nasty moment when I could see Gurney's blue McLaren coming straight for me, but he managed to stop and dodge around me. I baled out of the cockpit and ran. The whole accident had probably taken about four seconds.

'The combination of the aluminium monocoque and the seat belts saved me from any ill effects of the shunt — I wasn't even stiff the next day. But when I glanced along the path that the car had taken up the hill, I saw immediately that someone had been hurt. A corner worker had sustained some fairly serious injuries. A racing driver knows the risks he is taking and does his best to minimise them, but the risks that corner workers and photographers expose themselves to always appalls me, and I hate to see accidents happen like this.'

The lower left wishbone had broken, triggering the accident. The corner worker suffered broken legs.

The final race in the 1969 CanAm series was at Texas International Speedway, a tri-oval with internal roads making a combined circuit of 3 miles. Bruce used what had been the spare car after wrecking his racer at Riverside and while it was generally assumed that he would win the race and Denny would finish second, which would give him enough points to take the title, it wasn't quite that settled within the team.

'Nobody was really sure whether Denny or I would win the title, and we weren't very sure either, although we had sat down and looked at each other once or twice... Denny had been gradually getting faster in the CanAm car all year, but whereas last year I think I might have been able to beat him in a knock-down-drag-out fight in a CanAm car, I don't think I could now. So if Denny had wanted to, he could have won the Texas race and the championship. There are two ways of looking at this. You might say, well he drives for the team so he should drive to team orders, but in fact our team has never been that way. We've always endeavoured to find individuals in every area who would do the best possible job with no limitations, and if you set that sort of policy you don't map out a battle plan for them, you map it out *with* them.

'I won the CanAm series in 1967 and Denny won in it 1968 and for 1969 we had tacitly agreed to take turns while things were fairly easy for the sake of a happy team. As it turned out nobody had to make the final decision because Denny's engine didn't run the distance.'

Bruce won the 1969 CanAm championship J-Wax trophy with 165 points from Denny on 160. Chuck Parsons was a distant third with 81. It illustrated the total dominance of the McLaren team in CanAm racing in what was Bruce's last season.

22 CanAm co-drivers

The two-seat CanAm sports car provided a unique opportunity for mere scribes to find out exactly what it was like to power along at racing speeds, sitting alongside a driver in a car that was capable of going faster than a Grand Prix car. Denis Jenkinson had ridden with Stirling Moss in the works Mercedes 300SLR when they won the Mille Miglia in 1955, so he was not a man easily impressed. Like me, he was treated to a ride with Bruce McLaren. American writer Pete Lyons had covered the European Formula 1 season for *Autosport* in the late 1960s and later went home to cover the CanAm series with his magic prose. Peter Revson took him scorching around Riverside. Reading of the men who designed and fabricated these cars and the drivers who performed in them as the team grew in strength and success is a trifle remote from reality, but to be able to sample the speed as described by a mortal as opposed to a race hero, is a fascinating experience. Not better than being there, but certainly safer…

Denis Jenkinson, passenger
Jenks was sceptical about the big-banger CanAm sports cars. He wrote in *Motor Sport* in October 1964, that the makers should be spending all that effort and using the V8 American horsepower on pure single-seaters for Formula Libre events.

'My contention is that if they are going to race sports cars, then at least they should be able to carry two people at racing speeds, and in this way I persuade them to take me for rides! I would like to take this two-seater question further and suggest that riding mechanics should be carried in these sports cars when they are racing, and I can just see the RAC allowing that, which is a pity for I am all set for a dice, and I know lots of other people who would join me as racing passengers. The first McLaren, as it is called, was surprisingly comfortable, the level ride being outstanding and the suspension so soft and controlled that sitting on a fibreglass seat was no bother at all. Cockpit room was pretty cramped, and through St Mary's and the chicane I had the greatest difficulty in avoiding leaning on McLaren's left arm, which supports my contention that racing with passengers would develop much more civilised "sports cars". The Oldsmobile engine, running at 7000 rpm, was remarkably smooth, but gave a good punch in the back on acceleration, compared with the smooth torque of the V12 Ferrari in the 330P and the handling of the McLaren was remarkable for its smoothness and balance, there being very little wheel-twiddling or full-lock slides, the car being held on a very steady course, especially through the fast corners. Being a "sports car" as distinct from a prototype GT car, the windscreen was minimal and tailored for the driver, so that wind pressure at 130–160 mph was terrific and a lot of laps would have given me a pain in the neck. The chassis and suspension on this car are virtually to modern Grand Prix car specification, and its smooth ride was a most outstanding impression, which explains why Grand Prix drivers can sit in an unpadded cockpit on a sheet of aluminium or fibreglass.'

Eoin Young, passenger
In 1967 Bruce took me round Goodwood in the M6. My account follows:

'I'm rather short in the wheelbase and wide in the rear track, if you know what I mean, and the FIA hadn't taken into account that chubby chaps like me would be squirming down into the token passenger seat of things like Group 7 McLaren sports/racers when people like B. McLaren are testing...

'The mechanics had thoughtfully removed the fire extinguisher from its mounts where my bottom was about to be, and it had been rehoused with sticky tape on top of the side tank by my left shoulder. There were a couple of big bore water pipes alongside my left hip, going back and forth to the radiator. Under my left knee the arm of a front wishbone poked through the monocoque to a mounting point rather hazardously situated from my point of view.

'The green screen was sloped so gently it wasn't hard to see over it. McLaren hopped over the side screen and slid straight down behind the wheel, while I was trying to figure out which cheek I would roast on the water pipes. He flicked his safety straps over his shoulders and thoughtfully asked if the fact that he was securely strapping himself in made me nervous. I forced a confident if rather weak laugh.

'He switched on, pressed the button and the big 5.8-litre 500-horse Chevy V8 thundered into life behind our heads. He graunched the stumpy gearlever up on the right into first and I sat smugly glad that I hadn't made such a racket on Mr Hewland's gearbox. Then we were off with a rumble and a rush and Madgwick loomed as a neverending right-hander. He was peering at his wrist watch and I'm thinking, "For God's sake watch the road, man…"

'Those giant front wings in bright orange fibreglass makes it seem like peering down the cleavage of some sort of automotive pin-up girl. The road starts rushing by and we're on top of St Marys. Then it drops away to the left and I hope that he's better on left-handers than I am.

'The engine waffles away behind our heads. There's a little window in the front guard and I can see the fat, flat Goodyear riding up and down but then my mind is jarred back to the job in hand as I realise we're never going to make Woodcote at the end of the straight at this speed. We do. CHRIST! Someone's built a wall across the road. Take your partners for a fatal road accident. But it's just the chicane and a broad arrow on the wall points to the right where there seems to be no visible means of exit. But there is.

'As we thunder straight at the uncompromising wall some earnest lamp-rubbing on my part works the genie trick and a narrow gap opens at the end of the wall. We snick through and we're accelerating past the pits with such a burst that my borrowed helmet slams back against the chromed roll-over bar, completely destroying the composed "I do this every day" picture I was endeavouring to convey to the pit watchers. But the lap wasn't so bad. I think that big-banger racing can't be so hectic after all. I haven't seen him do anything yet that I couldn't do. Perhaps these fellers *do* get paid too much…

'I'm a bit uncomfortable sitting sideways and those two big central-heating pipes don't make things any better. My thigh feels as though it's alight. The water temperature gauge says 70 but it's obviously wrong. The bit going past my leg is easily 100. A couple more laps and I'm thinking of tapping the shoulder of the masked racer on my right and asking if I can have a go…

'Then he down-changes going into Madgwick and I think "Funny, he hasn't done that before…" Then it all starts happening and the scenery is blurring. I think his brain has snapped…perhaps the throttle has jammed… but he looks pretty composed about the whole thing. It's really a bit hard to work out what's happening in the McLaren mind even if he is just a crammed shoulder's width away. He might be chuckling hysterically to himself behind that Protex mask and taking a bead on the bank that nearly killed Stirling Moss at St Mary's…but we thunder at the right-hand sweep into St Mary's, down a gear, and defying all the laws of gravity and road-holding, we're skating down through the left-hander.

'There's starting to be a hot smell now — a sort of mixture of hot engine, brakes, rubber and just *SPEED*. Then the sharp right at Lavant looms like the end of the road and from what feels like 200 mph we're braking ridiculously hard and my knee feels as though it's slicing into the riveted dash panel.

'My crash helmet slams the roll-over bar again and we're charging away from Lavant, scrubbing through the funny kink after it and blasting out on to the straight as though we're on a drag strip. The road is flashing past underneath us like one of those drummed-up sequences in Cinerama, only this is real and I'm in it...I've become acutely aware that someone has loaded Woodcote into a cannon and fired it at us head-on...I'm watching the rev needle climbing absurdly steady to 5700...I convert that quickly into some impossible speed and then transfer my thoughts instantly back to personal self-preservation and Woodcote, which suddenly looks like a cul-de-sac. These are new brake pads he's trying out. What happens if he dives in deep and they don't work? I scan the bank for a soft spot and try to imagine what Masten Gregory would have done in my fraught situation (Masten was famous for jumping out of sports cars before they crashed)... I'm Graham Hill at the Nürburgring in practice for the German Grand Prix and the Lotus isn't going to slow enough for the corner and Colin Chapman's going to be *really* annoyed...then I'm back to me again and after forever McLaren is on the brakes and the car is arrested in flight, Woodcote is lined up and he's booting it through and out the other side.

'But he's easing off now and for the first time I realise that I'm suffering. My thigh is on fire from those damn water pipes and the left-hander in St Mary's is suddenly the best corner on the track as it eases me off those twin branding irons. I want McLaren to do another quick one, but then I weigh my enthusiasm against my burning leg and tap him on the shoulder, pointing to the pits. He eases back and pulls in and I'm trying to slide out of the cramped seat as professionally as McLaren slid into his, but I make a complete hash of it and collapse back into the narrow seat and the hot pipes...I clamber back to my feet and perform an impossibly agile leap over the curved-in Perspex screen.

'I check some of my pent-up queries with the still-masked McLaren. How fast on the straight? "160 mph." Hmmm. How fast through St Mary's? "Umm…about 110 mph." Ulp… I remember the Guild of Motoring Writers motor show test days at Goodwood when there were five or six more corners than there were today…damn tricky ones too…I wonder what happened to them? What was our lap time on the horrendous quick one? Team manager Teddy Mayer says 1:22. That's an average of 105.37 mph. That was the lap record that Stirling was chasing the day he parked his racer in the bank at St Mary's. The BARC used to award the Goodwood Ton trophy to everyone who could lap the circuit at over 100 mph. I wonder if they'd give me one as a sort of associate member?'

A year later Bruce invited me for a ride in the first M8A, but it was raining and I begged off. I was glad that I did. Bruce was tooling around Goodwood on dry tyres when he hit a puddle and lost it on the straight. I quoted Tyler's description in my *Autocar* column the following week: 'I was standing at the chicane and I could hear him coming out on to the straight. He changed to third, to fourth and then to fifth and then you could just hear this funny swoosh…swoosh…swoosh. I couldn't see him for the long grass, but I knew he'd spun it!'

Bruce had spun for some distance down the track and then cut a broad swathe through the tall grass, eventually knocking a wheel off. When I heard that story, I was very glad that I hadn't gone down to the testing session. It doesn't bear thinking about the fact that that spin had surely taken Bruce down part of his last-ever loss of control less than two years later.

On a lighter note, I was at Long Beach for the Grand Prix when I had a phone call from the owner of not one but two McLaren CanAm cars, who wanted me to come and see them. My best efforts at pleading lack of interest or pressure of journalistic work failed and the gentleman came to collect me at the Imperial 400 motel. As well as a late-model CanAm car in race trim, he had a 1966 Chevy-engined M6B, which he had made road legal.

In *It Beats Working* I wrote, 'I knew what was coming next. He asked me if I would like to go for a ride in it. Imagine driving on the freeway at 55 mph in a full-race CanAm sports-racing car with the hub-nuts of trucks spinning at head-height and the car itself effectively invisible to the drivers of these huge semi-trailers. It was a terrifying experience but the owner was *loving* it. After about 10 miles I was delighted to realise that he was aiming for the slip-road and we would be heading back home. Under the freeway he stopped, leaned across to me and shouted over the roar of the engine, "Mr Young, you must know more about these cars than anyone else I know, so it would be a pleasure if you would drive my car!"

'I probably knew *less* about driving a CanAm car than anyone else he knew, I had never driven one in my life and here I was struggling into the driver's seat to cope with the big, heavy-shifting Hewland gearbox, to say nothing of the rush-hour freeway traffic…'

I am unhappy to report that my first and last drive of a CanAm McLaren was not one of my better memories in a lifetime devoted to fast cars and the men who raced them. I knew my place.

Pete Lyons, passenger

Pete Lyons wrote with a pure enthusiasm about motor sport and his piece for *Autosport* on lapping Riverside with CanAm champion Peter Revson in an M8F in 1971 was reprinted in his excellent *CAN-AM* history. It was, he said, one of the greatest experiences in his life. 'Revson's gone now; so is Riverside, and the old, original Canadian-American Challenge Cup race series came to a sad end within three years of that vivid October day. I was a naively enthusiastic young motor sports reporter then, living in the Ford Econoline van that toted me and my typewriter some 40,000 miles a year to race tracks all over North America. A wretched experience, obviously, but it did afford the occasional bright spot. Like my rocket ride aboard the fastest road racer that had yet burned the face of the earth.'

I used to travel and stay with Denny Hulme on the CanAm series after Bruce's death and Pete would bring his completed race report and films to our motel before we left for the flight back to the UK on Monday mornings. I noted that Pete used a hyphen for Can-Am, whereas I always wrote it joined-up — CanAm. Let's agree that we're both right.

Pete wrote: 'A great hammer struck my spine, slamming my head back. I forced it down, and stared at the long black roadway between the orange wheel bulges. It was rushing like some demonic torrent frantic to enter the gates of hell. Small markings — stains, patches, pebbles — appeared as flickers and were gone like dust on a cine film. There was no longer any sensation of speed. We were going too fast.

'A bridge flashed overhead like an aircraft's shadow. The wide straight kinked to the left. Still absolutely on full bore, the McLaren bent into it. The world tilted on edge. To hold myself away from the driver's arms, I had to strain every tendon. Just ahead, the world ended in a boilerplate wall. The last time I'd seen the tachometer, it had been showing 6600. That had been 184 mph, but Peter Revson's foot had been hard down ever since. I couldn't look at it now. My eyes were stuck on that wall.

'It's like an insane bull. There is a shattering bellow going on, which I feel as much as hear. I feel it my chest. Everything behind me seems to be trying to push through to the front of me. The straight is nothing before such acceleration; it hurls back at us like a snapped rubber band.

'From the pits, the first corner is Turn 2, a 120-odd-mph right-hander entering a little valley which holds the esses. From the track you can't see all the way around Turn 2; it vanishes between dun-coloured slopes. The track is a dark grey band, and on it is a black arc. You know that arc is your lifeline. You must hit it precisely. It's all shooting back at you like falling off a mountain. It looks narrow. It's arriving very fast. Too fast, really, to think about.

'The engine's throb eases. Revson's hands press the wheel. The McLaren has darted around. It was over like a lash of a whip. For one instant there was a bucket-on-a-rope sensation, then that huge engine was driving again and we were straight.

'That was the only moment in the entire ride I felt any apprehension. That magnificent automobile had shrugged off that curve with such contempt that I surrendered myself completely. No twinge of doubt about the car's abilities ever formed again. I relaxed.

'The aerodynamics squash the car to the road, and it changes direction like a puma chasing a rabbit. Slashing through the esses is like being attacked on both sides at once.

'The brakes are the car's most phenomenal feature. Flying down into Turn 9, aiming squarely at that boilerplate wall at 190 mph, Revvie's right leg makes one strong pumping movement, and a tremendous force, like a giant octopus, tries to suck me down into the footwell.

'The long bottom gear pulls us up above 90 mph. There is a pause; my spongy body recoils forward, then...slam! I can see nothing but blue Californian sky. My flesh is melting into every rearward cranny of the cockpit. Another pause, another slam. The acceleration feels absolutely as strong as before.

'Revvie's hands are in constant twirling motion, but seldom does he need more than about one-sixth steering lock. It seems smoother than I expected.

'On one lap, trundling down through 7, he held up a finger to say, "Watch this." As the turn began to open out and we had begun to pile-drive forward again, he gave the wheel a big wrench to chuck the tail out and in the next instant slammed out the throttles. The whole massive stern of the car went into a severe tremble — tyre vibration. I could feel all the various sprung and unsprung masses joggling against each other rapidly. It was much the sort of feeling you'd expect should an aircraft piston engine suddenly lose a propeller blade. It was so strong a phenomenon that I could easily visualise the whole car shaking apart. As we snapped back straight and blasted away up the next piece of road, Peter turned his face to me, and I could see his eyes through his visor asking me if I understood just how serious a problem this tyre vibration is. I nodded vigorously. Two other times in the ride, at other places, this started to happen spontaneously, and I could feel Peter feathering the throttle to kill it.

'One overall impression of my ride remains: a sensation of having entered another world. A first-class racing driver allowed me to visit the place where he is home. During those few minutes we were in a capsule, a cocoon, shut away from the familiar values of action, reaction, velocity. The old world was still there all around us, but it had nothing to do with us. We were enclosed in our own world. Different laws applied. Everything was magnified. The most delicate movement on a control produced intense response. A manoeuvre which, from the outside, looks easy and gentle, is a maelstrom of violence from the inside. A place on the road which looks from the outside to be a disturbing bump is not even perceived from within the car; two places at Riverside that looked to be shallow elevation changes became to the race car a nasty spank on the bottom and a severe drop — at 185 mph, the worst bump on the circuit.

'Three times we flashed around. The better of the two lap times that were taken — using a point on the back straight — was 1:38.5. I was pretty impressed with that, as it was a mere 2 seconds off last year's best race lap... With all the factors slowing us down that day I felt Revvie had given me a damn fine ride — and I still felt so late in the day when he went out alone, to shake off the feeling of being a bus driver, and went 5 seconds faster. I had been taken up into his world as far as it was seemly for me to go. The farther reaches are his alone.

'But I most certainly was sorry to stop!'

23 The McLaren dream road car

Bruce had always been fascinated with the idea of having his name on the nose of a road car and the shapely M6GT was a prototype for his dream, but the project died with Bruce. The prototype was directly based on the M6 chassis that Bruce had driven when he won the CanAm title in 1967. Three works M6As were built at the Colnbrook factory and a further 28 customer copies were built at the Lambretta Trojan factory at Croydon.

In 1969 the team contemplated entering the Group 4 sports car championship using a GT version of the CanAm car. However, an FIA requirement was registered for a minimum of 50 identical cars to qualify for homologation, so the idea had to be abandoned, but not before an initial batch of GT bodies had been built. Those superfluous bodies gave Bruce the idea of building a prototype McLaren road car. Doing so would realise another of his boyhood ambitions. Plus, there was the exciting thought of turning it into a Le Mans entry.

The M6GT mirrored the M6A open racer, with its rigid, lightweight aluminium monocoque sporting bonded-in steel bulkheads and twin fuel cells contained in the side pontoons. The instruments, including the 160 mph speedometer, were by Jaeger and the lights were Lucas units. The headlights were operated manually by raising the fibreglass covers on the front wings. The German ZF 5-speed gearbox was used.

'The aim was to utilise all the parts we had readily available, so no expense was wasted on elaborate fancy items. Even the exhaust manifolds were standard Chevrolet cast iron, not the pricey four-branchers you might have expected,' recalled Phil Kerr, Joint Managing Director of McLaren Racing. 'Remember our intention was to get the prototype up and running as easily and inexpensively as possible, not to go for a balls-out full-blown supercar.'

The Chevrolet V8 breathed through a four-barrel Holley carburettor and the exhausts were a pair of Jack Brabham Len Lukey mufflers.

I rode with Bruce a few times in the red GT and the noise was shattering. After twenty minutes your head was ringing. Twenty minutes after getting out it was *still* ringing! Depending on the weather, you either fried or froze in the prototype, which was still very much a CanAm car with a coupe body.

The McLaren was a GT shape of a later age, formed in fibreglass, made at Specialised Mouldings and styled by Jim Clark (no relation). If the idea was to develop a rolling test bed to discover incipient problems before production, then the prototype could be deemed a huge success. There were plenty of problems. One report noted: 'The cockpit was far too cramped and impractical for everyday use. There was no luggage or storage space. Different wheel sizes front and rear means there was a problem when it came to carrying a suitable spare tyre. But worst of all was the noise. Apart from a lack of sound insulation inside, the rush of oncoming air over the top of the car, originating from the radiator ducting in the nose section, was very noticeable.'

Phil Kerr had fonder memories of the car, being involved with Bruce in the original project and later part owner of the vehicle. 'The M6GT was, in a way, surprisingly good on the road, given that it was built on a racing car chassis. There was some noise from the suspension, but other mechanical noise was acceptable for this type of car. There were extremes of heat and cold because there were no air ducts or wind-down windows. All of this was more than compensated for by the sheer performance of the car, even though it had a relatively mild LT1 Chevrolet small block 350 cubic inch engine, probably producing around 375 bhp. Bruce and I spent a lot of time talking to a range of companies, including Jensen, with a view to getting a more sophisticated version produced as a low-volume road car.

'Denny Hulme tested the car round Goodwood when we were down there testing the M8 CanAm car. The 700-horsepower M8 race car could lap around 1:10 and was doing about 180 mph on the straight. Denny did only a few laps with the M6GT on Goodyear rain tyres, but he was doing 1:14 laps comfortably. Bear in mind the M6GT had only just over half the horsepower and didn't have slicks.'

New Zealand racing mechanic and car builder Allan McCall remembers Bruce giving him jobs in 1969 'so that I could keep eating while I was building my first Tui Formula 3 car. Mike Barney and Gordon Whitehead, who had been with Bruce since Cooper days, were building the coupe in the new David Road factory. I helped them put in the headlamps and hang the doors and a few other things in the final stage of the build. We used Lotus Elan headlamp units for the basis of the pop-up lamps.

'When the car was finished I had the privilege of being the first passenger with Bruce. We ran the car down the reservoir road towards Staines and he took the car straight up to full song. I figured that was about 155 mph. Boy, he sure had faith in us. I personally was not quite so confident. My fingermarks are most probably still in the monocoque…'

Gordon Coppuck, who designed the McLaren at the Colnbrook factory, interpreting Bruce's ideas on paper also had the opportunity to drive it. 'When Bruce let me use it for a weekend, I needed ear muffs permanently affixed by the Saturday night. Driving round the reservoirs of Staines and Heathrow airport it seemed as if there was a hurricane howling at full strength, with the terrific roar coming up over the windscreen. I can still hear the sound of it in my ears even now!

'Of course the car was very low, just 41 inches high at roof level, so other road users had extreme difficulty in seeing it come up from behind.

The Ford GT40 gained its name by being just 40 inches from road to roof. It's very difficult to produce a sensible road car from a racing machine, so no wonder it had so many disadvantages...but what a tremendous car to drive!'

The unique M6GT McLaren was registered OBH 500H for road use in the United Kingdom and from mid-1969 Bruce used it as his personal transport, keeping it in his garage at home. He wowed all in the Brands Hatch paddock car park when he drove it down to the 1970 Race of Champions. Bruce, Denny and Gordon Coppuck did about 1600 miles between them in that car.

There was a suggestion that the market size for such a vehicle might be 150 cars per year and a design for a Mk 2 version was drawn up by Bruce and Jo Marquart early in 1970. This featured a more customer-friendly interior, with narrower sills for easier entry, proper drainage channelling around the door apertures, same-size wheels front and rear, and a modified cooling duct in the nose to reduce the noise.

In an interview early in 1970, Bruce talked about his plans for a road car programme that might, or might not, have been run past the other directors.

'We are taking a look at the road car project from all angles — financing the whole operation, markets, servicing depots and all that sort of stuff. Just to leap in and build a road car and try to sell it afterwards would be a bit stupid. You have to get everything else set up first because otherwise you run out of money very quickly. Suddenly you have a car built and nowhere to get it serviced, and do all the stupid things that BMC and other people have done for years. You can't buy a spare part for a Mini Cooper anywhere in America, it's just ridiculous — I could go on about that but I won't.

'The other problem is that I want to use the team that we have built up, designing and making the CanAm, the Formula 1 and the Indy cars. There are about six people who are really capable of coming forward with a reasonably good idea on any particular problem, and I would like to use these six people on the road car. This would mean that for 12 months the racing projects would have to stop. So it won't be this year and probably not next. It means that we have to be bigger, and to do, in a way, what Colin Chapman has done — have a second echelon of people to carry on with the racing and hope that the people to whom you are delegating the responsibility can handle it. I haven't yet, in an engineering sense, delegated complete responsibility to anyone, and this is bad. It has to be done soon — very soon. But it has to be someone I know and trust within the organisation, and if he makes his mistakes, well, he makes his mistakes…'

Teddy Mayer certainly did not share Bruce's road car dream; however, Phil Kerr did. Bruce and Phil had talked about a road car when they were still racing Austin Seven Specials in New Zealand: 'After Bruce's accident, the car sat in the factory for some time and Teddy was anxious that it should be disposed of, as he had no interest in or love of the project right from the start. I think he believed we should only be building racing cars and he was probably right. Denny (Hulme) and I eventually bought the car and sent it back to New Zealand where it was initially on display at a museum and looked after by Bruce's father, Les McLaren.'

The GT was later displayed at Kerr's Bruce McLaren Motors in Auckland and in 1986 it was extensively restored. However, the cost of maintaining it and insuring it was too high and the car was eventually sold. There was a notion that the car would be shown in New Zealand and in California and that Denny would demonstrate it, but the car was on-sold in a Christie's Pebble Beach auction for $1.32 million in 1990. OBH 500H was eventually acquired by Harry Mathews and is on display in his incredible collection of McLaren cars in Arvada, a suburb of Denver, Colorado.

∧
Get me to the race on time — in the hands of Bruce McLaren, even a Morris Minor had considerable speed.

>
A major step forward in racing car aerodynamics: Tyler Alexander cuts a hole in the nose of the Zerex Special, 1964.

El Gráfico

$ 8.-

BRUCE McLAREN
VENCEDOR DEL VII GRAN PREMIO DE LA
REPUBLICA ARGENTINA.

∧
After winning the 1960 Argentine Grand Prix Bruce became a cover-boy for the sport.

MONACO GRAND PRIX

AUTOSPORT

JUNE 8, 1962

2/-

EVERY FRIDAY
Vol. 24   No. 23

Registered at the G.P.O. as a Newspaper

BRITAIN'S   MOTOR   SPORTING   WEEKLY

IN THIS ISSUE
JOHN BOLSTER TESTS THE SKODA OCTAVIA SALOON
CLUB RACING AT SILVERSTONE AND SNETTERTON

∧
Autosport featured Bruce's 1962 Monaco win for Cooper.

∧

Bruce's 1962 win at Monaco was as good for Ferodo as it was for Cooper.   EOIN YOUNG COLLECTION

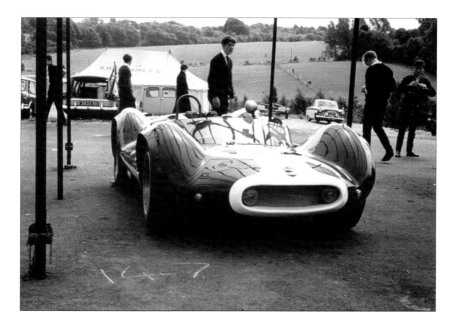

^
One year, two hemispheres, endless races. From driving the Cooper Oldsmobile at Brands
Hatch (top) to the Tasman Cooper at Pukekohe (bottom), 1964 was a busy year for Bruce.

Motor Racing

38c

'I find happiness in
Motor Racing...
the BOAC 500,
a racing driver's school,
a very special Fiat,
drive-yourself-round-
Brands Hatch offer...
and a fastgirl pull-out.'

'Don't forget yourself, McLaren.'

∧
Motor Racing and SportsCar magazine cover, 1968.

∧
Team chat, 1968: Teddy Mayer, Eoin Young, Bruce, Denny Hulme.

> Phil Hill, Bruce and Jimmy Clark
on the Pukekohe grid, 1965.

> John Cooper, a pivotal man in
Bruce's career, seen here in 2000.

24 The Indianapolis project

By 1969 the McLaren team had made a huge impression on the motor sport scene. They had dominated the CanAm sports car series for several summers, they were winning in Formula 1. What they hadn't tried was the famous Indianapolis 500. The team was at a CanAm race listening to the Indy race on the radio and they decided that they could build a car for Denny to win the '500'. Surely it couldn't be that difficult? After all, it was just another race, wasn't it? Not quite.

The Indianapolis Speedway was built in 1909 on the northwest side of Indianapolis, Indiana. It is the oldest race track in the world still being used in its original form. It was built as a 2.5-mile rectangle because this was the longest track format that could be fitted into the land available. The race was pegged at 500 miles because this was as far as a race could run in daylight hours. The first '500' ran in 1911 and it was run annually since, with breaks only during the war years.

The original course was made by covering a 2-inch layer of gravel with 2 inches of crushed limestone and taroid. This surface broke up, so it was replaced with 3,200,000 paving bricks and the circuit was known thereafter as 'The Brickyard'. The four, identical quarter-mile turns were banked at 9 degrees, separated by two long straights measuring five-eighths of a mile and two shorter straights of an eighth of a mile. It sounds simple, but it was incredibly complex in its irritating simplicity.

Bruce had actually driven at Indy in 1968 when, at the behest of Goodyear, he and Denny became involved in an ill-starred project to build a turbine car for the race. McLaren Racing was paid $50,000 to help with development and there was an additional $20,000 for Bruce's testing input. In fact, they were add-ons to someone else's programme and the McLaren personnel were extremely uneasy about what they saw as a wildly over-funded, under-designed car.

Before being allowed to race at the Speedway, Bruce had to pass his rookie test — he was the first driver ever to take his rookie test at Indianapolis in a turbine! The test involved starting out at low-speed laps and gradually raising that speed in increments. He also had to pass a medical and he was worried that he might fail the eye test, because he knew one eye was a lot weaker than the other. An Indy veteran showed Bruce how to place his left hand over his weak eye and read the chart, then put his *right* hand over the same eye and read the chart again. It worked perfectly.

The turbine was fundamentally difficult to adapt one's driving style to — not to say downright dangerous — and it was obvious to Bruce that he was compromising his integrity, but the Goodyear funds were badly needed by the team in 1968.

Their initial session at Indy completed, Bruce and Denny flew back to Spain for the Grand Prix, where they were relieved and delighted to hear that Goodyear had abandoned the turbine project, having buried over a million dollars for zero return.

It was said that the designer of the turbine car had come up with a device like the iris in a camera, which could increase the annulus intake once the car was on the track. This was outside the regulations and word had apparently leaked out to the authorities so the cars were suddenly withdrawn.

'The next day the turbines were gone,' Indianapolis historian Donald Davidson told me in 2004. 'They were loaded up in the middle of the night and everything had just completely disappeared. There was a message in chalk on one of the blackboards with an official statement…'

Indy, therefore, didn't hold the happiest of memories for Bruce, but taking his own car there would surely be different. The team planned to build a single-seater McLaren for Indianapolis based around the running gear of the CanAm car and fitted with a four-cylinder turbocharged Offenhauser motor. The 1970 return to Indianapolis was a total team project, with Denny, who had previously driven at the Brickyard, and Chris Amon as drivers. Bruce tested the new M15, as it was known, at Goodwood when it was ready to run and he had to teach himself to cope with what was a turbocharged, updated, antique engine.

'We had laid down what looked to be an almost impossible schedule to design and build an Indianapolis car ready for testing in a little over three months, but the factory responded splendidly and Colnbrook vibrated on Sunday afternoon to the sound of its first Offenhauser Indianapolis engine. And "vibrated" was the word. The four-cylinder Offy beloved by the US "circle racers" is quite an engine. Anybody who remembers the old 500 Cooper-Norton will know what I mean — it's like having four of those tied together. The engine was designed back in 1931 and our drawing office was so proud of their new aluminium monocoque chassis, which finishes just in front of the engine, that there was dark talk of sticking a little sign on the chassis at that point worded "1970 Stops Here!" '

I wrote in my *Autocar* column: 'It does seem strange that teams like McLaren put a lot of money and modern know-how into developing a brand new car for Indianapolis and then fit a four-cylinder engine like the Offenhauser that first saw the light of day in 1931 under the Miller label! It's almost like Colin Chapman slotting an updated 1930 4.5-litre blown Bentley engine into his new four-wheel-drive Lotus for Indy. Not quite like that, but you get the picture.

'The Offenhauser engine was developed in 1931 for Harry Miller and it carried his name until his company went under in 1938 and the Offenhauser company took over production. They in turn were taken over and the 1969 versions of the "Offy" are built by Meyer and Drake in Los Angeles.'

The engine had obviously undergone considerable development since the 1930s, and with the turbocharger fitted it produced a pretty reliable 600-plus horsepower from its 2.6-litres.

'We ran it the next day at Goodwood,' wrote Bruce, 'but the odd habits of the turbocharger meant it wasn't much of a car for road circuits. The turbocharger is run by exhaust gas, and the more exhaust gas you've got, the more intake mixture you push into the engine. This works the other way to start with — when you first open the throttle you haven't got much exhaust gas so that the fan in the turbocharger in the intake isn't pushing much in until you've had the throttle open for a little while to get some exhaust gas to speed the turbine which blows a bit more intake mixture in which creates more exhaust gas which creates a bit more intake pressure — *Phew!* — which creates a *lot* more exhaust gas which means suddenly you've spun off in the middle of Madgwick when it all comes in with a bang! And that's exactly what happened to Denny...

'Indy is a whole new ballgame. First of all, you don't run much below 160 mph and most of the time you're neared 200. In Grand Prix or CanAm it's the other way round — you're not much *over* 160 and this is the first thing that you notice.

'So that we would have some sort of yardstick to go by, we set the car up as a road racer at Goodwood prior to shipping it, so that if the engine had been responsive it would have been about the same way we'd expect a Grand Prix car to be. We hadn't been to Indy with one of our cars before and we didn't know much about it, but I was much more interested in finding out why and how a car is fast at Indianapolis for myself, rather than just copying all the trick things that people have developed over the years. I figured that we had plenty of time to learn — the best part of six months — but if this hadn't been the case, we wouldn't have had time to go through this learning process. I drove the car initially, but I soon realised my lack of experience at Indy was going to hurt just a little. It takes quite a long time to go really fast there. Make no mistake, it's a lot more than just four left-hand corners.

'There's a very definite art in getting through those high-speed turns correctly. You have to run a very precise line and pattern — at least I think so — to go fast. I got up to 162 mph fairly quickly, and I could imagine quite a few things that would make the car faster, but as Denny had been through all this before with the Eagles, we elected to have him start driving at that stage. Chris Amon was there with us too. One of the problems of testing at Indy is that they only allow one car out at a time, so if there were three or four cars there you would only get a quarter of the day. We got through about half of our experiments and Denny was lapping at just over 168. If we're lucky we'll find another two or three miles an hour, and we should be in the running next May. Two months ago, we were saying, "Right, remember now, it's just another race…" But there's never been a single race that we've got this excited about!'

The McLaren M15 had an aircraft manifold pressure gauge on the dash in addition to the rev counter, but Denny said he drove according to manifold pressure with the turbocharged Offenhauser at Indy and virtually ignored the rev counter. Once cars get up to speed at Indy they tend to stay in top gear all the time, so a rev counter isn't a great deal of use. The manifold pressure gauge read in inches of mercury and if the needle was registering anywhere between 60 and 874 inches Denny knew he had about 680 horsepower on immediate call, but if it dropped below 60 inches (about 15 lb of boost) he only had about 160 horsepower available.

Chris was ambivalent about the Speedway. He could run faster around Spa with its slow hairpin and trackside trees than he could at Indianapolis and this spooked him. Denny, on the other hand, was comfortable with everything about the Speedway, from the traditions of the railbirds, the old hands who had grown up at the Brickyard, to the strange art of lapping at extremely high speeds.

Unfortunately Denny fell victim to a freak accident while testing the M15 at Indianapolis. A fuel breather cap had popped open and the alcohol-based fuel was leaking, streaming back to the red-hot turbocharger and exploding in clear flames. Denny only became aware that he was burning when he felt the pain. He slowed as much as he could and then jumped out of the cockpit.

Later, sitting up in hospital at Indianapolis, drifting in and out of consciousness with the pain-killing drugs, his hands, feet and left forearm caked in white tacky dressings like icing, Denny was still able to chat and titter when Bruce and others in the team called to see him each day.

Denny's accident was enough for Chris. He had never been enamoured with the place and Denny's misfortune made up his mind for good. Bruce had never intended to drive himself in the '500', so the team signed up Peter Revson and Carl Williams. When Denny was driving, the team knew they were working with someone who had proven himself to be competitive in this special sphere of racing and they were able to alter the car accordingly, to his suggestions. Gordon Coppuck summed it up well: 'We always had a suspicion that if Denny had been able to drive he could have run quick enough to win the race, but we weren't sure whether the others were able to.'

Tyler described it as trying to sort out a Formula 1 car with a driver who could not tell them whether it was oversteering or understeering. It was a new world for Bruce, and a frustrating one, because he could do nothing on the cars. He valued the assistance and comments of an experienced driver like Bobby Unser, who tried the car for only four laps — the last two at 166 mph — and recommended alterations that produced an immediate improvement in Peter Revson's laptimes. After those four laps, Unser approached Teddy Mayer, asking if he could buy one of the cars.

It was the first time the McLaren team had been to Indianapolis and they left nothing to chance. In the heat of the afternoon on carburation day, Bruce was down there pushing the car down the pit lane and into the pit where the mechanics waited to simulate fuel stops and wheel-changes against the stopwatch. Since pushing the car was reckoned to be something even I could handle without making a mistake, I was press-ganged into helping. After half a dozen runs I was bushed, but Bruce wasn't even short of breath; he was already in a heads-together meeting with the mechanics sorting out a way to speed up the pit stop…

During the race, Revson ran well until he was sidelined with engine failure. Williams finished ninth. Bruce and Gordon were delighted when the Indiana section of the Society of Automobile Engineers presented Bruce with a plaque in recognition of his contribution towards progress at Indy.

The new cars had performed well enough for the buyers to be queuing up at the McLaren garage the next day. Two cars were sold to Gilmore Broadcasting for Gordon Johncock to drive.

On the plane home, Bruce and Gordon Coppuck sat together and discussed ideas for a new car for the 1971 '500'. 'We decided that we hadn't seen the concept of our new car and that we would have to investigate several basic shapes before coming to a decision,' said Coppuck. 'We wondered whether a wedge would be better, or a slim pencil shape, or a fat car. The M15 was what we called a "fat car". It was 45 inches wide, whereas our current Formula 1 car was only 26 inches wide…'

Jack Brabham was also on that flight and he spent some time with Bruce, discussing future plans. 'Bruce talked about retirement and said perhaps he would give up Formula 1 and just do testing and the CanAm series. My theory was that if you gave up, you gave up…'

The next day Bruce was killed in that freak testing crash at Good-wood.

25 The last season

By chance, I came upon the manuscript of an interview with Bruce written early in 1970, but there was no clue as to the identity of the journalist or whether it had ever been published. It is one of the last major interviews Bruce ever did. My feeling is that the writer was English, a trifle self-indulgently woolly as a journalist, an older acquaintance of Bruce's. Also, the fact that it was typed on foolscap paper suggested the writer was an older chap. Older than me, in 1970 anyway, as we always used quarto, then A4 paper, tapping away on manual typewriters in a pre-laptop era.

It is an interesting piece and I present it as written, as it conveys the spirit of the time, together with Bruce's comments on questions I probably wouldn't have asked and he probably wouldn't have answered at such length.

'Come to lunch on Friday,' said Bruce McLaren. So I went. Unfortunately, Bruce is at present on a self-imposed diet, convinced that good living in the United States has made him fat. Therefore 'lunch' consisted of two Limmits [slimmer's biscuits] for Bruce and a cup of vending machine coffee for me!

However, bravely fighting back the thought of the mixed grills or gammon and pineapple that I knew the rest of Bruce's gang were enjoying at the local pub, I switched on the tape recorder and concentrated on the business in hand — which was difficult. The McLaren factory is situated as close to the main runway at

London Airport as it can be without actually getting mixed up with the landing lights, and talking to Bruce in his first floor office, I was somewhat distracted by the Boeings and VC10s and DC8s and Tridents gliding past the window. With a landing or a take-off about every thirty seconds I thought the tape recorder would have a nervous breakdown, but it didn't; and Bruce didn't seem to notice the noise.

I launched into my investigation. What has the present-day Bruce McLaren, successful constructor, driver and businessman, in common with the young lad from New Zealand whom I first met twelve years ago? What is his engineering philosophy? What makes the McLaren team such a happy one? How does Bruce rate his chances at Indianapolis this year? How does he feel about New Zealand? Would he like to go back to live there?

'As far as I'm concerned, New Zealand is a great place. There are so many good beaches, and so many things you can do to keep you fit and bronzed and all those nice things you can't do in England. But I couldn't build racing cars there. I would be frustrated and bored stiff if I went back there at the moment. I would get a lot fitter in a hurry, but that is about all. At this stage I would not consider going back to New Zealand. What I'd like to do is tow England to somewhere just off the coast of California — that would be great!'

Except for this winter and last, Bruce has been going home every year for the Tasman series and to spend Christmas either with his family or his wife's. The McLarens come from the Auckland area of the North Island, and Pat from Timaru in the South Island.

'I met Patty very early in 1958 when I was touring the South Island with my racing car. We got along famously right away, and the next year when I came back for the racing season again we spent a lot of time together, and then next year we decided to get engaged. She came over to England with me in 1960 and we married in 1961.'

Now, with their daughter, Amanda, who is 4 and commonly called 'Mandy Muffet' by her father, the McLarens live in a beautiful, new house in Surrey. The design of *Muriwai* (which is the name of the beach where Bruce entered his first competitive event) is dignified and traditional, planned by Bruce and Patty to house themselves, Amanda, a much-hoped-for second child, the nanny-housekeeper who takes over when Pat is away, and Tyler Alexander, McLaren's American Chief Mechanic and close friend who has lived with them for years. The new house is the main outward symbol of Bruce's enormous success as a constructor/driver, situated in one of England's most expensive real estate areas, surrounded by wealthy neighbours and landscaped gardens.

This does not change Bruce at all, except that he appreciates the financial security and is modestly proud of his achievements.

'I often think,' he says, pensively, 'when we go out to dinner now — what I spend on dinner without blinking an eye would have kept me going for about two months when I first came over here. I appreciate what I have, far more for remembering the times when I was down to my last £20 or £30 in the world, apart from my racing car. The only thing I had was racing. I had nowhere to live, apart from hotels, and I had to have enough money to pay the hotel bills or else go out on the street. It was reasonably nasty!'

Bruce could barely have failed to become involved with motor racing, because his father had been a well-known competitor in motorcycle racing, and later in rallying, hill climbs and sprints. He also owned a garage service station, and built his own motorcycles and later refurbished cars, from his stock of bits and pieces. Bruce, as a small boy, used to build himself 'trolleys' — basically four wheels and a slab of wood that you can use for whizzing down hills — from the huge collection of old parts dating from the 1920s, some new and some used, stored underneath the service station.

'When I was nine or ten I used to draw more racing cars at school than anything else. It was the beginning of becoming a draughtsman, I suppose. But all my other interests were in physical pursuits, especially football. I was captain of the Junior School football team. I was the second best fighter in the class; the other chap was bigger than me. And we used to have cycle races up and down the hills. I mostly won those, particularly downhill!'

At the age of ten, just when he was due to move on to secondary school, Bruce suffered a setback which must have had a profound psychological effect on him. After a series of falls — from horses, walls and trolleys — he was found to be suffering from a disease of the hip-joint called Perthes' Disease. The only cure at that time was a long spell of complete rest, and Bruce was hospitalised for two years. All his sporting pastimes came to an abrupt halt. During his stay in hospital, and his year on crutches convalescing, he began to take an interest in reading about cars and the design of cars.

'By the time I was ready to go back to school, I chose to go to an engineering school where the main subjects were maths, science, English and history, and where part of the curriculum was engineering workshop practice. In other words, we were taught to use a file, a hacksaw, a lathe and drills and so on. By this time I was about 13 and my father was rebuilding an Austin 7 Ulster just out of boxes of bits, so I took an interest. I helped with the rebuilding and then began to drive it — just around the back yard at home.'

Gradually, Bruce learned to handle the car like a veteran, building up to his first power-slide on the rough surface of the yard — and narrowly missing the side of the house. His father was racing and rallying an SS Jaguar, a 1936 coupe, and the Austin intended for racing at an airfield circuit called Seagrove, near Auckland. Bruce passed his driving test first time at the age of 15, and spent Christmas and summer holidays 'belting the Austin around on loose-surfaced roads and began to learn something about tail-slides'. At the end of 1952 he took part in his first competitive event, a hill climb, and came second in his class. From then on he entered events of all kinds with the Austin, often competing against his father, who was faster. This fact prompted Bruce to 'show the old man how to do it', and the encouragement he received from his father was a major factor in the development of Bruce McLaren, racing driver.

Meanwhile, McLaren the engineer was proceeding from engineering school to the Engineering Department of Auckland University.

'Part of my training at secondary school was technical drawing, so I had some good basic training in that, but my favourite subject was what we term engineering mathematics — mathematics applied to the broad scope of engineering. I became good at that partly because I was interested, and partly because there was nothing else to do at that time. I couldn't play any sport for a while (though I eventually got back to swimming and rowing), so the only hobby I could have was something connected to school. The subjects that applied to motor racing and engineering were horsepower formulae, and centrifugal force formulae, and all the things that cover the design of a racing car. I'm still reasonably good at maths today, though I don't get much practice at it. But I can tell immediately if someone is stressing something overmuch in the drawing office, or if someone has made a mistake in the calculation of the load we ought to get on a particular wheel under a certain amount of acceleration or something. You start looking at things, and they either look strong or weak. It comes more from experience than anything else, but you have to learn good engineering practice first.'

So out of the apparent disaster of his years in hospital came many of Bruce's most useful qualities. The enforced inactivity made him want to stretch himself to the limits, physically and mentally. Although he was left with a pronounced limp because one leg is shorter than the other, he developed strong arms and shoulders to compensate, and the will to overcome difficulties — useful attributes for a racing driver. The study of mathematics, which would probably in other circumstances have seemed a chore designed to keep him away from the rugby football field, became a pleasure. And there is nothing in the world more calculated to make people determined to pack as much as possible into their lives as lying in a hospital bed wondering if they will ever walk again. I know. I've been through the experience myself.

By the time Bruce went on to the School of Engineering at Auckland University, the ingredients for success were already mixed and ready to work, though perhaps not in the way his professors expected.

'My university career was not very distinguished because now I was going to races at weekends with my Austin 7. I even had a confrontation eventually with the chemistry professor. He said, 'You will have to choose between motoring racing, McLaren, or engineering.' I said, 'Yes, sir.' He thought I meant engineering, and I didn't tell him I didn't. I chose both, I reckon. Now I'm waiting for them to give me an Honorary degree!'

Bruce made this remark jokingly and accompanied it with a hearty laugh, but I got the impression he is very well satisfied with the way things have turned out. From the chemistry professor's point of view, McLaren is eating his cake and having it, which is nice for McLaren. The New Zealand government thinks very highly of him too — it is significant that out of the world's top ten Grand Prix drivers, three are Kiwis, and the number of racing mechanics from those two small islands is staggering. As Bruce explains it, there are two main reasons for this.

'In the fifties, when John Cooper and Colin Chapman were creating the British motor racing industry as we know it today, we in New Zealand were having four international motor races a year — well promoted, well attended, from a population of under 3 million people. It is the equivalent of having four inter-national motor races in Surrey! If you did that you would find that a lot of people in Surrey would be racing mechanics or racing drivers and what have you, and that is the main reason why there are so many New Zealanders in the sport now.

'The other factor was that the New Zealand Grand Prix Association which ran the races, was far-sighted enough to say, "Let's get something big off the ground, let's not create obstacles, let's do it, let's put on the best show we can." And they went further than that. Having put on a show that people were keen to come to see, even from Europe, they wanted to put some-thing back into the sport, and they did this with the "Driver to Europe" scheme. I was the first to be sent over under the scheme in 1958, and I brought one mechanic with me, and it snow-balled after that. Other New Zealanders thought, "Well, England isn't all that far away, after all, and McLaren seems to be doing all right, so we ought to go." '

Bruce makes light of his early racing days now, and calls it 'old history', but it was a considerable advance from the Austin 7 via an Austin Healey to a real racing car, a 1750 cc single-seater Cooper which his father bought him when his potential became clear. It is sufficient, perhaps, to say that Bruce was competent and fast enough to drive in some grand company, including Stirling Moss and Jack Brabham, in New Zealand in 1957, and to justify his selection for the 'Driver to Europe' scheme. (It had been a bit of a toss-up between Bruce and another young driver called Phil Kerr, who later became Brabham's business manager and is now joint managing director of Bruce McLaren Motor Racing Ltd.)

That first year in Europe with his own Formula 2 Cooper was 'good fun but terribly worrying', says Bruce.

'In fact, I *learned* to worry that year. I had a £3000 racing car, and engine bills to meet all the time, and I was on the ragged edge of my bank account. In fact, my mechanic, Colin Beanland, had to buy the Ford Zephyr that we towed the thing around with, and I was only able to pay his wages after we had been a bit lucky and had a win or something. I know I got £600 from a second place at Casablanca, and I thought I was made — £600 then was like a million now. It would go in half a day here. Ridiculous. But at that time…!'

In the summer of 1958 Bruce made a sizeable impression on the motor racing scene by winning the Formula 2 section of the German Grand Prix at the Nürburgring and coming fifth overall.

'I went slowly in practice because I had no idea where the road went, and I was a bit cautious. At that stage I was still driving my own car and I couldn't afford to bend it. Anyway, I was slow, and no one considered I was in the running. But in the race I went

30 seconds a lap quicker, faster than Phil Hill in a Ferrari and Edgar Barth in a Porsche. Barth was supposed to be the fastest mortal man around the 'Ring at the time, and blowing him off was very satisfying.'

The very first races Bruce won in Europe were at minor meetings at Brands Hatch and at Silverstone.

'It was like winning a CanAm race — there was no opposition. In other words, Moss and Brooks weren't there. I don't feel I've really won a race unless I have beaten the best guys in road racing, and the best then were Moss, Brooks, Stuart Lewis-Evans and Jack Brabham.

'Unfortunately, my basic caution has stayed with me from those early days, when to shunt the car would have meant the end of my motor racing. I know I am considered to be the perfect Number 2 in a team, the eternal runner-up. That aggravates me. I'd much rather win, of course, but the ability isn't always there. Sometimes it is, sometimes I can do it. I wish I could do it *all* the time, but I have no illusions. I know I can't. Andretti, Stewart and Rindt all seem to be able to go faster than I can, most of the time. Denny can go faster than I can. He used not to be able to, but he certainly can now. He seems more on form than he used to be. He's just plain better. Jack Brabham is amazing — he has this tremendous ability to put one great lap together. Jacky Ickx comes and goes. I had a long dice with Ickx at the British Grand Prix, and it wasn't until my car got on to empty tanks at the end of the race that he got by. Up to that stage I stayed in front of him; but I had to try as hard as I could.

'However, I think I have won more races than I have lost by being sensible. In 1959, for instance, I began the season with my first works Formula 1 drive, for Coopers — Jack Brabham being number one. I was under instructions not to bend the car, and I drove carefully and sensibly, and gradually got faster and faster, but always carefully, and I finished every race up to the British Grand Prix. At the British Grand Prix I had a big dice with Stirling Moss and I thought, right, that's it, I've arrived! So after the British I went every race like the clappers, and six in a row I didn't finish. Things broke, largely gearboxes, engines — all sorts of things. The next race where I drove reasonably, I finished. I just followed Jack and kept to his pace, which was just behind Moss, and I won the race when Moss and then Jack dropped out.'

When Jack left Cooper to build his own cars, Bruce became number one driver, but Cooper fortunes suffered with the change of Formula 1 from 2.5 to 1.5-litres, and there wasn't much Bruce could do about the downward trend. First Ferrari, then BRM, then Lotus were supreme. The sole Cooper Grand Prix win in the years '61 to '65 was at Monaco in 1962, when Bruce went into the lead after Graham Hill's car broke down seven laps from the end.

Bruce stayed with Cooper until the end of the 1.5-litre formula, each year achieving a placing around the middle of the World Championship table. But for a long time the engineer in McLaren had been struggling to get to grips with a car of his own. No doubt Brabham's successes in all three formulae inspired him to have a go.

'I learned a tremendous amount from Jack when we were at Coopers, though not much in terms of engineering. I would often try to get him talking about what sort of car he would build if he were going to build one — way back in 1959 and '60. I used to say, "What's your ideal racing car? Do a sketch on a piece of paper." But he never would. He wouldn't talk about it at all. He was *very* good at putting things together — I was reasonably good.

I used to build a chassis quite well. Towards the end, just before I left Coopers, a lot of their design came from the stuff that I made, and I used to be quite capable of building all the bits on a car. I couldn't do it to the standard of our guys now. But I miss it. To be able actually to make something is awfully nice.'

This desire to 'make something' had been with Bruce since his earliest childhood — the days of the trolleys and the model aeroplanes — and manifested itself in attempts to alter some of the established ways of thinking at Coopers in the early 1960s. But he was up against strong opposition from Charles Cooper, John's father, who held the view that drivers should drive and not interest themselves in development or design. Charles was so furious with one motoring journalist for suggesting that Coopers were becoming old-fashioned, and that Lotus were streaking past them in the design field, that he forbade him to 'darken their doorstep'. He was also furious with Jack Brabham for leaving Coopers, and never quite forgave him. Bruce is not the person for any kind of 'scene', but he, too, is fairly stubborn in his own way, and he knew the path he would take if it could be made financially possible.

McLaren Motor Racing Ltd was formed at the end of 1963 to enter cars for the newly formed Tasman Series. Bruce won the title, but his friend and teammate, American Timmy Mayer, was killed during practice for the final race. This was a great shock for Bruce and for Timmy's brother, Teddy. These two now came together to form a business partnership which continues to this day. Teddy is a law graduate, and is an equal shareholder in the company with Bruce, as well as being his exceedingly busy racing manager.

Bruce has some very definite ideas on design and development, which reflect his temperament and are in turn reflected in his cars. I remarked that he had been compared quite often with Colin Chapman, and asked him what he thought of that.

'I think Colin Chapman is a lot cleverer than I am. In fact, I know he is. He is a very sharp, quick thinker. Chapman will innovate for the sake of innovating. I am not at all interested in building the fastest car. I think you have to be capable of getting on the front row to be sure of winning a race, but I'm all for reliability too. We haven't yet built our ideal Formula 1 car — but we're working on it! We have a new one for 1970 but we don't think this is the ideal, either. We'll probably never reach it, because you are learning all the time. I know a lot more now than I did last year. I will know a lot more next year than I know now. We used to get to every September and say to each other, "How did we manage to build cars knowing as little as we did?"

'Keith Duckworth of Cosworth Engineering says "development is only necessary because of the ignorance of the designers"; but if, in fact, we look at the development of his own engine we find that there have been problems arising from some factors that he forgot when he was designing it, brilliant man though he is. Of course, it has been developed. If development were not necessary the Wright Brothers would have designed the VC10. You design to the very best of your ability, but changing circumstances enforce both changes in design and sometimes changes in philosophy. Very few designers can say they are going to design a part, and here is a list of every possible factor that he should take into account. There will be something he has forgotten, there will be something he will see after he has completed the design and he will say, "There was no way we could have known that," and that is why prototypes are built in engineering.'

Bruce is convinced that he saves a lot of time by building prototypes, and irons out a lot of problems more quickly and more practically in this way.

'I always say first of all, particularly in motor racing, you are designing to a time deadline. What you have to do is come up with a car that is slightly better than someone else's, but you have got to do it *now*. The time factor is terribly important. At the factory, after we have spent a certain amount of time on a design, I'll say, "Let's build a prototype." You can maybe do the initial design in a week, but to do the detail and sort out every possible little problem might take another three months. The prototype will only take you a month and sort out the problems for you. There's no way you can design a car ten years in the future. But you can design next year's car and get it *running* — that's the philosophy around here, anyway.'

I asked Bruce a question I had put to Keith Duckworth 18 months before, a matter that I think is of some importance in assessing an engineer. At what stage does he decide that a design is not going to work and he should consign the whole project to the wastepaper basket?

'I wish you wouldn't talk about the four-wheel-drive car like that!' said Bruce, laughing the familiar, infectious, chuckling McLaren laugh. This was exactly the subject I wanted to raise, but I hadn't expected Bruce to be so frank about something which had become a comparatively delicate subject in motor racing.

'We didn't race it again after Silverstone (Derek Bell drove it in its British Grand Prix debut), but we kept struggling. We are throwing good money after bad, unfortunately, but we followed up, we thought we ought to give it a fair test, and we investigated a lot of factors. We might resurrect it in the future. It is difficult to face up to the fact that a design is basically wrong — you keep pushing the thought away. But sometimes it dawns on you very suddenly…

'Sometimes when the mechanics are actually putting a car together, they say, "It's all right for you, sitting upstairs in your office." But it is a lot harder sitting upstairs trying to decide what the hell you are going to do about some terribly important matter than just going downstairs and making something. It is for me, anyway. I don't get around the cars enough any more. I can, just by virtue of the amount of experience I have had, generally pick the right way to do something on the car. But, though I've always had a reasonably inventive turn of mind if it's prompted, I can't sit down cold and be imaginative. I can, if there's the germ of an idea, take it and expand on it. Improve on it? Well, maybe. Sometimes. Occasionally if we are rushed, particularly if we are making a mock-up or something, I can see the way a particular piece of metal should be bent, or beaten, or cut, and I am quite happy to pick up the hacksaw, or whatever, and do it. Unfortunately, it doesn't happen very often.'

We discussed Denny's victory in Mexico and Bruce's own rotten luck in not starting at all in the US and Mexican Grands Prix.

'Yes, in the last few races we were very unfortunate. Plain bad luck. Denny was especially unlucky, considering how many front-row grid positions he achieved last year. What happens is that once you get down on luck — or once you get on top of it — you tend to stay that way for a while. It is as though success breeds success. Everyone works a little harder if you're winning, everyone has just that little bit fresher outlook and attitude. Whereas when things are bad, one says, "Oh, hell, I'd do the nut and bolt up again and go home." When things are going well one might say, "I'll do this nut and bolt up again, and check it carefully and we might win the next one. No, I don't like that...I'll put in a *fresh* nut and bolt." It is simply that success gives everyone more confidence.'

The 1970 McLaren Formula 1 car is now complete and ready for extensive testing. The CanAm programme goes ahead with its already legendary record to promote confidence, and now McLarens enter a new field — Indianapolis. After trials at Phoenix and the Speedway, the odds on a McLaren victory are shortening. Bruce himself gives it a 10-to-1 chance, even if they were to run it as it was back in November, and a 1-in-3 if they satisfactorily complete the development work and modifications that are now being undertaken. Bruce regards the CanAm car as a very advanced item, 'although it looks so simple. Our 1969 Formula 1 car was pretty old-fashioned in its basic thinking, but the M8 is a fairly advanced car, all the design philosophy is very good and the detail execution is excellent. I think last year's Formula 1 Matra was a very well-thought-out and well-designed car, but there are very few features on that car that we don't have in one way or another on the M8 CanAm car.'

This is as near to boasting as I've ever heard Bruce come, and one can only agree that he has every reason to be proud of his CanAm record. It has made him a lot of money, given him a status in America that he went out and built for himself, having the foresight to see that here was a field which other European designers had not taken very seriously. As rewards in CanAm races are dependent upon results, not many teams from this side of the Atlantic would have taken up the challenge as Bruce did and 'got something off the ground'. If you ask him why the CanAm cars have been so successful, he says 'Because there was no opposition,' and that is largely true. But there is a good deal more to it than that. The subject deserves a book to itself, but to put a finger on it briefly, it has a lot to do with the personalities of Bruce, Denny, Tyler Alexander, and the rest of the group, which is more like a close-knit family unit than a racing car team. They are all around the same age, they like each other and they share a similar sense of humour. Bruce says of Denny 'I understand him and he understands me,' and that, Bruce implies, is what it's all about.

The question of a McLaren road car has been under consideration for some time. As the enterprise has grown, people have speculated as to whether McLaren will become another Colin Chapman. The short answer is 'Not just yet.' Bruce has a few problems to iron out first, not the least of them being when he might have the time! A full season of Formula 1 racing is practically a full-time job in itself, including test sessions and there are to be 13 Grands Prix this year, plus several international Formula 1 meetings. There will be 11 CanAm races. The Indianapolis 500. And the factory to run. Bruce seriously considered giving up some or all of his Formula 1 racing this year, depending on whether Chris Amon would join Denny in the team. But Chris decided to go to March and I don't think Bruce was all that disappointed to find that he had his twelfth Formula 1 season to look forward to.

Bruce discussed his enthusiasm about the way his team worked. 'A lot of detail is delegated. I can go away for weeks and a darned good car will be built here, but that is basically because if a guy has been here for two or three years and he is not prepared to think the way I would like him to, then it is better if we part company. If he stays then we get the cars that I like and I am not fussy, not trying to change him all the time. This is the way we think right now — get it done, get it done simply, get it done *early*. Strong and efficient is better than delicate and beautiful as far as I am concerned...'

The Bruce McLaren I first met in 1958 has not changed much, though he has more to say and he has learned a lot about the problems of making a racing car. He was always a happy, enthusiastic person, thoughtful but never morose, modest, easy-going, and *very* hard working. Success in America has made him more businesslike — he values himself more highly. There is precious little time left nowadays for anything that could remotely be called a hobby. His work is his hobby...and his bread-and-butter...and his kicks. He loves swimming and water-skiing, playing with Amanda and teasing the cat; but I think he is happiest after a test day at Silverstone or Goodwood (or Phoenix or Riverside or Indy) when things have gone well and the orange McLarens, immaculate as always, are capable of taking on the opposition and beating it. The competitive urge in Bruce is as strong as in most racing drivers.

Did he really mean it when he said he had thought of retiring from Grand Prix racing? I asked on my way out.

'Oh yes...if we could have got Amon, I think I would have done only about half the Formula 1 races. But if I had turned out to be faster than him, I would have kept on going!'

'69 M7A McLaren F1

'68 M8A McLaren CanAm

M6GT McLaren Road Car

Austin Ulster

58

'65 M1B McLaren CanAm

114

Cooper Bobtail